YOUNG

writers guide

2nd Edition

R O D N E Y   M A R T I N

YOUNG WRITERS GUIDE
Published by Era Publications,
220 Grange Road, Flinders Park, SA 5025 Australia

© Rodney Martin, 2000
Graphic design by Lisa James
Technical design by Barry Wallis
Printed by C.O.S Printers Pte Ltd, Singapore
First edition published 2000
Second edition published 2002

National Library of Australia Cataloguing-in-Publication data:
Martin,R.D.(Rodney David),1946-.
Young writers guide.

Rev. ed.
ISBN 1 86374 637 4.
ISBN 1 86374 792 3 (CD-Rom).
1.English language -Rhetoric -Handbooks, manuals,etc. -
Juvenile literature. 2. English language - Grammar -
Handbooks, manuals, etc. 3. Report writing - Handbooks,
manuals, etc. - Juvenile literature.
I. Title.

808.042

This publication is also available on CD-ROM.

For worldwide distribution details of
this book see the Era Publications website:
www.erapublications.com

15 14 13 12 11 10 9 8 7 6 5 4 3 2 (2002)

Contents

Foreword

Writers and editors do not need to remember all the words and rules in their language. They could not – it would be too difficult. Instead, they use references to help them solve problems in writing.

The main references that writers and editors use are:
- the **dictionary** for information about word meanings, spelling, pronunciation and parts of speech;
- the **thesaurus** for information about vocabulary – synonyms and antonyms;
- the **style guide** for information about punctuation, capitals, word usage, grammar, type, symbols, text structure and other details about writing.

This book is a style guide. It explains and gives examples of the English language in use, and techniques for writing.

A style guide is a reference work, not a grammar textbook. You do not need to learn all the information in it. Use it to look up information whenever you need help in writing. It has ideas on planning and organising different types of writing.

This book has a section on word histories – interesting stories about where words came from. Sometimes these stories help us to understand the meanings of words, or why they are spelt the way they are.

Various English references differ in their opinions about the English language and its 'rules' for writing. If you have a view that differs from the content in this reference, your written comments or questions are welcome. If you find that something you want to know is not included in this guide, please contact the author. Email, fax and post details are on the publisher's web site below.

Use your style guide often and you will soon find that it makes writing easier and more interesting. It will give answers to many problems you meet.

Rodney Martin MBA, B Ed, Adv Dip T
www.erapublications.com

How to use this style guide

Headwords
Information in the guide is written under headings called 'headwords'. These headwords are listed in alphabetical order. To find information on a topic, look for that topic as a headword.

A headword does not begin with a capital letter unless it is a proper noun – the name of a particular person or thing.

Subheadings
Many headwords have subheadings. The subheadings are listed after the introduction to a topic. They help you to go straight to the details you want within a topic. The following example has a small list of subheadings. Subheadings begin with a capital letter and are a smaller type size than headwords.

participles

Participles are forms of verbs. Verbs have two *participles* – a present participle and a past participle. They are described under the following headings:
> **Present participles**
> **Past participles**

Present participles
Present participles end with the letters *–ing*
> jumping, laughing, diving, running, hiding, giving, having,writing

Past participles
The past participles of many verbs end with the letters *–ed*.
> jumped, dived, laughed

Entry
A headword and all of the information under that headword is called an 'entry'. Here is an example of an entry. The labels explain each part.

Headword	Definition	Example	Explanation
This is the topic you search.	Explains the headword.	Shows the topic used in a sentence. The examples sometimes come from books.	Gives further information about the example.

active voice

In grammar, the word *voice* is used for two forms of verbs – *active* and *passive* . Writing that is in the active voice has active verbs.

You **ruined** my painting!

In this example, the verb *ruined* is an active verb. The subject *You* does the action *ruined*. Therefore this sentence is in the active voice.

See also **active verbs; passive verbs; passive voice; verbs: Active and passive verbs.**

Writing tip

Why writers use active voice

The active voice makes your writing sound more exciting because it keeps a story moving along.

Readers identify with the characters in stories. If the hero feels strong, then the audience feels safe. If the hero feels scared, then the audience can also feel scared.

If the verbs linked to the characters are in the active voice, then the characters seem to be stronger or more interesting. In the passive voice, things happen *to* the characters, so the characters seem to be less powerful.

A writer can alter how you feel by using either active or passive voice.

Cross-reference	Boxes
Shows where you can get more information.	Give interesting extra information on a topic. The headings might be: *Writing tip* *Amazing but true*! *Hint* or *Did you know?*

Examples

Examples in each entry show how a topic is used in a text. The word(s) or mark(s) explained are printed in bold type.

knew / new

When the rope broke, I **knew** that I would need help.

The examples are often sentences and paragraphs quoted from children's literature. If so, then the name of the book or author is listed at the end of the example.

> Twinkle, twinkle little bat,
> How I wonder what you're at!
> Up above the world you fly,
> Like a tea tray in the sky.

Lewis Carroll

A complete list of books and their authors and illustrators is given in Appendix 2.

An example is sometimes a complete sample of writing. Writing samples usually have a dot point list before or after. The dot points explain the organisation, grammar and word usage in that writing sample.

Cross-references

Cross-references are notes that show you other places to look within the Guide to find information.

For example, to make sure that you are able to find information on words such as *knew / new*, the guide lists both words as headwords. The information on *knew* and *new* will be under the headword **knew / new** because *knew* comes first in the alphabet. The headword **new** will also have a cross-reference sending you to **knew / new**. So, no matter whether you search for *knew* or *new*, you will find the information.

---

knew /new

Knew is the past tense of the verb *to know* .

When the rope broke, I **knew** that I would need help.

New is an adjective. It means 'young, fresh, recent, not old'.

I found it difficult to make friends at the **new** school.
The **new**-born giraffe was wobbly on its legs.
The grocer put the **new** apples on display.
Her **new** shoes were very shiny.

See also **adjectives; verbs:Tenses (time)**.

---

new

See **knew / new** .

Cross-references are also given whenever further examples or information on a word or topic might be helpful. Cross-references show the headword in bold type.

See also **adjectives.**

Cross references sometimes lead you to subheadings under a headword. This is shown by the headword followed by a colon, then the subheading.

See **verbs: Tenses (time)**

Tenses (time) is a subheading under the headword **verbs**.

When more than one headword is listed in a cross-reference, then they are separated by a semicolon. In the example **knew / new**, there are cross-references for information on the special words *adjective* and *past tense*. These words were used in the explanation for *knew / new*. They are listed in the cross-reference at the end of the entry.

See also **adjectives; verbs: Tenses (time)**

This means that you can find out about the words *adjective* or *past tense* under those headwords and subheadings if you need to.

Cross-references sometimes show a headword and more than one subheading. When this happens, the headword and a colon are followed by subheadings separated by commas.

See **verbs: Finite and non-finite verbs, Regular and irregular verbs, Simple and compound verbs.**

Pronunciations

Letters or words bracketed by slashes or obliques / / show pronunciations or sounds.

Loose is an adjective. It means 'not tight'. It is pronounced /loos/ to rhyme with *juice* .

a / an

A and *an* are called *indefinite articles*. The following topics explain how to use these words.

> **Use with consonant sounds**
> **Use with vowel sounds**
> **Use with words beginning with the letter *h***

Use with consonant sounds

A is used before words that begin with a consonant sound.

> **a** word
> **a** dark cloud
> **a** history book
> **a** once-only offer
> **a** university student

In these examples, the words *word*, *dark*, *history*, *once* and *university* all begin with consonant sounds.

Use with vowel sounds

An is used before words that begin with a vowel sound. In English, it is difficult to say two vowel sounds alongside each other, such as, *a orange*, *a empty*. It is easier to say:

> **an** orange
> **an** empty box
> **an** hour

Use with words beginning with the letter *h*

Many years ago it was common for English speakers to drop the *h* sound in words beginning with that letter. For example, *history* was pronounced /*istory*/. A few words beginning with *h*, such as *herb* and *hotel*, came from French, where the beginning letter *h* is not pronounced.

When the *h* sound was not pronounced, people used *an* before such words.

> **an** 'istorical (historical) fact
> **an** 'erb (herb)
> **an** 'otel (hotel)

Today, people often pronounce the *h* in these words. So it makes sense to use the word *a* before them.

> **a** historical fact
> **a** herb
> **a** hotel

Some people still prefer the old custom of using *an* before words beginning with *h*, but this is a personal choice and not a matter of being 'correct'.

abbreviations

As a rule, if you pronounce the letter *h*, then use *a* before it — if you don't, then use *an*.

See also **articles**; **consonants**; **determiners**; **silent letters**; **vowels**; WORD HISTORIES: **herb**, **hotel**.

Hint

a / an

The beginning *sound* of a word tells you whether to use *a* or *an* — not the beginning *letter*.

Although the letter *h* is a consonant, it is silent in the beginning of some words (*hour, honest, honour*). These words begin with a vowel sound. So the word *an* is used before them.

> **An** hour had passed.

The word *once* begins with a vowel letter *o*, but has a consonant sound /w/. So the word *a* is used before it.

> This was **a** once only chance.

See also **consonants**; **vowels**.

---

abbreviations

Abbreviations are shortened forms of words. There are several kinds of abbreviations. They include *acronyms*, *clipped words*, *contractions, initials* and *Latin abbreviations*. Writers use them to give more information in less space.

> *Dr, eg, PS* and *pram* are all abbreviations.

See also **acronyms**; **apostrophe (')**; **clipped words**; **contractions**; **Latin abbreviations**; **shortened words**.

See under the following topics for further information about abbreviations:
When to use
Capitals
Full stops
Correspondence
Number(s)
No (Number)
Millions
Ordinals
Titles of people

When to use

Abbreviations are used mostly in titles, addresses, business names, tables, charts, maps, directories, business and nonfiction writing, footnotes and bibliographies. They are used much less in stories.

Most writers do not begin a sentence with an abbreviation unless it is an acronym in capitals or the title of a person.

> **UNICEF** gives emergency help for children in disaster areas.
>
> **Mr** and **Mrs** Plunket worked for a first aid organisation.

Writers use abbreviations only when they are sure the reader will understand them. Some abbreviations (for example *Mr, Mrs* and *Dr*) are so well-known that they are used in any writing.

Writers use abbreviations in reference texts. Abbreviations make it possible for the author to put a lot of information in a smaller space.

> **fever** A body temperature higher than the normal $37.2°$**C**/98.4°**F**. Can be caused by illness, **e.g.** infections

A children's medical encyclopedia, p. 12

In this example from a reference book, the author uses *C* for 'Celsius', *F* for 'Fahrenheit', ° for 'degrees' and *e.g.* for 'for example'.

Writers need to explain uncommon or special abbreviations.

> Animal-rescue workers from the Royal Society for the Prevention of Cruelty to Animals (**R.S.P.C.A.**) checked the animals on the film set.

In this example, the writer writes the full form of the abbreviation *R.S.P.C.A.* then places it in brackets. The writer can then use the letters *R.S.P.C.A.* again and readers will understand what it means. The abbreviation *R.S.P.C.A.* is also called an *acronym*.

See also **acronyms**; **bibliography**; **correspondence**.

Capitals

If an abbreviation is used together with a proper noun, for example a person's name, a business name or an address, then it should begin with a capital letter.

*   Captain Bilgewater (**Capt** Bilgewater)
*   Cracker Company (Cracker **Co**)
*   7 Silver Crescent (7 Silver **Cr**)

Some words that do not have capitals as full words, do have them when they are an abbreviation.

*   P.S. is a shortened form of the word *postscript.*
    > **P.S.** I'll be calling on you later in the month.

- TV is a shortened form of the word *television*.
  I shouldn't watch **TV** all the time.

See also **clipped words**; **Latin abbreviations**; **nouns**: **Proper nouns**.

Full stops
Some writers use a full stop at the end of each part of an abbreviation.
  Dr. Roberts works for the **R.S.P.C.A.**
Some writers prefer to write abbreviations without full stops.
  Dr Roberts works for the **RSPCA**.
The modern trend is to use full stops in abbreviations less often.

Correspondence
Abbreviations are used in many parts of correspondence, including addresses, dates, greetings, the main body of the letter and the signature.
The following abbreviations are commonly used in correspondence:
- am (ante meridiem — before midday)
- & (and)
- Apr (April)
- Apt (Apartment)
- Assoc (Associates; association)
- Assocn (Association)
- Attn (Attention)
- Aug (August)
- Ave or Av (Avenue)
- Bldg (Building)
- Blvd (Boulevard)
- Bros (Brothers)
- Cc (copied to, copies)
- Cnr (Corner)
- Cntr (Centre)
- Co or Coy (Company)
- Corp (Corporation)
- c/o or c/- (care of)
- Cres or Cr (Crescent)
- Crk or Ck (Creek)
- Crt (Court)
- Ct (Circuit)
- Dec (December)
- Dr (Drive)
- eg (exempli gratia — *for example*)
- encl (enclosure)
- et al (et alii — Latin for *and others*)
- etc (et cetera — *and so on*)

abbreviations

- Feb (February)
- Fl (Floor)
- Fri (Friday)
- Gdns (Gardens)
- Hwy (Highway)
- ie (id est — *that is*)
- Inc (Incorporated)
- Jan (January)
- L (Lake)
- Ln (Lane)
- Ltd (Limited)
- Mar (March)
- Mon (Monday)
- Mt (Mount)
- NB (Nota bene — Latin for *note well*)
- No (Numero — *number*)
- Nov (November)
- Oct (October)
- Pk (Park)
- pm (post meridiem — *after midday*)
- PO (Post Office)
- POA (price on application)
- POB (Post Office Box)
- PPS (Post Postscript)
- PS (Postcriptum — *postscript*)
- Pty (Proprietary)
- Pte (Private — *army rank*)
- Pte (Private (Singapore) — *company*)
- R (River)
- Rd (Road)
- RSVP (please reply)
- Sat (Saturday)
- Sept (September)
- Squ or Sq (Square)
- St (Saint)
- Sun (Sunday)
- Tce (Terrace)
- Thurs (Thursday)
- Tues (Tuesday)
- Viz (Videlicet — *namely*)
- Wed (Wednesday)

See also WORD HISTORIES: **am**, **ampersand (&)**, **Cc**, **eg**, **etc**, **ie**, **pm**, **PS**, **RSVP**, **viz**.

Number(s)

No (Number)

No is an abbreviation of the Italian word *numero*, which means 'number'. In writing, it should always be followed by a numeral so it is not confused with the word *no*.

>Meet me at **no 2** Sycamore Street.

The plural of the abbreviation *no* is *nos*.

>Serial **nos 15–23** were needed to complete the card collection.

The abbreviation *no* is used in memos, personal writing, notes, tables, captions, addresses and references. It is not often used in formal writing.

Sometimes a full stop should be used with the abbreviation *no*, especially where it might be confused with the negative word *no*.

>**No** one answer is correct.
>**No.** 1 answer is correct.

Millions

The letter *m* is an abbreviation of the word *million*(s) in amounts of money.

>$5**m**
>US$2.4**m**
>£3**m**

Ordinals

Ordinals are words that show the position of something in a sequence.

>Their team came **first** in the race.
>He was seated **second** from the left.
>On the **tenth** day they reached home.

Ordinals can be abbreviated by writing them as numerals.

>**1st**, **2nd**, **3rd**, **4th**

>**1st** degree burn: reddening of skin. **2nd** degree burn: blistering of skin. **3rd** degree burn: damage to skin and flesh.
>
>*A children's medical encyclopedia, p. 21*

This example is from an encyclopedia. The author used the abbreviations *1st*, *2nd* and *3rd* to save space. Reference texts often have abbreviations for this reason.

Ordinals are sometimes abbreviated when used in lists or headings.

>**1st** prize: a trip to London.
>**2nd** prize: a digital camera.
>**3rd** prize: a box of chocolates.

Ordinals up to the word *ninety-ninth* are usually not abbreviated within a text.
> This was the **first** time Jenny had met her aunt, even though it was her **fourth** visit to Greystones.

Writing tip

When to use ordinals

Writers often use ordinals in explanations. This is because explanations describe how or why something happens. The writer needs to say what happens first, then what steps happen after that, right up to the last step. Ordinal words are not usually abbreviated in explanation texts. (See also **explanation**.)

The writing process

First, the writer needs to think about the audience and the purpose of the writing. The **second** step is to decide the topic of the writing. Then the writer does the pre-writing activities, including research and planning.

Titles of people
Titles of people are words such as *Capt*, *Dr*, *Mr*, *Mrs* and *Prof*. A title is abbreviated when it is used with a person's name (a proper noun).
> A large number of people gathered to honour **Dr** Laverton.

If a title word is a common noun, then it is not abbreviated.
> I made a telephone call to the **doctor**.

Here is a list of abbreviated titles:
- Capt (Captain)
- Col (Colonel)
- Dr (Doctor)
- Hon (Honourable)

This title is used for politicians who have been elected to government. The word *the* is usually written before it and it may be followed by *MP*.
> The **Hon** Janet Masters, MP

- Messrs (Messieurs — a French word which is the plural of *Mister*)
- Mme (Madame)
- Prof (Professor)
- Rev (Reverend)
- Sr (Sister)
- St (Saint)
- MP (Member of Parliament)
- Mr (Mister)
- Mrs (Mistress)

Although *Mrs* is an abbreviation of the word *mistress*, it is pronounced /missus/.
• Ms
This word is not really an abbreviation, but a blend of the words *Miss* and *Mrs*. *Ms* is pronounced /muhz/.

See also **contractions**; **nouns**: **Common nouns**, **Proper nouns**, WORD HISTORIES: **Messrs (plural form of Mr)**, **Miss**, **Mr**, **Mrs**, **Ms**.

absolute adjectives

See **adjectives**: **Absolute adjectives**.

abstract

An abstract is a kind of summary, often only one or two paragraphs long. It usually summarises the main points of a lecture, a study or a research report. The following text is an example:

The Penicillin Puzzle
The question Who discovered and developed penicillin? is not easy to answer. Newspapers, books, journals, diaries, interviews and even the personal notes of scientists who worked on penicillin, all provide information. Different sources provide different points of view about the answer to any question. The book *The Penicillin Puzzle* discusses the question Who discovered and developed penicillin? It reports on the people and events that were involved, and who was given the credit and recognition.

In England, Fleming is the person most commonly associated with the history of penicillin. In Australia, Florey is more often recognised. Fleming, Florey and Chain were recognised with the Nobel Prize. But other important contributors are rarely remembered. To understand what has happened in the past, people need to ask questions and seek answers from different sources. In the end, they must decide for themselves.

The penicillin puzzle (abstract)

Notes about the abstract:
* In the first paragraph, the author introduces the topic and the content of the book.
* In the second paragraph, the author briefly mentions some key points from the main part of the book and summarises its conclusion.

abstract nouns

Abstract nouns are the names of ideas — things we can think about, feel or imagine, but not touch.

These words are abstract nouns:
>anger, beauty, laziness, doubt, eagerness, friendship, greed, loneliness, victory, defeat, generosity

For more information see **nouns**: **Abstract nouns**.

accept / except / expect

Accept is a verb. It means 'to take what someone gives you' or 'to be satisfied with a situation'.
>There are arguments for nuclear power but many people do not **accept** that it is neccesary.

Except is a preposition. It means 'not including' or 'apart from'.
>Everyone (**except** me, that is) followed the new fashion.

Further examples:
>All the dogs at the show behaved well **except** mine.
>The day was great **except** for the rain that sent everyone running.

Expect is a verb. It means 'to think that something is likely to happen'.
>The astronauts **expected** the journey to the moon and back to take eight days.

Further examples:
>Do you **expect** me to wait on you?
>I didn't **expect** him to be.

See also **prepositions**; **verbs**.

access / excess

Access can be used as:

- a noun meaning 'a way of entering a place'
   The ramp gave people in wheelchairs **access** to the building.

- a verb meaning 'to reach or get'
   The person in a wheelchair used the ramp to **access** the building.

Excess can be used as:
- a noun meaning 'too much'
   The clothes that would not fit in the suitcase, were **excess**.

- an adjective meaning 'beyond what is needed' or 'more than is allowed'
   The passenger with the very heavy suitcase had to pay for **excess** baggage.

See also **adjectives**; **nouns**; **verbs**.

accessary / accessory

Accessary is used only when referring to people. It means 'someone who knowingly helps someone to do something'.

A person who helps someone to commit a crime is called an **accessary** to the crime.

Accessory is used only when referring to things. It means 'something that accompanies something else, but is not essential'.

A handbag, a belt or a scarf is an **accessory** to someone's clothing.

acronyms

Acronyms are words made by joining the first letters of a group of words.

The acronym *NASA* was made from the first letters of the words *National Aeronautics and Space Administration*. Some other acronyms are:
- scientific words and inventions
   CD-ROM (Compact Disk Read Only Memory)
   scuba (self-contained underwater breathing apparatus)
   laser (light amplification by stimulated emission of radiation)

- places and organisations
   UK (United Kingdom)
   NZ (New Zealand)
   WHO (World Health Organisation)
   ASEAN (Association of South East Asian Nations)

- computer industry words
    PC (Personal Computer)
    LAN (Local Area Network)

It is possible to pronounce some acronyms as words:
    Qantas (Queensland and Northern Territory Aerial Services)
    Anzac (Australian and New Zealand Army Corps)
    Shatec (Singapore Hotel and Tourism Education Centre)

Other acronyms, however, are spoken as individual letters:
    CD (Compact Disk)
    DVD (Digital Versatile Disk)
    TV (television)

See also **abbreviations**.

Information on how to use acronyms is under the following headings:
    When to use
    Capitals
    Plurals
    List of acronyms

When to use
Acronyms like *sonar, laser, scuba, CD, CD-ROM* and *OK* are used in any writing. They don't need to be explained because most people know what they mean.

Technical or unfamiliar acronyms should always be explained when they are first used. Writers usually do this by first using the full words, then they write the acronym in brackets. After this, the acronym is used rather than the full words.

Smith & Co have improved their computer systems by installing a **Local Area Network (LAN)**. Mr Smith said the **LAN** will improve the company's efficiency.

Dr Foster worked for the **World Health Organisation (WHO)** for ten years. Her first job with the **WHO** was in Africa.

Acronyms for places or organisations, such as ACT, UK, US and WHO, are mostly used in addresses, labels, charts, maps and nonfiction writing.

Mr Tom Sheridan
33 East Ave
Canberra **ACT**

Writing tip

Using acronyms

Acronyms can be useful for simplifying your writing. They allow you to use fewer words to say something. However, take care not to use too many acronyms or your readers may not understand what you are saying. It can make your writing sound as though you are using jargon. It annoys readers who do not already know the meanings of the acronyms you are using.

See also **jargon**.

Capitals

Acronyms for places and organisations are usually written in capitals without full stops.

> **UK** (United Kingdom)
> **USA** (United States of America)
> **UNICEF** (United Nations International Children's Emergency Fund)
> **WHO** (World Health Organisation)
> **MITA** (Ministry of Information and the Arts)

However, some writers do use full stops in acronyms for countries.

> She really wanted to visit a special museum in Washington D.C., **U.S.A**.

Some acronyms that were originally written in capitals, for example ANZAC, are used so much that they become ordinary words. When this happens, only the first letter of the acronym has a capital.

> **Anzac** (Australian and New Zealand Army Corps)

Acronyms are sometimes written in lower case, especially the names of inventions or scientific words.

> **radar** (radio detection and ranging)

Some acronyms are clever words created for fun to describe people or situations. They are usually written in lower case.

> **dinky** (double income no kids yet)
> **snag** (sensitive new-age guy)

Plurals

Acronyms in capitals have the letter *s* (lower case) added to form the plural.

> The manufacture of foam cups creates **CFCs** that attack the ozone layer.
> They played **CDs** at the party.
> The **VIPs** arrived in a limousine.

List of acronyms
- ACT (Australian Capital Territory)
- aka (also known as)
- AIDS (Acquired Immune Deficiency Syndrome)
- Anzac (Australian and New Zealand Army Corps)
- asap (as soon as possible)
- AWOL (absent without leave)
- CB (citizens' band — radio)
- CD (compact disk)
- CD-ROM (Compact Disk Read Only Memory)
- COD (cash on delivery)
- dinky (double income no kids yet)
- HQ (headquarters)
- IQ (intelligence quotient)
- JP (Justice of the Peace)
- laser (light amplification by stimulated emission of radiation)
- midi (musical instrument digital interface)
- NSW (New South Wales)
- NT (Northern Territory)
- NY (New York)
- NZ (New Zealand)
- OK (Old Kinderhook)
- PC (personal computer)
- posh (portside out starboard home)
- Qantas (Queensland and Northern Territory Aerial Services)
- quasar (quasi-stellar)
- radar (radio detection and ranging)
- R&R (rest and recreation)
- RSPCA (Royal Society for the Prevention of Cruelty to Animals)
- SA (South Australia)
- scuba (self-contained underwater breathing apparatus)
- sonar (sound navigation and ranging)
- TV (television)
- UK (United Kingdom)
- UN (United Nations)
- USA (United States of America)
- VIP (very important person)
- WA (Western Australia)
- WHO (World Health Organisation)
- WWW (World Wide Web)
- WW1 (World War 1)
- WW2 (World War 2)

See also WORD HISTORIES: **OK**, **posh**, **television**.

active verbs

A verb is active when the subject of the sentence does the action.

> The whale **dived**.

The whale is the subject of the sentence here. The whale did the diving, so *dived* is an active verb.

> The sea **had begun** to freeze around the ship.

The sea is the subject of this sentence. The sea is doing the action. So *had begun* is an active verb.

> Some fungi **glow** in brilliant colours at night.

Some fungi is the subject of this sentence and it is doing the action of the verb *glow*. So *glow* is an active verb.

> Ahmed **was** on his bike.

In this example, the verb is *was*. It is a form of the verb *to be* (*am, are, is, was, were, will be, will have been*). *Ahmed* is the subject of the sentence, and *Ahmed* was doing the action of *being*. So *was* in this sentence is an active verb.

See also **passive verbs**; **verbs**: **Active and passive verbs**.

active voice

In grammar, the word *voice* is used for two forms of verbs — *active* and *passive*. Writing that is in the active voice has active verbs.

> You **ruined** my painting!

In this example, the verb *ruined* is an active verb. The subject *You* does the action *ruined*. Therefore this sentence is in the active voice.

See also **active verbs**; **passive verbs**; **passive voice**; **verbs**: **Active and passive verbs**.

Why writers use active voice

The active voice makes your writing sound more exciting because it keeps a story moving along.

Readers identify with the characters in stories. If the hero feels strong, then the audience feels safe. If the hero feels scared, then the audience can also feel scared.

If the verbs linked to the characters are in the active voice, then the characters seem to be stronger or more interesting. In the passive voice, things happen *to* the characters, so the characters seem to be less powerful.

A writer can alter how you feel by using either active or passive voice.

addresses

A mailing or delivery address usually includes:
- the title and name of the person
- the name of the business (if appropriate)
- street number and name (or post office box number)
- suburb
- town or city
- state, province, shire or region
- post code
- country (if international)

Abbreviations are used in addresses to save space. Capitals are also used in addresses because most of the words are proper nouns.

The use of abbreviations and capitals in addresses is explained under the following headings:
Abbreviations in addresses
Business names
Job titles
Care of (c/o or c/-)
And others (et al)
Ampersand (&) and hash (#)
Capitals in addresses
Business letters
Personal letters

addresses

Abbreviations in addresses

Addresses are usually shortened to fit into a small space on an envelope, a label, a letter, or in a list or directory (eg telephone or business directory). The words that are often shortened are titles, post offices, streets, regions, provinces, states, and shires, counties and sometimes countries.

> **Mr** Sherman Hayes
> Wonderbike **Co Pty Ltd**
> **PO** Box 916
> WOOLASTON **NSW**
> AUSTRALIA 2025

> **Ms** P Adams
> Elm Rd
> Andover **HANTS** SP11 9HY
> **UK**

Business names

Words that describe a company are often shortened. Common abbreviations in business names are:

- & (and)
- Assoc (Associates or Association)
- Bros (Brothers)
- Co (Company)
- Corp (Corporation)
- Inc (Incorporated)
- Ltd (Limited)
- Pte (Private) (Singapore)
- Pty (Proprietary)

For example:

> Smith **Bros Inc**
> Smith **&** Black **Pty Ltd**
> Smith **& Assoc Ltd**

Job titles

Job titles are often abbreviated in addresses. For example, *Chief Executive Officer* is shortened to *CEO*.

> Ms T G Penny, **CEO**

Further examples:

- Exec (Executive)
- GM (General Manager)
- Jr or Jnr (Junior)
- MD (Managing Director)
- Mgr (Manager)
- PA (Personal Assistant)

- Pres (President)
- Sec (Secretary)
- Sr or Snr (Senior)
- VP (Vice President)

Care of (c/o or c/-)

Letters or parcels can be addressed to a person 'care of' another person, organisation or business. The words *care of* are abbreviated to *c/o* or *c/-*.

Ms Diane Sharp
c/o Helping Hand Society
15 Beach St
OCEAN VIEW QLD 4521
AUSTRALIA

And others (et al)

When a letter is addressed to more than two people, the Latin abbreviation *et al* can be used.

Messrs R & B Smith **et al**
Smith Bros Inc
PO Box 64
NEW YORK NY 200649
USA

Ampersand (&) and hash (#)

The *ampersand* (&) can replace the word *and* in addresses. The *hash* (#) symbol can replace the words *suite, unit, level* or *floor* in addresses.

Drs M **&** S Ridzak
#6, 415 Glenorchy Blvd
NEW YORK NY 10602
USA

See also **ampersand (&)**; **Latin abbreviations**; WORD HISTORIES: **ampersand (&)**.

Capitals in addresses

Business letters

Because business letters are often sent in window envelopes, the address on the letter becomes the address on the envelope. In these letters, businesses often prefer not to use full capitals for the address, because it looks out of balance with the type in the rest of the letter inside the envelope.

Mr S Hayes
Wonderbike Co Pty Ltd
PO Box 916
Woolaston NSW 2067

Post offices do prefer addresses written in full capitals to make it easier for postal sorting machines and workers to read them.

> WONDERBIKE CO PTY LTD
> (ATTN MR S HAYES)
> PO BOX 916
> WOOLASTON NSW 2067

Personal letters
The title, names and street in personal letters often begin with a capital, while the suburb or city and the state are in full capitals.

> Mr Sam Sharrad
> 14 Shipster St
> BRADFIELD SA 5161

Post offices in most countries do prefer the whole address in personal letters written in full capitals for the same reason given above in *business letters*.

See also **capitals**.

adjectival clauses

Adjectival clauses are clauses that act like adjectives — they add meaning to nouns and pronouns.

> Police were chasing a man **who passed a bundle to a girl**.

The adjectival clause *who passed a bundle to a girl* describes the noun *man*.

> The bird had an incurable disease, **which stops new feathers from growing**.

The adjectival clause *which stops new feathers from growing* describes the noun *disease*.

See also **clauses**.

adjectival phrases

Adjectival phrases are phrases that act like adjectives — they add meaning to nouns and pronouns.

> He was the winner **of the cup**.

In this example, the adjectival phrase *of the cup* adds meaning to the noun *winner*.

Further examples:

> She gazed at the colours **of the sunset**.
> The searchlight picked out the planes **in the night sky**.

Authors sometimes use more than one adjectival phrase to add meaning to a noun.

They followed the yacht **with the red flag at the top of its mast**.

In this example, three adjectival phrases describe the noun *yacht* — *with the yellow flag* — *at the top* — *of its mast*.

See also **phrases**.

adjectives

Adjectives are words that add information to nouns or pronouns. They are important in writing because you can use them to add detail and make meanings clearer for the reader.

Adjectives describe the colour, size, number or any other aspect of a noun or pronoun.

He was a **tall, thin, proud young** man …

The adjectives *tall, thin, proud* and *young* describe the size, personality and age of the noun *man*. They give the reader a good idea of what the man looks like and how he behaves.

Further examples of adjectives:

The shark moved through the water like a **huge black** shadow.

Fungi grow in **damp, mild** places.

See also **nouns**; **pronouns**.

Further information about adjectives is under the following headings:

Adjectives before and after nouns

Attributive adjectives (before the noun)
Predicative adjectives (after the noun)

Adjectives of degree

Positive, comparative and superlative degree
Ways of making comparative and superlative degrees
Absolute adjectives

Compound adjectives
Verbal adjectives

Adjectives before and after nouns

Attributive adjectives (before the noun)

Attributive adjectives are placed before the nouns they describe.

Suddenly, from a bag, he pulled out his **smelly old** sneakers.

In this example, the adjectives *smelly* and *old* are placed before the noun *sneakers*.

The rain made a pattering sound on the **old iron** roof.

In this example, the adjectives *old* and *iron* are placed before the noun *roof*.

Predicative adjectives (after the noun)
Predicative adjectives are placed after the noun or pronoun they describe. They are also usually placed after the verb.

>The cub was **secure** and **warm** — resting in the den.

In this example, the adjectives *secure* and *warm* describe the noun *cub*.

>The predator was **helpless** now.

In this example, the adjective *helpless* is placed after the noun *predator*.

Some adjectives are always placed after the noun they describe. They are never used as attributive adjectives.

>The cupboard was **ajar**.
>They are **asleep**.
>All the passengers were **aboard**.

See also **predicate**; **pronouns**; **verbs**.

Adjectives of degree

Positive, comparative and superlative degree
There are three different forms of adjectives of degree — *positive degree, comparative degree* and *superlative degree*.

Adjectives in the *positive degree* describe things or people by themselves.

>He was a **tall, thin, gangly, irritable young** man …

The adjectives *tall*, *thin*, *gangly*, *irritable* and *young* are in the positive degree. They do not compare the man with anything.

Adjectives in the *comparative degree* compare two things.

>She bought a new pair of jeans a bit like yours only **darker**.

The adjective *darker* compares one character's jeans with another character's jeans.

Adjectives in the *superlative degree* compare more than two things.

>Lina wore the **most perfect** jacket I had ever seen.

In this example, the adjective *most perfect* is in the superlative degree. It tells how perfect Lina's jacket was compared with many other jackets. (Notice how the author has the character say *most perfect*. This shows that the character is emphasising a point, but it doesn't really make sense — see **absolute adjectives** to find out why.)

>The clown costume was voted the **craziest** idea at the party.

adjectives

In this example, the adjective *craziest* is in the superlative degree and tells how crazy the costume was compared with many other costumes.

Ways of making comparative and superlative degree
The suffixes -*er* and -*est* are used to make adjectives of degree. These suffixes are usually used with adjectives that have only one or two syllables.

Positive	Comparative	Superlative
old	older	oldest
wild	wilder	wildest
strong	stronger	strongest
short	shorter	shortest
hungry	hungrier	hungriest
narrow	narrower	narrowest
happy	happier	happiest
easy	easier	easiest
busy	busier	busiest

The words *more* and *most* can be used before some adjectives to make the comparative and superlative degrees. This usually happens when an adjective has more than two syllables.

Positive	Comparative	Superlative
beautiful	more beautiful	most beautiful
desperate	more desperate	most desperate
dangerous	more dangerous	most dangerous
wonderful	more wonderful	most wonderful
delicious	more delicious	most delicious
difficult	more difficult	most difficult

Some adjectives **change to different words** for the different degrees.

Positive	Comparative	Superlative
bad	worse	worst
good	better	best
many	more	most

Absolute adjectives

Absolute adjectives do not have a comparative or superlative degree. They cannot be used to make comparisons.

> The bird was **dead**.

The word *dead* is an absolute adjective. Something that is dead cannot be 'deader' or 'more dead' or 'deadest'.

Absolute adjectives are a common trap for writers. For example:

> It was the **most perfect** diamond they had seen.

Something is either *perfect* or it is not. Something cannot be *more* perfect than perfect.

Further examples of absolute adjectives:

> empty, full, infinite, eternal, everlasting, final
> first, second, third … last
> pure, unique, top (top player), bottom (bottom rung)
> square, horizontal, circular, complete, entire, total, whole, equal

See also **suffixes**.

Writing tip

Beware the double degrees!

A common mistake in speech and writing is to use two different forms of comparative or superlative with one adjective.

> The inland taipan is the **most deadliest** snake in the world.

In this example, the writer has used the word *most* as well as the suffix *-est*. The snake can be the *most deadly* or the *deadliest* — but not both!

> This game is **more easier** to play than that one.

The game can be *easier* to play but not *more easier* to play.

Compound adjectives

Compound adjectives have more than one part. These parts are joined by hyphens.

> **Forty-three new-born** babies were saved from the floods.

In this example, each adjective (*forty-three* and *new-born*) has two parts.

See also **hyphen (-)**.

Verbal adjectives

Verbal adjectives are participles (-*ing* words) used as adjectives.

They raced each other in their **roaring** cars.

In this example, the participle *roaring* describes the noun *cars*.

See also **participles**.

adjectives of degree

See **adjectives**: Adjectives of degree.

adverbial clauses

Adverbial clauses are clauses that act like adverbs — they tell *how, when, where* or *why* something happened.

They collided **where the two roadways joined**.

The clause *where the two roadways joined* tells where *they collided*.

When I was little, I became lost in the city.

The clause *When I was little* tells when *I became lost*.

You must be fit **so that you remain healthy.**

The clause *so that you remain healthy* tells why *you must be fit*.

See also **adverbs**; **clauses**.

adverbial phrases

Adverbial phrases are phrases that act like adverbs. They tell *when*, *where*, *how* or *why* things happen.

It wouldn't arrive **before noon**.

The phrase *before noon* adds meaning to the verb *wouldn't arrive*. It tells when *it wouldn't arrive*.

You can make a kit **with paper, wood and string**.

The phrase *with paper, wood and string* tells how something is *made*.

Further examples of adverbial phrases:

Four days after the launch, Apollo 11 entered lunar orbit.

In the distance stood a tall cathedral.

The mist formed **like a curtain**.

See also **adverbs**; **phrases**.

adverbs

Adverbs are words that give information about verbs, adjectives and other adverbs. They are useful in writing because they add meaning and interest. There are different types of adverbs.

See under the following headings for more information about adverbs.

Adverbs telling how, where and when
Adverbs of manner (how)
Adverbs of place (where)
Adverbs of time (when)
Adverbs of degree
Adverb modifiers
Negative adverbs
Making adverbs

Adverbs telling how, where and when

Adverbs of manner (how)
Adverbs of manner tell *how* something happens.
Officials **quickly** called for the emergency services.
In this example, the adverb *quickly* tells *how* the officials called.

Further examples of adverbs of manner:
happily, well, hopefully, amusingly, sneakily

Adverbs of place (where)
Adverbs of place tell *where* something happens.
He chased all the stray dogs **away**.
In this example, the adverb *away* tells *where* he chased all the stray dogs.

Further examples of adverbs of place:
here, there, everywhere, outside

Adverbs of time (when)
Adverbs of time tell *when* something happens.
I'll tell them **tomorrow** that the trip has been cancelled.
In this example, the adverb *tomorrow* tells *when* they will be told.
Further examples of adverbs of time:
ever, often, usually, soon, today, yesterday, now, later, immediately

See also **explanation**; **ordinals**.

adverbs

Adverbs of degree

Like adjectives, adverbs have three degrees of comparison — *positive, comparative* and *superlative*.

The comparative and superlative degrees are often made by adding the suffixes -*er* and -*est*, or the words *more* and *most*, to the adverb.

Positive	Comparative	Superlative
soon	sooner	soonest
productively	more productively	most productively
happily	more happily	most happily
eagerly	more eagerly	most eagerly
often	more often	most often

Some adverbs, however, change to different words for the different degrees.

Positive	Comparative	Superlative
well	better	best
badly	worse	worst
much	more	most

Adverbs in the *comparative degree* compare two things.

My dog barks **louder** than yours.

In this example, the adverb *louder* is in the comparative degree and tells how one person's dog barks louder than another person's dog.

Adverbs in the *superlative degree* compare more than two things.

Of all the dogs in town, my dog barks **loudest**.

In this example, the adverb *loudest* is in the superlative degree and tells how my dog barks compared with other dogs in general.

See also **suffixes**.

Adverb modifiers

Some adverbs are modifiers — they affect the meaning of adjectives or other adverbs.

The roses were **quite** nice.

In this example, the adverb *quite* weakens the meaning of the adjective *nice*.

They sang **quite** loudly.

In this example, the word *quite* weakens the meaning of the adverb *loudly*.

Other examples of adverb modifiers:
>rather, almost, only, just, slightly

See also **intensifiers**; **modifiers**.

Negative adverbs

The word *not* is a negative adverb.
>We did **not** finish the job.

The adverb *not* is often joined with a verb to make a contraction *didn't* (did + not = didn't).
>We **didn't** finish the job.

See also **contractions**.

Making adverbs

Adding the suffix *-ly* to a word often changes that word to an adverb.
>Slow (adjective) + -ly = **slowly** (adverb)

Further examples:
>fortunately, purposely, really, actually, angrily, hopefully

Did you know?

Three interesting facts about adverbs

1. Not all adverbs end with the suffix *-ly*, as the following examples show.

>soon, later, never, yesterday, today, tomorrow, now

2. The letters *ly* on the end of a word are not always the suffix *-ly*. In the following sentence, the word *silly* is an adjective.

>That was a **silly** decision.

3. Often, the same word can be an adverb, an adjective or a noun. It depends on how the word is used. Note the different uses of the word *yesterday* in these sentences.

>There will never be another **yesterday**. (*noun*)

>These **yesterday** cakes cost less than the fresh ones. (*adjective*)

>The package arrived **yesterday**. (*adverb*)

See also **adjectives**; **adverbs**; **nouns**; **suffixes**.

advertisement
See **argument**: **Advertisements**.

advice / advise
Advice is a noun. It means 'helpful, useful information'.
> The expert gave them some **advice** about their garden.

Advise is a verb. It means 'to give someone useful information'.
> The expert **advised** them about their garden.

See also **nouns**; **verbs**.

affect / effect
Affect is mainly used as a verb. It means 'to cause a change'.
> Rubella can **affect** unborn babies.

Further examples:
> How did the war **affect** what happened?
> If they spray poisons by air, it could **affect** people's health.

Effect is usually used as a noun. It means 'a result or an outcome'.
> The fire had a terrible **effect** on the forest.

Further examples:
> The scientists tested the medicine's **effect** on animals.
> CFCs have a harmful **effect** on the ozone layer.

See also **nouns**; **verbs**.

affixes
Affixes are word parts. They are used to change the meaning of root words and how they are used. There are two kinds of affix in English — *prefixes* and *suffixes*.

Prefixes are joined to the beginning of a word. Suffixes are joined to the end of a word.

Unhealthily is an example of a word with several affixes.
* *heal* is the root word. It is a **verb**.
* *-th* is a suffix. It changes the verb *heal* to a **noun** — *health*.
* *-y* is a suffix. It changes the noun *health* to an **adjective** — *healthy*.
* *-ly* is a suffix. It changes the adjective *healthy* to an **adverb** — *healthily*.
* *un-* is a prefix that means 'not'. It changes the meaning of the word *healthily* to a **negative adverb** — *not healthy*.

See also **adjectives**; **adverbs**; **negatives**; **nouns**; **prefixes**; **suffixes**; **verbs**.

ago / before

Ago is an adverb of time. It means 'in the past'.

> He had a scar on his arm where he had burned it years **ago**.

Before is used as:

* a conjunction that joins phrases in a sentence, meaning 'earlier than'
  > It was good enough when I was a boy — **before** all this new-fangled technology came along.

* a preposition that begins a phrase, meaning 'in front of' or 'ahead of'
  > **Before** the procession, she made her way up the hill.
  > The criminal stood **before** the judge.
  > The team played **before** a record crowd.

* an adverb of time, meaning 'at an earlier time'
  > They had been there **before**.
  > He had not won the prize **before**.
  > She had tried **before**, but not this hard.

See also **adverbs: Adverbs of time (when); conjunctions; phrases; prepositions**.

Hint

Before

The word *before* can be used in front of or after the word *long* (or other words and phrases meaning a time).

Long **before** the time of books, people enjoyed telling tales.

Before long they entered the streets of London.

Long ago, **before** the time of books, people enjoyed telling tales.

Note in the last example, a writer would write *long ago* but not *ago long*.

---

ago / since

Ago is an adverb of time. It means 'in the past'.

> He had visited the same place years **ago**.

Since is a conjunction. It means 'from the time when'.

> It was a month **since** they had met.

In this example, the word *since* joins the two clauses *It was a month* and *they had met*.

Further example:
> Nothing had happened **since** the winter snow first came.

Since can be used as an adverb. It means 'from that time'.
> I lost my good pen, so I have used a pencil ever **since**.

In this example, the word *since* tells when *I have ever used a pencil*.

See also **adverbs**: **Adverbs of time (when)**; **conjunctions**.

Writing tip

Ago and *since* do not go together

It is a common error for writers to use the words *ago* and *since* together in a sentence.

> It was six weeks **ago since** the children had seen each other. (X)

There are two ways in which this sentence might be written correctly, by using either *ago* or *since* — but not both!

> It was six weeks **ago** that the children saw each other. (✓)

> It was six weeks **since** the children had seen each other (✓).

---

agreement

Agreement is a term used in grammar. It describes the link between the subject and verb of a sentence. For a sentence to make sense, the subject and verb must 'agree' with each other:

- in number (*singular or plural*)
- in person (*first person* — I am, *second person* — you are, *third person* — she/he is).

The following topics give more information about agreement:
> **Agreement in number**
> **Agreement in person**
> **Agreement and gender**
> **Agreement for collective nouns**

Agreement in number

To agree in number, a sentence with a singular subject must have a singular verb.
> **Tami was** late for school.

The subject of the sentence (*Tami*) is singular. It agrees with the verb (*was*), which is also singular.

agreement

A sentence with a plural subject must have a plural verb.

Tami and James were late for school.

In this example, the subject (*Tami and James*) is plural. It agrees with the verb (*were*), which is also plural.

We was late for the lesson. (X)

In this example, the pronoun *We* is plural, but the verb *was* is singular. So the subject (*We*) and the verb (*was*) do not agree in number.

We were late for the lesson. (✓)

This example has a plural pronoun (*We*) together with a plural verb (*were*), so they agree in number.

See also **mass nouns**; **plural**; **singular**; **singular words**; **subject**; **verbs**.

Hint

Rules on agreement *can* be disobeyed in dialogue

Authors sometimes disobey the *agreement in number* rule.

"Well, 'Ansy me luv, there's rules see."

Hannah, p. 28

In this example, the character is a market seller in old London. The verb *is* (*there's* = there is) and the subject *rules* do not agree. For agreement, it would need to be either:

there are rules (*plural*), or there is a rule (*singular*).

However, if the subject and verb did agree, the speech of the character would not sound right. The author wrote the way the character would actually speak.

See also **dialogue (US: dialog)**.

Agreement in person

The subject and verb in a sentence must also agree in person (*first, second* or *third* person). Agreement in person is very important between pronouns and the verb *to be*. There are different forms of the verb *to be* for each person.

agreement

Singular	Present	Past
First person — I	am	was
Second person — you	are	were
Third person — he, she, it	is	was
Plural		
First person — we	are	were
Second person — you	are	were
Third person — they	are	were

> **I am** hungry. (✓)
> **I are** hungry. (X)
> **I is** hungry. (X)

In these examples, the subject *I* (first person singular) is in agreement with the verb *am* (first person singular). *I* does not agree with the verb *are* (second person singular) in the second sentence. *I* does not agree with the verb *is* (third person singular) in the last sentence.

Further examples:

> **You are** hot in the sun. (✓)
> **You was** hot in the sun. (X)
> **You is** hot in the sun. (X)
> **You am** hot in the sun. (X)

In these examples *you are* agrees in person. *You was, You is* and *You am* do not agree in person.

See also **anyone**.

Agreement and gender

Often, in nonfiction writing, a writer needs to refer to a person, but doesn't especially mean a male or female person. For example:

> Anyone who wants to play tennis this weekend should write (**his** or **her**?) name on the list below. (**He** or **She**?) will be put into a team. The team captains will meet (**him** or **her**?) at the courts at noon.

The writer has the problem of deciding whether to say either *he/him/his* or *she/her* — or mention both by writing *he or she*. Here is another example:

> An oral history is a record of a person's memories of **his or her** life.

Writing *her or his* or *his or her* becomes clumsy when it needs to be repeated. It is becoming common for writers to use the plural *they* and *their* instead.

> Anyone who wants to play tennis this weekend should write **their** name on the list below. **They** will be put into a team. The team captains will meet **them** at the courts at noon.

31

The following example disobeys the old rule of agreement in number because it uses the plural pronoun *their* with the singular noun *a person*.

> An autobiography is a record of a person's memories of **their** life.

This use of *their* solves the clumsy use of *he/she*, because *their* can mean male or female. It treats males and females equally. However, because it does break an old rule, some people do not approve of this style. We will have to wait a little longer to discover whether it becomes common in English writing.

See also **gender**.

Agreement for collective nouns

A collective noun is a word that describes a group of people or things (eg *herd, class, crowd, team*).

A collective noun is usually treated as a singular word in writing. This means it needs a singular verb for agreement. In this example, the collective noun is *team*.

> The research **team was** ready to begin tests on humans.

When the subject of a sentence has a collective noun plus other parts, then the sentence always needs a plural verb.

> **Tom, Kari and the research team were** busy collecting data.

The subject of this sentence is *Tom, Kari and the research team*. So the plural verb *were* is used.

See also **nouns**: **Collective nouns**.

allegory

When authors use the characters and plot in a story to communicate a message about life, the story is called an *allegory*. Allegories can be written as poems or narratives. The message the author wishes to communicate is woven throughout the story.

In his book *Animal Farm*, George Orwell writes about animals on a farm, but the story really communicates a message about people in society. Fables are also a very simple type of allegory.

See also **fable**; **narrative**; **parable**; WORD HISTORIES: **allegory**.

alliteration

Alliteration is the repeated use of a beginning consonant sound in words in a sentence or phrase. Writers use alliteration to make their writing sound more interesting.

> He was a **lean, lanky, lithe little** man who **loved** to make speeches.

In this example, the author repeats the /l/ sound.

The **snake slipped** and **slithered** to the ground and **slid** under a rock.

In this example, the author makes an alliteration by repeating the /s/ sound (*snake, slipped, slithered, slid*) to build a 'snakey' image.

With just **one whack** of the **whip** he could turn the herd.

In this example, the author repeats the /w/ sound (*with, one, whack, whip*). Note that not all the words in this alliteration begin with the same letter (w). The word *one* begins with the letter *o* — but it has a /w/ sound. Alliteration is the repetition of *sounds*, not *letters*.

See also **adjectives**; **consonants**; **slogan**.

allot / a lot

Allot is a verb. It means 'to give out or to dispense'.

The leader had to **allot** jobs to the team members.

A lot is a noun phrase. It means 'many'. Note that it is written as two words.

The leader had **a lot** of jobs to do.

See also **noun phrases**; **verbs**.

all ready / already

All ready is a phrase. It means 'everything or everyone is prepared'.

The children jumped into bed, **all ready** for a story.

Already is an adverb. It means 'at this time' or 'before'.

We were **already** a day late with our homework.

Some children had done their homework **already**.

See also **adverbs**; **phrases**.

all right / alright

When *all right* means 'okay', it can be spelled *all right* or *alright*. Both are correct.

"Are you feeling **alright** Olivia?" Sasha whispered.

When I think of home, I know that everything's going to be **all right**.

When *all right* means 'all is correct', it is written as two words — *all right*.

They finished their test, and their answers were **all right**.

When the levels of the fence posts were **all right**, the farmer began to attach the wire.

alright is all right

Alright began its life as *all right*. People often make words shorter if they can, or reduce phrases to words. Many people once thought that *alright* was incorrect. As people become used to a word, they often accept it as a formal word. *Alright* and *all right* are both correct forms of the same meaning.

See also WORD HISTORIES: **goodbye**.

all together / altogether

All together is a phrase meaning 'everything or everyone is in one place or time'.

> They went to the beach **all together**.

The words *all* and *together* do not always go together — they can be separated in a sentence.

> They **all** went to the beach **together**.

Altogether is an adverb. It means 'entirely, on the whole, generally'.
> They were not **altogether** happy with the service.

See also **adverbs**; **phrases**.

all ways / always

All ways means 'every way' or 'each direction'.

> **All ways** out of the cave were blocked.
> The painter was a perfectionist — fussy in **all ways**.

Always is an adverb telling when something happens. It means 'at all times'.
> Rachel had **always** wanted to travel.
> The class **always** looked at the clock, waiting for a break.

See also **adverbs**.

aloud / allowed / loud

Aloud is an adverb. It means 'with noise' or 'noisily'.

> They read the book **aloud**.

In this example, the word *aloud* tells how *they read*.

Allowed is the past tense of the verb *to allow*. It means 'to permit or let'.
> We weren't **allowed** to feed the animals at the zoo.

Loud can be used as an adjective. It means 'noisy'.
> Jennifer Higginsbottom has a **loud** voice.

Loud can be used as an adverb. It is usually linked with the preposition *out*.
> Each morning the teacher read bits of the newspaper out **loud**.

See also **adjectives**; **adverbs**; **verbs**: **Tenses (time)**.

alternative spellings

Many English words have more than one acceptable spelling. When there is more than one spelling for a word, it is important to choose a spelling, and keep to it in that piece of writing.

Words like *colour* and *color* are different because of the difference between traditional English (UK) spelling and American (US) spelling. Other examples like this include:
> centre/center, realise/realize, travelling/traveling, labour/labor

In many parts of the world, eg Australia, Canada and New Zealand, both UK and US spelling is acceptable.

Words like *auntie* and *aunty* are different because the spelling of some words changes over many years. Some people keep the old spelling and others accept the new spelling. Other examples like this include:
> axe/ax, waggon/wagon, judgement/judgment,
> acknowledgement/acknowledgment,
> programme/program, tranquillity/tranquility

Many words had different spellings when the first dictionary writers recorded them. If each spelling was very popular, then the dictionary writer sometimes kept both forms of the word. *Leaped* and *leapt* are examples of this.

More detail on alternative spellings is given under the following headings:
> **-ed / -t (spelled, spelt)**
> **-eled / -elled (modeled, modelled)**
> **-er / -re (center, centre)**
> **-fs / -ves (hoofs, hooves)**
> **-log / -logue (dialog, dialogue)**
> **-ie / -y (auntie, aunty)**
> **-ise / -ize (organise, organize)**
> **-oes / -os (haloes, halos)**
> **OK / okay**
> **-or / -our (color, colour)**

alternative spellings

-ed / -t (spelled, spelt)

The past tense of some words can end with either -ed or -t. Leaped and leapt are examples of this. It is a matter of personal choice. Both are correct, but -ed is preferred in writing; -t is more common in speech.

Some examples are:

> burned/burnt, dreamed/dreamt, kneeled/knelt, leaped/leapt, learned/learnt, smelled/smelt, spelled/spelt, spilled/spilt, spoiled/spoilt

See also **verbs**: **Tenses (time)**.

-eled / -elled (modeled, modelled)

Many English words end with the letters -el (travel, model, level etc). When suffixes are added to these words, there are two ways they can be spelt.

In UK English, the letter l is doubled when adding suffixes.

> travelled, travelling, traveller

In US English, the letter l is not doubled when adding suffixes.

> traveled, traveling, traveler

-er / -re (center, centre)

Some words like centre have two forms of spelling. In traditional UK English spelling, they end with the letters -re. In US English spelling, they end with the letters -er.

The following table shows some examples:

UK spelling	US spelling
centre	center
fibre	fiber
sabre	saber
sceptre	scepter
spectre	specter
theatre	theater

-fs / -ves (hoofs, hooves)

Some nouns ending with f can have either -s or -ves added to make them plural.

> scarf — scarfs or scarves
> wharf — wharfs or wharves
> dwarf — dwarfs or dwarves
> hoof — hoofs or hooves

-ie / -y (auntie, aunty)

The spelling of some words ending with -ie or -y (aunty and auntie) are equally accepted in different parts of the world.

> I took a photo of my **auntie's** place.
>
> 'She's wearing my favourite hat!' said **Aunty** Di.

Other **ie/y** words like this include:

> cabbie/cabby, yabbie/yabby, yuppie/yuppy

Other word groups that have equally accepted spellings include:

> **a/ah** (savanna/savannah, veranda/verandah)
>
> **e/i** (despatch/dispatch, encase/incase, encrust/incrust, encumbrance/incumbrance, endorse/indorse, enquire/inquire, liquefy/liquify)
>
> **i/y** (gipsy/gypsy, pigmy/pygmy, siphon/syphon, tire/tyre)

See also **tire / tyre**.

-ise / -ize (organise, organize)

Many verbs in English end with the letters -ise and -ize. Some of these words can be spelt either way. Some can be spelt only one way. Here are the main points to remember about how to spell these words.

Words which end only in -ize

There is only one verb in this group which must end with -ize. It is:

> capsize

Words which end only in -ise

Some verbs in this group *must* end with -ise. They are:

> advertise, advise, compromise, despise, devise, exercise, improvise, revise, supervise, surprise, televise

In America, people prefer to use the -ize spelling. This means they have to remember the group of words above that *must* have -ise.

In the rest of the English-speaking world, people choose either -ise or -ize. If they choose -ise, they have to remember the one word (capsize) which is the exception.

Writing tip

-ise or -ize?

-ise is easier to remember because there is only one exception (capsize).

-log / -logue (dialog, dialogue)

There is a group of nouns in English which can end with either -*log* or -*logue*. The -*log* spelling is used in US English. The -*logue* spelling is used in UK English.

UK spelling	US spelling
analogue	analog
catalogue	catalog
dialogue	dialog
epilogue	epilog
prologue	prolog

See also WORD HISTORIES: **dialogue**.

-oes / -os (haloes, halos)

Some nouns that end with *o* can have either -*s* or -*es* added to make them plural.

> banjo — banjoes or banjos
> dingo — dingoes or dingos
> flamingo — flamingoes or flamingos
> halo — haloes or halos
> lasso — lassoes or lassos
> mango — mangoes or mangos
> mosquito — mosquitoes or mosquitos
> zero — zeroes or zeros

See also **plural**: **Nouns ending with -o**.

OK / okay

The word *OK* is usually written in capital letters. Full stops are sometimes used (*O.K.*). It is also spelled *okay*, especially when used as a verb.

> The quality inspector **okayed** the computer at the factory.
> '**OK**! Let's go,' they cried.
> 'Is it **okay** if I borrow your bike?'

Like OK, there are many individual English words that have more than one correct spelling, but do not fit into any pattern found in other words. For words like this, you should use your dictionary to check acceptable spellings, then keep to one spelling within any piece of writing.

See also **verbs**; **wagon / waggon**; WORD HISTORIES: **barbecue**; **OK**.

-or / -our (color, colour)

English words that can end with -or or -our are different spellings of the same words. Here are some of the most common examples:

> armor/armour, behavior/behaviour, color/colour,
> endeavor/endeavour, favor/favour, flavor/flavour, harbor/harbour,
> honor/honour, humor/humour, labor/labour, odor/odour,
> rumor/rumour, savior/saviour, splendor/splendour, valor/valour,
> vapor/vapour, vigor/vigour

Both the -or and -our spellings of these words are correct. Different English-speaking countries have different spelling preferences.

* -or is more common in the USA.
* -our is more common in the UK.
* In Australia, Canada, New Zealand, South Africa, Singapore and most other English-speaking countries, both -or and -our are used, but -our is the most common.

If you choose the -our spelling, take care with the following words which do *not* keep the letter *u* with some suffixes.

> glamour — glamorous
> honour — honorary (but honourable)
> humour — humorous
> labour — laborious, elaborate
> vapour — vaporise, evaporate
> vigour — vigorous

Many words ending in -or do not have an alternative spelling.

> donor, error, horror, interior, junior, major, manor, mayor, minor, mirror, motor, razor, sailor, senior, tailor, terror, traitor

For other information on English spelling, see **-ei- / -ie-**; **spelling**; **tire / tyre**; **wagon / waggon**.

ambiguity

Ambiguity is writing that can have more than one meaning. So the reader can think the text means one thing, when the writer intended it to mean something else.

Writers usually try to avoid ambiguity. Newspaper headlines are sometimes ambiguous because they are so short.

> Squad Helps Dog Bite Victim

This headline meant that the squad helped the victim of a dog bite. However, the reader might think that the squad helped the dog to bite the victim!
It is often difficult for writers to find ambiguity in their own writing. This is partly the job of an editor.

Editors of newspapers do not have much time to check all the text in a newspaper. This is one reason why so many newspaper headlines can be ambiguous.

Ambiguity can happen because many words and phrases have more than one meaning. This is why these newspaper headlines are ambiguous:
- General Macarthur Flies Back to Front
- Include Your Children When Baking Cookies
- Police Begin Campaign to Run Down Jaywalkers
- Safety Experts Say School Bus Passengers Should Be Belted
- Teacher Strikes Idle Kids
- Enraged Cow Injures Farmer with Axe
- Kids Make Nutritious Snacks
- Grandmother of Eight Makes Hole in One
- Milk Drinkers are Turning to Powder

Ambiguity can happen because some words have more than one function or purpose in a sentence. Present participles (-*ing* words) are one example.
- Police to Stop Looting
- Teacher Says Children are Revolting

Sometimes writers intentionally use ambiguity to create jokes. Puns are often used in this way.

> If everyone owned a horse, the world would be more stabilised.

Ambiguity can happen because certain words are placed in the wrong order in a sentence. The words *only* and *even* are common examples of this.

> **Only** children are allowed to use the computer games.
> Children are **only** allowed to use the computer games.
> Children are allowed to use the computer games **only**.

See also **grammar**: **Word order and links**; **only**; **participles**.

among / between

The key to these words is to understand the history of the words *between* and *among*.

Among refers to a group of more than two people or things.

> The tourists walked **among** the penguins.
> Insects, birds, molluscs, frogs, worms and so on, live **among** the leaf litter.

Between refers to a group of two individual people or things.

> They ran **between** the two finishing posts.
> Juanita stood **between** Jose and Jacinta.

When used with 'divide' or 'share':
* *among* is used only with plural nouns or pronouns.
  The food was **shared among** the **refugees**.
  The children chose to **divide** the prize **among themselves**.
* *between* is used only when two people or things are involved.
  The food was **shared between the two** refugees.
  The **twins** chose to **divide** the prize **between themselves**.

See also **plural**; **nouns**; WORD HISTORIES: **among**; **between**.

ampersand (&)
See **symbols**: Ampersand (&); WORD HISTORIES: **ampersand (&)**.

an
See **a / an**.

analogy
Writers often liken one thing to another, to explain an idea. This is called 'making an *analogy*'.

> Grandma says **children are like library books**. You only get a loan of them for a while and then you have to return them. I think she means when kids grow up and leave home.

One wild weekend with my grandmother, p. 27

In this example, Grandma compares children to library books. She then explains why they are alike.

In her novel *Voices*, Edel Wignell tells two stories: one about humans, and one about penguins. As the story progresses, the reader discovers that the author is actually comparing the child-rearing practices of humans and penguins. She also draws the reader's attention to the fact that both animals and humans communicate with each other in very individual ways.

anecdote

Wignell makes the following points in her analogy:

Humans	Emperor penguins
A scientist is studying penguins in Antarctica. While he is working away from home, his wife has a baby.	The female penguin lays her egg; the male looks after it while the female makes a long journey to the sea for food.
While the scientist is away, his wife and daughters raise the baby. They tape record the baby's voice for his father to hear later. The scientist wonders how his son is growing.	The female penguins reach the ocean and feed until they are full. Then they make the long journey back to the males; they do not know if their chicks have hatched.
The scientist returns home, and father and baby hear each other's voices for the first time. Their voices seem strange to each other at first, but the baby soon learns to recognise his father's voice.	As the penguin chicks hatch from the eggs, they hear their father's voice. They learn and remember how it sounds. The females return from their trip in time to feed the chicks. Among thousands of birds, each adult penguin recognises its mate's voice.

anecdote

An anecdote is a short, often funny re-telling of an incident. Anecdotes are a type of recount text.

> The first trick Fritz ever performed was a success.
> *"It was with a bowl of eggs. The top one was raw. I cracked it into a glass and drank it! All the other eggs were hard-boiled. Then I started to juggle the other eggs over the heads of the audience. The eggs dropped to the ground because I could not juggle. Everyone cried, 'Look out!' but were relieved to find that the eggs were hard-boiled and did not splatter."*

Entertainers, p. 19

In this example, a clown named 'Fritz' tells an anecdote about how he began his work as a clown. Notice how the first sentence is in the third person, because the author is writing about Fritz. The rest of the anecdote is in the first person (*I*) because Fritz is telling the story about his own experiences.

See also **person**; **recount**.

annotation

Annotations are notes written alongside text, drawings or photographs. They may be written in a book, on paper, or in a computer file. Annotations are used to give the reader extra information or an explanation about a text or illustration. They may also be used to remind a reader of ideas or thoughts about the text. Annotations are usually brief and can include sentences, sentence fragments or lists. Authors and illustrators often write annotations on their drafts.

In the following example, Amanda Graham, the author and illustrator of *Lovely Lunch*, added annotations to her sketches. They remind her of ideas she had for finishing her story. Notice how the annotations are very informal because she was writing to herself.

See also **formal / informal writing**; **sentences**; **sentence fragments**; WORD HISTORIES: **annotation**.

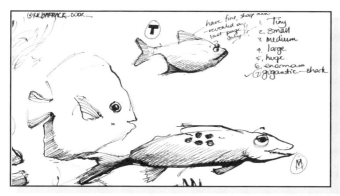

Lovely lunch (sketches)

antecedent

An *antecedent* is a word or phrase (usually a noun) that is replaced by a pronoun later in a sentence. This word is used in grammar to describe how nouns and pronouns work together.

     Andrew stood on his toes, balancing **himself** with **his** walking stick.
In the example above, the pronouns *himself* and *his* replace the proper noun *Andrew* later in the sentence. So *Andrew* is the antecedent of the pronouns *himself* and *his*.

     Out came a shy **child, who** immediately hid behind the door.
In this example, the pronoun *who* replaces the noun *child* later in the sentence. So *child* is the antecedent of the pronoun *who*.

See also **nouns**; **pronouns**.

antonyms

Antonyms are words that are opposite to each other in meaning. Some examples are:

> right/left, up/down, over/under

Most words do not have antonyms that are exactly opposite in meaning. For example, whether *big* is opposite to *small* depends on what the writer means by 'big' (*tall, heavy, fat, wide* etc) and 'small' (*short, light, thin, narrow* etc). Careful writers pay attention to the shades of meaning in words.

Many antonyms are formed with prefixes.
> happy/unhappy

Authors and editors often use a thesaurus to find synonyms and antonyms. This is so they can use more interesting words in their writing.

See also **prefixes**; **synonyms**.

anyone

Anyone is a singular word. It refers to only one person. Therefore, in a sentence, the word *anyone* needs to be linked to a singular verb if the sentence is to have agreement.

> **Anyone** who ran in the heat **was** de-hydrated at the end of the race.

In this example, *anyone* is used with the singular verb *was*. It would be incorrect to write:

> **Anyone** who ran in the heat **were** de-hydrated at the end of the race.

See also **agreement**; **singular words**.

apostrophe (')

The apostrophe is a punctuation mark ('). It is used in writing for two main reasons.

It is used in shortened words and phrases called *contractions*. It shows where letters have been left off a word or phrase.

> isn't

Isn't is a contraction of the phrase *is not*. The apostrophe shows that the letter *o* was left out of the word *not*.

apostrophe (')

The apostrophe is also used to show that something or someone owns something. This is called the *apostrophe of possession*.

> The **dog's collar** was loose.

In this example, the apostrophe shows that the *collar* belonged to the *dog*.

See also WORD HISTORIES: **apostrophe**.

Further information is under the following topics:
Apostrophe for contractions
Apostrophe of possession
    Apostrophe for abbreviations
When not to use the apostrophe
    Plural nouns
    Possessive pronouns
    Titles of works and company names

Apostrophe for contractions
The apostrophe shows where letters have been left out in contractions.

> Staying with my aunt is really quite exciting. **It's** a bit like being at a late night party except I **haven't** lost my voice yet. **I've** stayed with her before because **she's** so much fun.

In this example, the apostrophe shows where letters have been left out in the contractions *it's* (it is), *haven't* (have not), *I've* (I have) and *she's* (she is).

See also **contractions**.

apostrophe (')

This table shows some common contractions using the apostrophe.

Phrase/word	Contraction	Phrase/word	Contraction
are not	aren't	that had; that would	that'd
cannot	can't	that will	that'll
could not	couldn't	that has; that is	that's
could have	could've	there had; there would	there'd
did not	didn't	there will	there'll
does not	doesn't	there has; there is	there's
do not	don't	they are	they're
had not	hadn't	they had; they would	they'd
has not	hasn't	they have	they've
have not	haven't	they will	they'll
he had; he would	he'd	was not	wasn't
he has; he is	he's	we are	we're
he will	he'll	we had; we would	we'd
here is	here's	we have	we've
I am	I'm	we will	we'll
I had; I would	I'd	were not	weren't
I have	I've	what is; what has	what's
I will	I'll	what had	what'd
is not	isn't	who had; who would	who'd
it had; it would	it'd	who has; who is	who's
it will	it'll	who have	who've
it has; it is	it's	who will	who'll
let us	let's	will not	won't
shall not	shan't	would have	would've
she had; she would	she'd	would not	wouldn't
she will	she'll	you are	you're
she has; she is	she's	you had; you would	you'd
should not	shouldn't	you have	you've
should have	should've	you will	you'll

apostrophe (')

Apostrophe of possession

The apostrophe of possession shows that something belongs to something or someone.

> Last weekend I stayed at my **auntie's** home.

In this sentence, the apostrophe is placed after the word *auntie*, because auntie owns the home.

> Last weekend I stayed at my **aunties'** home.

In this example the apostrophe is placed after the word *aunties*, because more than one auntie owns the home — it is plural.

Further examples of the apostrophe used with plural words:

> Today it is the **males'** turn to do the cooking.
> They searched for **birds'** eggs.

See also **plural**.

Hint

Where to place the apostrophe of possession

To find out where you should put the apostrophe of possession, ask yourself 'Who owns it?', then place the apostrophe after the answer.

> Michael cleaned his mothers car.

Who owns the car? His *mother*.

> Michael cleaned his **mother's** car.

> The class cleaned their mothers cars.

Who owns the cars? Their *mothers*.

> The class cleaned their **mothers'** cars.

Apostrophe for abbreviations

The apostrophe of possession is used with abbreviations such as TV.

> The **TV's** remote control would not work. The **CD's** case was cracked.

See also **abbreviations**.

When not to use the apostrophe

Plural nouns
It is a common error for writers to use an apostrophe with plural nouns when they do not 'possess' anything.

> The **team's** played in the rain. (X)
> The **teams** played in the rain. (✓)
> They brought ten **CD's** to the party. (X)
> They brought ten **CDs** to the party. (✓)

Possessive pronouns
The apostrophe is never used for possession in pronouns.

> The dog chased **it's** tail. (X)
> The dog chased **its** tail. (✓)
> **Your's** is the best writing in the class. (X)
> **Yours** is the best writing in the class. (✓)

Titles of works and company names
It is a modern trend to not use the apostrophe of possession in the titles of works, or company names — but this is still a matter of personal taste.

> Young **Writers** Guide
> They shopped at John **Martins** store.

Oddity

A tricky apostrophe of possession

Sometimes the letter *s* is not written after an apostrophe of possession mark — even when it is in the singular form.

> "This dog is my best friend," said Joe, stroking **Chips'** ears.

Joe is stroking the ears of his dog, *Chips*. The word *Chips* ends with the letter *s*. Another *s* has not been added after the apostrophe because the author thought *Chips's* would be clumsy to say. However, it would not be incorrect to write *Chips's*. It is a matter of personal style.

---

appendix

An appendix is a section of information, additional to the main text of a book. It is placed at the back of a book. It is separated from the main text because it would make the book unenjoyable or too hard to read if the writer tried to fit it all within the main text.

> **Appendix: Some facts about whales**
>
> All whales are mammals and so have warm blood. They mate and produce live young which drink milk from the mothers.
>
> In place of arms, whales have flippers. All whales have a tail with two horizontal sections called flukes. Some whales have a back (dorsal) fin.

Baleen, p. 39

Baleen is a fiction book about a fierce whale character. The appendix gives factual information about whales, so readers can appreciate the story more. However, if the author wrote this information within the story, it would interrupt the story for the reader.

See also WORD HISTORIES: **appendix**.

argument

Argument is persuasive text. In an argument, a writer tries to persuade an audience to accept a point of view. The writer gives an opinion on a topic, then presents reasons to explain or support the opinion. An argument text is also called an *exposition*.

There are three main parts in an argument:
* *Introduction*

Explain the topic or issue and state a position. You may give some background information. To get the audience's attention, use a dramatic exclamation or question, or a funny situation — anything that will make the audience stop and read or listen.
* *Argument*

Present reasons and evidence to support the argument. Also try to convince the audience by appealing to their feelings. Statements are used in arguments. Ideas in the argument are often linked through words like *therefore, so, because, unless* and *finally*.
* *Conclusion*

Sum up the argument and perhaps suggest actions to the audience. Questions are often used in the conclusion to make the audience feel they need to give an answer. Commands are also used to tell the audience what to do.

See also **exclamations**; **question mark (?)**; **sentences**: **Commands**.

The following topics describe three kinds of argument:

Advertisements
Letter to the editor
Discussion
  Debate
  Interviews

Advertisements

Advertisements are arguments from one point of view. The writer tries to persuade the audience to buy something or act in a particular way.

The author does four key things in the following advertising poster/billboard:

- gets attention (introduction)
- gives information (introduction)
- appeals to the readers' emotions (argument)
- demands action (conclusion).

Introduction

The author gets the readers' *attention* by using a dramatic question as the heading. When someone asks a polite question, the audience usually feels they should give an answer, or read on to find the answer.

The author gives the readers *information* by using statistics (sets of figures) to make the text sound scientific so readers believe the argument. The author also uses a comparison (*enough to go around the world*) to build a picture that amazes readers and holds their interest.

How many dolphins' lives did this can of tuna cost?

Fishing fleets from some countries use drift-nets to catch fish. During 1990, in the Pacific Ocean they set more than 47,000 km (29,000 mi) of net each day — enough to go around the world.

Driftnets don't catch only fish. They also trap and kill thousands of seals, dolphins, small whales, sea turtles and seabirds.

When you buy canned fish, check to see where it came from. Don't buy fish from countries that use driftnets. It costs too much!

Issues: Dolphin poster

Argument
The author tries to make readers feel *emotional* about the topic, because most people act on emotions. Notice the verbs (*trap, kill*) and the nouns (*seals, dolphins, whales, turtles, birds*). Why did the author leave out nouns like *sharks, jellyfish, stingrays*? Because they are unlikely to get the readers' sympathy.

Conclusion
The author speaks directly to readers by using the second person pronoun (*you*), instead of the third person (*they*). This makes the readers feel personally involved. The author also uses a *command* to tell them what to do about the problem — what *actions* to take.

When **you** buy canned fish, **check to see where it came from**.
The author finishes with a short exclamation that emphasises the main point and concludes the argument.

It costs too much!
See also **compare and contrast**; **nouns**; **sentences**: **Commands, Exclamations, Questions**; **person**; **pronouns**; **verbs**.

Letter to the editor
The 'letters to the editor' section in newspapers and magazines is a good example of argument text. Usually there is only one point of view in each letter — the writer's view.

Letter to the Editor
Save our Forest

Our government plans to turn Waterfall Gully into a theme park. Waterfall Gully is the only natural forest area left in our city. It should not be developed as a theme park.

Theme parks are common in other cities. Natural forests are not. Waterfall Gully is a unique part of our city, with magnificent old trees and beautiful scenery. We should be promoting this as a perfect environment for bushwalking and ecotourism. Research shows that tourists are attracted to the natural beauty of places like Waterfall Gully.

The government's plan is an excuse to let timber companies cut down our ancient trees. What took hundreds of years to grow would be destroyed in just a few weeks. The loss of the forest would also mean the loss of animals that depend on the trees.

Use the natural forest to attract tourists, not chainsaws! Leave Waterfall Gully alone.

D.S. Grace, Happy Valley

Issues: Letter to the editor

Introduction
The letter has a heading that is a command, to give it urgency and authority. The letter begins with a short statement to introduce the topic of the argument.

Argument
The author states an opinion about the topic and presents evidence (research) to support the opinion. The author gives facts about trees and animals to support the argument, and to make the audience feel sad about the loss of the trees.

Conclusion
The author reminds the reader what the topic is, and sums up the argument. This is a command to give the argument emphasis and authority.
Letters to the editor are signed with the name, and suburb or town of the author.

See also **sentences**: **Commands**, **Statements**.

Discussion
Discussion texts are arguments that include *more* than one point of view about a topic. They usually discuss situations which have no simple answer. The author often plans the writing around key questions or issues.

Debate
A debate is an argument between two points of view. In a debate, two individuals or groups argue for and against a topic. Each side tries to persuade an audience that it has the better argument. This gives the audience a chance to compare the two points of view.

In the following example, environmentalists and mining companies put their points of view about mining in Antarctica. The writing is presented as a voting paper, so the audience can respond by voting for the argument it prefers.

argument

ANTARCTICA — TO MIND IT . . .	WHAT DO YOU SAY?
	MIND IT? ☐ OR MINE IT? ☐
OR TO MINE IT?	

ENVIRONMENTALISTS ARGUE THAT:	MINING COMPANIES ARGUE THAT:
• Mining always changes an environment in a big way. In Antarctica, even small changes would destroy wildlife.	• Antarctica has a lot of oil and other minerals. People need these resources.
• Accidents, such as oil spills, are certain to happen.	• Mining companies could be told to obey strict safety rules. They could prevent accidents.
• Like a freezer, the Antarctic weather stops waste from breaking down. Waste disturbs wildlife breeding areas.	• Mining companies could remove their waste.
• Antarctica should be a world park. The land, and the sea around it, should be left as a wilderness.	• Mining companies could do research that would help the world.
• Antarctica should be a place of peace. People may fight over territory if they mine it.	• Countries who have an interest in Antarctica have signed a treaty. They are already working together peacefully.

Issues: Antarctica poster

• *Introduction*

The debate is introduced by a question that is the topic of the argument.

• *Argument*

One side (*environmentalists*) gives a number of different reasons to support the argument that Antarctica should not be mined. The other side (*mining companies*) argues against each argument presented by the environmentalists. Notice how the environmentalists use the word *should* (being definite) while the mining companies use the word *could* (being careful not to commit themselves with the word *would*).

- *Conclusion*

Usually a judge or judging panel decides which group gave the better argument in a debate. In this example, the readers are asked to vote so that a decision can be reached. The author uses a question in the second person (*you*) to speak directly to the readers or voters.

What do **you** say? Mind it? OR Mine it?

See also **could / should / would**; **modal verbs**; **sentences**: **Questions**.

Interviews

An author may interview people to gather information for a discussion text. When each person has given an opinion on the topic, the author tries to summarise their points of view and decide where there is agreement or disagreement. Sometimes people can decide to agree to disagree.

Discussions are sometimes conducted on television, with a chairperson who asks the questions, controls the discussion and gives a summary.

The following extract is from a book about waste disposal.

- *Introduction*

Notice how, in the introduction, the author has chosen interviewees who are unlikely to have the same point of view on the topic. This makes sure there will be a debate.

The author has chosen three questions that focus on *what, how* and *who*. Each person is asked the same questions. The author uses open questions that cannot be answered with a *yes* or *no*.

This text is about opinions — not facts. People are arguing their own points of view.

See also **sentences**: **Questions**.

- *Argument*

The opinions given by the six different interviewees form the argument in the text. The author allows different opinions or arguments to be considered. This is why it is a discussion — a balance of different viewpoints on a topic.

- *Conclusion*

At the conclusion of the discussion, the author must make a summary of the viewpoints given by the interviewees, or allow each interviewee to give a summary statement.

INTRODUCTION

This book discusses the problem of waste disposal from different points of view.

Six people, who play different roles, were interviewed about their opinions on the following questions:
- What are the problems with waste disposal?
- How should these problems be solved?
- Who is responsible for solving these problems?

Interviewee	Role
Ron Patrick	*Plastics manufacturer*
Phillip Graham	*Government health inspector*
Dudley Williams	*Manager of a waste disposal company*
Lynette Thorstensen	*Greenpeace spokesperson*
Romeo Panazzolo	} *Householders*
Maria Panazzolo	

Viewpoints on waste, p. 3

See also **pronouns**: **Interrogative pronouns**.

articles

Articles are short words that begin noun phrases (eg *a brown dog*). There are only three articles in English — the definite article *the*, and the indefinite articles *a* and *an*. Further information is under the following headings:

Definite article
Indefinite article

Definite article

The word *the* is called 'the definite article', because it points to a particular, definite thing.

The broken windmill

In this phrase the writer is being definite — pointing out a particular windmill.

Indefinite article

The words *a* and *an* are called 'indefinite articles', because they do not point to particular things.

> **A** broken windmill.
> **An** old, broken windmill.

The writer is not being definite in these phrases — they could mean *any* windmill.

See also **a / an**; **determiners**; **noun phrases**.

as / like

The words *like* and *as* have confused writers for a long time. In traditional, formal English grammar, they were supposed to be used in quite different ways.

The following examples show what is considered to be correct or incorrect in formal writing:

> The car sounded **like** it needed a service. (X)
> The car sounded **as though** it needed a service. (✓)

In the first example, *like* has been used as a conjunction. (It joins two clauses.) In formal writing, it should not be used as a conjunction. The word *as* can be used as a preposition, especially when it is used with *if* or *though*.

Like can be used as a preposition.

> The coyotes howled **like** a siren.

In this example, *like* begins the phrase *like a siren* so it is a preposition.

As, especially *as if* or *as though*, can be used as a conjunction (to join clauses).

> The coyotes howled **as if** they were sad.

In this example, *as if* joins the two clauses *The coyotes howled* and *they were sad*.

assonance

Assonance is the repetition of the same vowel sound in a number of words. It can make writing more interesting and memorable.

> They **clasped** the **last** photo taken of their mother.

In this example, the words *clasped* and *last* have the same /ar/ sound in the middle.

See also **slogan**.

assure / ensure / insure

Assure is a verb meaning 'to promise or convince'.

> The doctor **assured** me it was a serious illness.
> "This isn't my writing," he **assured** her.

Ensure is a verb meaning 'to protect, to guarantee or to make sure'.

> Life jackets should be kept in boats to **ensure** the safety of passengers.

Insure is a verb meaning 'to promise to replace something or the value of something if it is lost'.

> The home owners had to **insure** their house for fire damage.

Note: in the USA, the word *ensure* is used to mean *insure*.

> The home owners had to **ensure** their house for fire damage.

See also **verbs**.

asterisk (*)

The asterisk is a punctuation mark. In the days of typewriters, it was commonly used as dot points in lists. Today, with word processors, various dot points have become the common marks used to show items in a list.

The asterisk is more commonly used today as a symbol for footnotes.

See also **notes**.

attributive adjectives

See **adjectives**: Attributive adjectives (before the noun).

audience

All writing is created for an audience, even if it is people writing to themselves. However, most writing is created for a wider audience than just the writer. It might be for just one other person, such as a relative, friend, business person or government official. It might be for the rest of the world — film and TV scripts and books can reach audiences of millions of people.

Even personal diaries sometimes find a much wider audience. *The diary of Samuel Pepys* is famous because, long after his death, his personal writing gave historians important information about how people lived in the 1600s.

Another personal diary is *The diary of Anne Frank* about the experiences of a Jewish girl in Europe during World War 2.

The following topics give information about writers and their audiences.

General audiences
Special audiences
Purpose
Topic
Theme
Format (mode)
Text type (genre)

General audiences
A general audience could be anyone who reads or listens to a text. Most newspapers and TV news items are written for a general audience. When writing for a general audience, writers use common words that most people would understand. They do not use specialist words unless they can easily explain them in the writing.

Special audiences
Some audiences are particular groups of people, such as a coin collectors' club, a sports club, a doctors' association or a computer society. Each of these audiences has a special interest that the members share. They also share knowledge of specialist words (sometimes called *jargon*) used by such groups. For example, coin collectors would understand the meaning of the words *misstruck*, *over-stamp* and *mint*. Doctors would understand words like *prognosis* and *in vivo*. Therefore, when writing for special audiences, writers know they can use specialist words because the audience will understand them.

See also **jargon**.

Purpose
All writing is created for a purpose — to have a particular effect on an audience. When a writer has a definite purpose, it is easier to plan the writing. However, for the writing to be successful, the author must *engage* the audience. This means that the audience must get some satisfaction from the writing.

There are four main purposes for writing:
• To *inform*
Nonfiction writing informs an audience. The writer can interest the audience with fascinating facts presented in an interesting way.

- To *entertain*

Fiction writing entertains an audience by appealing to the audience's imagination. The writer can interest the audience with laughter, sadness, suspense, curiosity or excitement.

- To *persuade*

Persuasive text (*argument*) persuades an audience to think or act in a certain way. The writer can influence the audience by getting their attention, giving information, opinions or evidence, calling on their feelings and urging them to take action.

- To *challenge*

Reflective writing encourages people to think about issues or ideas. The writer can interest the audience by asking questions, making statements and presenting more than one point of view on a topic. Philosophers, historians, some religious writers and poets can encourage their readers to think about the environment or the meaning of life. Writers sometimes use discussion texts to do this. They challenge the way the reader thinks.

See also **argument**: **Advertisements**; **discussion**; **report**; **tone**.

Topic

The topic is *what* a piece of writing is about. Writers are often asked 'Where do you get your ideas from?' Writers get their ideas for topics from their personal experiences, observation and research; from things they do, see, hear, taste, smell, feel, read and remember. These ideas give them topics to write about.

Everyone has experiences — writers remember details about their experiences and are able to communicate them in different ways. Even fantasy begins with an experience of some kind. Ideas for nonfiction writing come from knowledge and research. The following examples describe how two authors each found their ideas for a book.

Example: *Letters to Leah*

Josephine Croser, the author of *Letters to Leah,* got the idea for the story when her young daughter was saddened by the death of a classmate in a road accident. Josephine tried to write a story that would help young readers understand grief. This was her topic. The book is about a girl who has lost her best friend.

Example: *The first lunar landing*

Rodney Martin, the author of this book wanted to write about an important event in modern history. He remembered how excited he felt on the day that men first walked on the moon. So, years later, he researched the event to get ideas for the book. The topic of the book is the journey of the Apollo 11 team to the moon and back.

Theme

After choosing a topic, authors decide *what they want to say about that topic* — they choose a focus. This is called the *theme*.

Example: *Letters to Leah*
The topic of this book is 'losing someone you love'. The theme is 'how a person might learn to cope with grief'.

Example: *The first lunar landing*
The topic of this book is 'the Apollo 11 mission'. The theme is 'what we learn from great pioneering achievements in history'.

Example: *Baleen*
The topic of this book is 'whales.' The theme is 'why some whales have no teeth'.

Example: *Viewpoints on waste*
The topic of this book is 'waste disposal'. The theme is 'what are the problems and who is responsible for waste disposal?'

Format

There are different formats for writing; for example, *letters, lists, journals, dialogue* (speech) and *verse* all have different formats. Different formats can be used for fiction and nonfiction, and for formal and informal writing.

Text type

Once the audience and purpose of a piece of writing have been decided, the author chooses a suitable text type (sometimes called *genre*). Text types are the different ways writers organise text to suit different purposes. The main text types or genres are *argument, discussion, explanation, narrative, poetry, procedure, recount, report* and *review*.

See also **argument**; **correspondence**; **dialogue (US: dialog)**; **discussion**; **explanation**; **journal**; **narrative**; **poetry**; **procedure**; **recount**; **report**; **review**.

auntie / aunty

See **alternative spellings**.

autobiography

In an autobiography, an author recounts what has happened in his or her life.

The following example is the introduction from the book *Me, an author? An autobiography* by Amanda Graham, an author of children's books. In this extract, Amanda writes about her family and her early life.

In the beginning

My story began on 29th September 1961. My parents, Ondrea and Wesley, and my brother, Stephen, were living in Elizabeth, South Australia, when I was born. My sister, Susan, was born three years later.

I can't remember much about Elizabeth except for the icecream van that drove around the streets in summer time.

Me, an author? An autobiography, p. 4

- Autobiographies are usually in the first person (*I, my*) because they are written from the point of view of the writer.
- Autobiographies are mostly written in the past tense because they recount events. (*began, were living, was born, drove*)
- The information in an autobiography is usually in chronological order — the order in which things happen in time.

See also **chronological; person; verbs: Tenses (time); recount**: **Autobiography**; WORD HISTORIES: **autobiography, chronology**.

auxiliary verbs

Auxiliary verbs are words that can be used with participles and other verbs to make verb phrases. They can be thought of as 'helper verbs'.

The following words are auxiliary verbs:

> am, is, was, are, were, has, have, had, could, should, would, will, shall, be, been, being, can, may, must, might, do, did, does, done

> She **was** standing near a doorway.

In this example, the auxiliary verb (*was*) helps the participle (*standing*) to form the verb phrase *was standing*.

More than one auxiliary verb can be used to form a verb phrase.

> It **could have been** worse.

In this case, two auxiliary verbs (*could* and *have*) help the participle (*been*) to form the verb phrase *could have been*.

See also **participles**; **verbs**: **Auxiliary verbs**; WORD HISTORIES: **auxiliary**.

awe / oar / or / ore

Awe can be used as a noun or a verb meaning 'wonder' or 'fear'.

> They were **awed** by the sights, sounds and smells of the market.
> "It's huge," said Angela, over-**awed** by the sight.

Oar is a noun meaning 'a paddle used to row a boat'.

> They could not row the boat because they had dropped their **oars** in the water.

Or is a conjunction used to join words, phrases or clauses in a sentence.

> Was Kim going to help **or** was he going to hinder the team?
> They didn't know whether to go left, right **or** straight ahead.

Ore is a noun meaning 'earth that is mined for metals'.

> The hillside was rich in iron **ore**.

See also **clauses**; **conjunctions**; **nouns**; **phrases**; **verbs**.

ballad

A ballad is a poem or song that tells a story, often about sadness, love, adventure or heroism.

To write ballads, writers often use:
* short four-line verses
* a rhyming pattern of A B C B
* a strong rhythmic pattern of light and heavy beats (called *iambic rhythm*).

> **Robin Hood and the Widow's Sons**
> There are twelve months in all the year,
> As many people say,
> But the merriest month in all the year
> Is the merry month of May.
>
> Now Robin Hood is to Nottingham gone,
> With a link a down and a day,
> And there he met a simple widow,
> Was weeping on the way.
>
> "What news? What news, poor simple widow?
> What news have you for me?"
> Said she, "There's my three sons in Nottingham town
> Today condemned to die."
>
> Now Robin Hood is to Nottingham gone,
> With a link a down and a day,
> And there he met with a simple old beggar,
> Was walking along the highway.

Extract from 'Robin Hood and the Widow's Sons', Anonymous

See also **iambic foot**; **rhyme**; WORD HISTORIES: **ballad**.

bare / bear

Bare is an adjective. It means 'empty, uncovered or unclothed'.

The room was **bare** — no furniture, no curtains, no rugs.
Bare is also found in compound words: *barefaced, barefoot, bare-headed.*

Bear can be a noun meaning 'a large mammal of the family *Ursidae* — for example, black bear, grizzly bear, polar bear'.

The polar **bear** is carnivorous.

Bear can also be a verb. It can mean 'to carry'.

The guests were **bearing** gifts for the young girl.

Bear, meaning 'to carry', is also found in compound words:
overbearing, load-bearing
He has an **overbearing** personality.

The verb *bear* can mean 'to endure or have patience'.

They could not **bear** to wait any longer.

See also **adjectives**; **compound words**; **nouns**; **verbs**.

bean / been

Bean is a noun meaning 'a vegetable'.

> There are many kinds of **beans** — broad **beans**, haricot **beans**, green **beans**. They are a vegetable that is an important source of protein.

Been is the past participle of the verb *to be*. It is used with other verbs to make a verb phrase.

> She had **been** waiting at the bus stop for two hours.

In this example, the verbs *had* and *waiting* link with *been* to form the verb phrase *had been waiting*.

See also **auxiliary verbs**; **nouns**; **participles**; **verbs**: Tenses (time).

before

See **ago / before**.

between

See **among / between**.

between you and me

Many people say 'between you and I' in speech. This is incorrect grammar because in English, all prepositions, such as *between*, are followed by the *objective* case of nouns and pronouns. *I* is in the *subjective* case: *me* is in the *objective* case. So the correct form is 'between you and me'.

See also **case**; **prepositions**; WORD HISTORIES: **between**.

bibliography

A *bibliography* is a list of books and other references an author has used to get information for a piece of writing. This list is usually placed at the back of a book.

A common order to write the details for each book in a bibliography is:
- author's family name
- author's given name or initials
- title of book (usually in italics)
- name of publisher
- place of publication (city, country)
- date (year of publication)

biography

The following bibliography from *The penicillin puzzle* uses this order:

> Bickel, Lennard, Florey, *The Man Who Made Penicillin*, Melbourne University Press, Melbourne, 1995.
> Birch, Beverly, Scientists Who Have Changed The World: Alexander Fleming, Exley Publications, Watford, 1990.
> Hughes, Howard. W., Pioneers of Science and Discovery: Alexander Fleming and Penicillin, Priory Press, London, 1974.

The penicillin puzzle, p. 24

See also WORD HISTORIES: **bibliography**.

biography

A biography is a recount of a person's life, written by another person. The information in a biography is based on events that really happened (factual information).

Cousteau: An unauthorized biography

This biography, written by Kevin Comber, is about some of the important achievements of Jacques Cousteau during his life.

Some points to note about biographies:

- They are usually written in the past tense.
- The information is usually organised in chronological order.
- They are usually written in the third person — using the pronouns *he*, *she*, *they*.

See also **chronological**; **person**; **recount**: **Biography**; **verbs**: **Past**; WORD HISTORIES: **biography**.

blank verse

Blank verse is verse without rhyme, but it does have regular rhythm. Often, this rhythm has five stressed beats to a line. In the following example, the stressed beats are in bold.

> I **will** not **change** my **horse** with **any** that **treads** ...
> When **I** be**stride** him, I **soar**, I **am** a **hawk**.
> He **trots** the **air**; the **earth** sings **when** he **touch**es it.

William Shakespeare (King Henry V)

Blank verse should not be confused with *free verse*, which does not have a regular rhythm.

See also **iambic foot**; **free verse**.

blurb

A blurb is a short piece of writing on the cover or jacket of a book, or a poster about a movie or other creative work. The purpose of a blurb is to make people interested in a book, film or other product. It is usually written by an editor or a marketing person.

A book blurb has just enough information to give a reader an idea of what the book is about. It is usually written by editors or advertising people. They often ask questions to appeal to the reader's curiosity. They also give 'juicy' clues about the content of a book or movie to make it sound more interesting. There are many writing techniques used in blurbs to promote a product.

The following examples are from the covers of fiction and nonfiction books:

> **The mystery of the missing garden gnome**
> Who took Uncle Stanley's garden gnome? Who sent the puzzling postcards from far away? The disappearance of the gnome caused an uproar in Gilly's family. Can she solve the mystery? Can you?

The mystery of the missing garden gnome, back cover

- In this blurb, the writer used questions to arouse the reader's curiosity.
- A brief piece of information is given about the topic of the story.
- The writer changed from the third person (*she*) to the second person (*you*) in the last question. So the author involved the readers by speaking directly to them.

> **Hannah**
> Josephine Croser has created a moving story, set in eighteenth century London, in which a young girl discovers inner strength as she fights to survive homelessness. When Hannah's father is abruptly taken away at Covent Garden, she is left to fend for herself in a strange city.

Hannah, back cover

- This blurb gives the reader a brief picture of the time and place of the story.
- The adjective *moving* suggests that the story will satisfy the reader.
- The phrases *inner strength* and *fights to survive homelessness* suggest that the hero of the story will be worth reading about.
- The final sentence of the blurb gives the impression of drama and suggests that the story will be exciting.

> **Be a puppeteer!**
> This book shows you how to make your own puppets. You can entertain people with zany puppet shows. It's great fun!

Making puppets, back cover

- The writer speaks directly to the reader using the second person (you, your).
- The blurb briefly tells readers what they can find in the book and that it is nonfiction.
- The writer tries to attract readers by appealing to their emotions, stating the good feelings they could get from the book (*You can entertain people, zany puppet shows. It's great fun!*)
- The exclamation mark is used to emphasise the word *fun*.

> **The penicillin puzzle**
> Penicillin was the world's first manufactured antibiotic. Because of penicillin's power to stop infections, it was called the 'wonder drug'. Who discovered penicillin? Who developed it as a medicine? Who was given the recognition?

The penicillin puzzle, back cover

- This blurb, for a nonfiction book, begins by giving information about the book's topic.
- Phrases like *world's first* and *wonder drug* are used to make the topic sound important.
- The writer uses questions to arouse the readers' curiosity — you will find the answers only if you read the book.

See also **adjectives**; **exclamation mark (!)**; **person**; **phrases**; WORD HISTORIES: **blurb**.

borrow / lend / loan

Borrow is a verb meaning 'to *get* something *from* someone on the understanding that you will return it'.

> They **borrowed** a wheelbarrow from their neighbour. They promised to return it the same day.

Lend is a verb. It means 'to give something to someone on the understanding that you will get it back'.

> Their neighbour was willing to **lend** them a wheelbarrow.

Loan is usually used as a noun. It means 'the thing that someone borrows or lends'.

> The bank gave them a **loan** so they could buy a house.

See also **nouns**; **verbs**.

bought / brought

Bought is the past tense of the verb *to buy*.

> He **bought** or borrowed many books about art.
> Sharon **bought** supper for her children on the way home.

Brought is the past tense of the verb *to bring*.

> Mrs Mills **brought** flowers to the hospital.
> Have you **brought** my parcel from the post office?

See also **verbs**: **Past**.

Hint

bought / brought: just think of the letters that begin each word

bring = **br**ought
buy = **b**ought

---

brackets ( )

Brackets are used in writing to surround words or thoughts. They are also called 'parentheses'.

The different forms of brackets are described under the following headings:
Round brackets
> *To add information*
> *Quotations*
> *Numbers and letters*

Square brackets
Curly brackets
Slash brackets
Punctuation and brackets

Round brackets ()

Round brackets are the most common brackets. They are used in different ways.

To add information

Round brackets are used to add information, which could be left out without changing the meaning of the sentence. Try reading these sentences without the words in brackets. The meanings do not change — but the text in brackets gives you extra information that adds meaning to each sentence.

brackets ( )

Tiny floating animals (mainly crustaceans) live in great numbers in the sea.

The company sent me a letter with a prize (a book).

Quotations
Round brackets are used to show where quotations come from.
'Our problem is we are a throw-away society'. (Sarah Williams)

Numbers and letters
Round brackets are used for numbered or lettered lists.
Depending on your destination, the methods of passenger travel, in order of speed, are:
(1) plane
(2) train
(3) car
(4) ship

Sometimes only one round bracket is used.
The most popular types of fiction at the local library were:
a) romance
b) action thriller
c) science fiction

Square brackets [ ]
Square brackets enclose words that are not part of a writer's text — for example, words added by an editor to explain something about the writing. This happens mostly in nonfiction writing.
Later, I received a letter from my older brother **[Rodney]**. I had not seen him for years.
In this example, the text was taken from an interview with someone. The person being interviewed did not say the name of the brother. The editor added the word in brackets to make sure the reader would understand who the brother was.

Curly brackets { }
Curly brackets (sometimes called *braces*) are mostly used in mathematics. They are also used in lists or charts to group items.

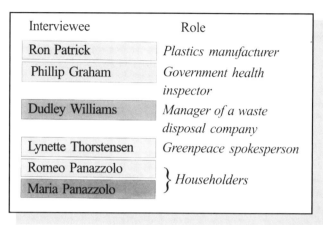

Viewpoints on waste, p. 3

In this example, the bracket groups two interviewees under one heading.

Slash brackets

Slash brackets (sometimes called *diagonal brackets*) enclose letters that represent a sound, for example the /oo/ sound in *foot*.

Her name is Anna Smyth, with an /i/ sound as in 'wife'.

Slash brackets are also used in computing, for example, in web site addresses.

http://www.erapublications.com/children's/

They are also used for dates written in numerals.

8/9/98

Hint

Beware when writing dates

Take care when using slash brackets in dates. In the United States the date is written in the order of *month/day/year*. In the United Kingdom, New Zealand, South Africa and Australia, the order is *day/month/year*.

3/12/99 means *March 12, 1999* in the United States

3/12/99 means *3 December 1999* in the other countries

See also **dates and time**.

Punctuation and brackets

If brackets are used at the end of a sentence, but are still part of that sentence, then the full stop is placed *outside* the second bracket.

> The Moon is about as old as Earth (about 4,600 million years old).

If the words in brackets are the whole sentence, then the full stop is placed *inside* the bracket.

> The astronauts expected the journey to the Moon and back to take eight days. (See *Apollo Mission Profile* on the back cover.)

See also **full stop (.)**.

brake / break

Brake can be used as:

- a noun meaning 'a device used to slow or stop something from moving'
  She put her foot on the **brake** pedal.

- a verb meaning 'to slow or stop something from moving'.
  The driver began to **brake** gently before the school crossing.

Break can be:
- a verb meaning 'to crack, snap, or separate into two or more pieces'
  If you drop the plate it will **break**.
  As the days grew warmer, the ice began to **break** up.

- a noun meaning 'a crack or a place where something becomes separated into two or more pieces'
  He used a special glue to fix the **break** in the plate.

- a noun meaning 'a rest or a holiday'.
  They had only one day of their **break** left to relax on the beach.
  The workers took a lunch **break**.

See also **nouns**; **verbs**.

breath / breathe

Breath is a noun. It means 'air that is taken into the lungs'. It is pronounced /breth/ as in *death*.

> He took a deep **breath** then dived.
> Johnny held his **breath** underwater.

Breathe is a verb. It means 'to draw air in and out'. It is pronounced /breeth/ as in *seethe*.

> She **breathed** in the perfume of the flowers.
> Poisonous gases made it difficult for people to **breathe**.

See also **nouns**; **verbs**.

bring / take

Bring means 'to fetch, move, carry or transport something *towards a named place or person*'.

> When he comes home from Hong Kong, he could **bring** me a radio.

In this example, the speaker thought that a radio could be delivered to her or him.

> Why don't you **bring** your friend here to dinner?

In this example, the speaker is asking whether someone would fetch a friend to a particular place where the speaker is.

Take means 'to move, lead, carry or transport something *away to another place or person*'.

> Tomorrow I will **take** a lantern and explore the tunnel.

In this example, the character intends to carry a lantern to another place to explore.

> The mother duck **takes** her ducklings walking.

In this example, mother duck leads her ducklings to another place.

Hint

bring or take?

Remember, the word *bring* involves someone shifting something **towards** another place or person.

The word *take* involves someone shifting something **away** to another place or person.

---

brought

See **bought / brought**

bullet points (•)

Bullet points (also called *dot points*) are dots that are used to list items in a text. The list of items usually has a short sentence or phrase to introduce the list. Bullet points have become more common in writing since the invention of word processors.

> When playing in the sun, it is advisable to wear:
> • sunscreen on exposed skin;
> • a hat to shade your face;
> • a top to cover your body.

- A colon is used at the end of the introduction phrase.
- A semicolon is used at the end of each item in the list except the last (this is because the items are phrases and clauses).
- The last item ends with a full stop.

See also **colon**: **Lists**; **report**: **Classification** (writing sample); WORD HISTORIES: **bullet points (•)**.

business letters

See **correspondence**: **Business letters**.

callout

Callout is another name for a speech balloon or speech bubble. Callouts show what characters in a text are saying or thinking (dialogue).

Callouts are also used to show thoughts. Instead of a 'tail' pointing to the speaker, thoughts have a series of little 'bubbles' leading to the speaker.

In the following example, the author uses illustrated characters to speak to the reader. Their speech is shown in callouts. Each callout has a 'tail' which points to the speaker. If a speaker is making more than one statement, then the callouts are linked or overlapped.

Writers often use callouts when a text is mainly dialogue. Some examples of this are comic strips and cartoons.

See also **dialogue (US: dialog)**.

To find out how the advertisers try to convince you to buy the toy you can ask:

What words or pictures do they use to make me want the toy?

Can I enjoy playing with the toy without all the accessories advertisers want me to buy?

How are movies, cartoons, comics and books used to sell particular toys?

What do you learn about being a boy or a girl?

What does the toy tell you about the ways boys and girls could behave, dress and play?

Consumer guide to toys, p. 17

can / may

Can is a verb. It means 'to be able to'. It can be used as part of a compound verb.

> You **can** ride my horse while I am on holiday.

May is a form of the verb 'might'. It means 'to be allowed to' or 'is possible'. It can be used as part of a compound verb.

> You **may** borrow my book.
> I **may** get there in time.

Today, in English, people tend to use *can* and *may* to mean the same thing. However, *may* is generally used in more formal or polite language, if the meaning is about being allowed to do something.

See also **verbs**: **Compound**.

capitals

Capital letters make some words stand out on a page and seem more important than other words around them. They are sometimes called *upper case* letters.

capitals

When the first letter of a word is a capital, then the word is *capitalised*. A word that has all letters in capitals is in *full capitals*. Capitals are used for many purposes in writing.

See also WORD HISTORIES: **capital**.

Further information is under the following topics:

Direct speech
Government
Headings and subheadings
Numbers
Personal pronoun *I*
Proper nouns
Relations (family)
Religion
    God(s) and holy persons
    Holy days
    Religious groups/churches
    Sacred books
    Words for holy beings
Scientific terms
    Astronomy
    Plants and animals
    Weather
Sentence beginnings and parts
Time and calendar terms
    Days and months
    Holidays and special days
    Periods in natural history
    Time zones
Titles of works
    Major use of capitals
    Minor use of capitals
    Full use of capitals
Trends and rules for using capitals
    Email
    Emphasis

Direct speech
A capital letter is used for the first word of each sentence in direct speech.

      "**He's** too young to drive a car," said the police officer.
      "**Monkeys** live in rainforests," said the zookeeper.

Sometimes, direct speech is not written at the beginning of a sentence — but the first word of the direct speech is still capitalised.

> I smiled mysteriously and replied, "**That's** not how I would do it."
> Rosa began, "**Daddy's** away on business, but…"
> He said, "**Each** time we try we get better at it."

Writers sometimes interrupt direct speech with other words. If the direct speech continues in the same sentence, then the second part of the direct speech does not begin with a capital letter (unless the first word is the personal pronoun *I* or a proper noun).

> "Because," he shouted, "**you've** got stolen property of mine!"
> "But," cried Ahmed, "**this** show is booked out."

When direct speech is interrupted with other words, and the spoken words continue in a new sentence, then the second sentence of the direct speech begins with a capital letter.

> 'You lost it!' I snapped. '**From** now on I do things my way.'

In this example, you know that *From now on* is the beginning of a new sentence, because there is a full stop after the word *snapped*.

See also **direct speech**; **nouns**: **Proper nouns**; **pronouns**: **Personal pronouns**.

Government
Words like *government, federal, national, state, province, shire* and *city* are given a capital letter when they refer to a *particular* government, country, region or city.

> Both the **Australian Federal Government** and the **State Governments** are responsible for education in that country.

These words are not capitalised if they refer to government generally (not a particular government or region etc).

> Education is funded by **local government**.

Headings and subheadings
Headings and subheadings are capitalised. This is common in nonfiction texts.

Whales
Toothed whales
> There are about thirty known species of toothed whales, the largest of which is the sperm whale.

In this example, the main heading is in larger type than the subheading. However, both headings are capitalised, no matter what the type size is.

capitals

Numbers
Words and letters that include a numeral are often capitalised.

> The neighbours in **No. 31** called the police because we were making so much noise at our party.

> The children wondered what the teacher had planned for the class of **5D** that afternoon.

Personal Pronoun *I*
The word *I* is a personal pronoun. It is always capitalised.

> As I walked home I made a mental list of what I had to do.
> I'm not responsible for the actions of others am I?
> My grandparents couldn't believe how much I'd grown.

See also **pronouns**: **Personal pronouns**.

Proper nouns
Capitals are used for all proper nouns (the names of particular people, places and things).

* awards and competitions
  > Cousteau made a film called *The Silent World*. It won an **Academy Award**.
* brand names and trademarks
  > **Magi-Clean**
* business names
  > The customer wrote a letter of complaint to **Crispy Chips Pty Ltd** about the quality of their product.
* business titles (when written together with the name of the person)
  > Yours faithfully
  > Sherman Hayes, **Director**
  However, if the word is not used as part of a title, then it does not have a capital.
  > Sherman Hayes is a company **director**.
* events
  > All schools were closed for **Anzac Day**.
  > They arranged to meet on **New Year's Eve**.
  > I wish we could go somewhere over **Easter**.
* institutions
  > When I came to the city I attended **Cabra College**.
* military groups and events
  > Armstrong had been a test pilot, and Aldrin and Collins were pilots in **The United States Airforce**.
  > During the **Gulf War**, over seven hundred oil wells were set on fire or damaged by soldiers.

- names of buildings (famous and public)

    Historians are still studying **Stonehenge** to learn about the people who built it.

    The final concert scene in the movie 'Shine' was filmed in the **Adelaide Town Hall**.

- names of organisations and offices

    We spent many months training and packing stores at the **Australian Head Office** in Hobart, before beginning our 6,000km journey to Mawson.

- names of people

    Herman Hill

    Elizabeth Ashley-Warner

- names of pets

    I've got a dog. His name is **Nelson**.

- names of places

    They travelled throughout South-East Asia.

    Snakes are not found in the **Arctic Circle**, **Ireland**, **New Zealand** and **Antarctica**.

- nationalities

    A **Russian** tourist ship stopped at the port.

- nicknames

    '**Buzz**' Aldrin was the second person to step onto the moon.

- official titles (when written together with the name of the person)

    President John F. Kennedy of the United States of America.

- titles such as *mister, doctor, uncle, aunt, captain, lady* and *sir* when used with a person's name

    "Not in my backyard!" gasped **Uncle** Roger.

    "But these trees are beautiful, Roger," replied my aunt.

    "Oh Sandra!" spluttered my poor uncle, "They grow huge roots."

    "Does it really matter? It's pretty, isn't it Andy dear?" said **Aunt** Sandra, turning to me.

- vessels (transport)

    In 1950 Cousteau was given a ship, called **Calypso**.

Relations (family)

The words *dad, mum, grandmother* and *auntie* etc are written in lower case, unless they are the first word in a sentence, or they refer directly to a particular person.

"**Mum**, **Dad**, I think you had better come quickly," she shouted.

The words *mum* and *dad* are capitalised in this example because they refer directly to particular people who are characters in a story.

Would you believe it, my **mother** is changing her career!

The word *mother* is not capitalised in this example, because the writer does not refer to the person directly.

Religion
The following religious terms are capitalised:

God(s) and holy persons
The names of gods and holy persons in any religion are capitalised. The word *God* is also capitalised if it means the only god in a religion.

> The survivors of the crash thanked **God** for their lives.

Holy days

> On **Easter Friday** the family went to church.

Religious groups/churches

> **Baptist Church, Buddhism, Christianity, Hinduism, Islam, Judaism**

Sacred books

> **Bible, Dead Sea Scrolls, Koran, Talmud, Veda**

Words for holy beings

> The Australian Aborigines of a particular area tell tales of the **Rainbow Serpent**, a **Creator Ancestor** from their Dreaming.

> **Allah, Buddha, Christ, Jehovah, Mohammed**

See also WORD HISTORIES: **holiday**.

Scientific terms
Capitals are used for the following scientific terms:

Astronomy

The names of particular planets, stars, moons and asteroids are capitalised. However, the words *sun* (our sun), *earth* and *moon* (our moon) are only capitalised when mentioned in relation to other planets.

> Gravity holds the **Moon** in orbit around **Earth**. And it holds the planets in order around the **Sun**. It would take about nine months for a spacecraft to travel from **Earth** to **Mars**.

If earth is not mentioned in relation to other planets, then it is lower case.

> Greenpeace is concerned about how we treat planet **earth**.

Plants and animals

Plants and animals have scientific names, usually written in italics. The genus name (first name in italics) is capitalised.

> ***Amanita** muscaria*, also called Fly Agaric, is a poisonous fungus.

There are different rules for capitalising the common names of plants and animals (eg blue whale). The *Young writers guide* uses capitals for proper nouns only.

> The khaki **Campbell** is a kind of duck that can be kept in a backyard. In this example, *Campbell* is capitalised because it is the name of the first person to breed these ducks.

Weather

When cyclones, typhoons or hurricanes are given human names, only that name is capitalised.

> Darwin was almost destroyed by cyclone **Tracy** in 1974.

Sentence beginnings and parts

Authors do not always express ideas in complete sentences. Sometimes a single word, phrase, or clause begins with a capital letter.

Captions and legends

The sentences in captions and legends are often written in note form. They always begin with a capital, but they do not always end with a full stop.

See also **captions and legends**.

Exclamations

An exclamation — whether it is a word, phrase or a sentence — begins with a capital letter.

> "**Yuck!**" screamed Jessie. "**That's** the worst food I've ever eaten!"
> He ran for the home base and dived just in time. **Safe!**
> "**Well** done, my friend! **What** a wonderful meal!"

See also **exclamations**.

capitals

Lists

Most lists have two parts — the *introduction* (a sentence or phrase) — and a *list of items*.

A sentence or phrase that introduces a list always begins with a capital.

> **Don't** put fish aquariums:
> • in a room when you spray for insects;
> • next to a heater;
> • under an airconditioner.

Items in a list are not always complete sentences. The items in the list do *not* begin with a capital if they are sentence fragments.

> The problems with waste include:
> • **the** amount of waste created by our 'throw away society';
> • **space** needed to dispose of waste;
> • **the** expense of waste disposal;
> • **damage** to the environment;
> • **toxic** waste.

Items in a list *do* begin with a capital if they are complete sentences.

> Six people, who play different roles, were interviewed about their opinions on the following questions:
> • **What** are the problems with waste disposal?
> • **How** should these problems be solved?
> • **Who** is responsible for solving these problems?

See also **report**: **Classification**; **sentence fragments**.

Phrases

When an author uses a phrase as a complete idea, the first word of the phrase begins with a capital.

> **Wow**! **What** a disaster. **Panic** in the kitchen.

Authors use phrases in direct speech because that is how people often speak. Such phrases are often capitalised.

> "**Any** news?" asked Dad.
> "**Not** yet."

Poems and verse

The first word in each line of a poem or verse often begins with a capital letter, even if it is not a sentence beginning.

> TO SAMUEL KNOTT
>
> **Here** lies the body of Samuel Knott;
> **His** father was Knott before him.
> **He** lived Knott,
> **He** died Knott,
> **And** underneath this stone he lies,
> **Knott** christened, Knott begot,
> **But** most of all, forgot not.

Anonymous

Time and calendar terms

The following time and calendar terms are capitalised:

Days and months
> Her birthday this year is on the first **Monday** in **May**.

Holidays and special days
> The family held a party to celebrate **New Year's Day**.

Periods in natural history
The name of a particular period in natural history is capitalised, but the words *period* and *era* are not.
> Tyrannosaurus rex lived in the **Jurassic** period.

Time zones
> The national broadcast was planned for midday **Eastern Standard Time**.

Titles of works

The following titles are capitalised:
- books, magazines, journals, newspapers, periodicals, newsletters, recipes and manuscripts
> The most popular book that week was, **An Atlas of Space Travel**.
- computer software
> They loaded the new program, **An Interactive Encyclopedia of Science** onto their computer.
- films, videos and television programs
> Cousteau made a film called **The Silent World**.
- pictures, paintings, drawings, photographs, sketches, posters, cartoons
> The **Mona Lisa** painting had special security at the gallery.
- plays, ballets and other works performed on stage
> At age fifteen, she danced in the ballet, **Coppelia**.
- poems
> **The Cats of Kilkenny**

- songs
  > Jacqui played her best-known classical piece called **Fur Elise** then Rachel followed with **Greensleeves**.

There are three ways to capitalise the titles of works and sections or chapter headings of works.

Major use of capitals
All words are given capitals except the articles *(a, an, the)*, conjunctions (*and, so, or, if* etc) and prepositions (*to, from, with, for* etc).
> **The Tiger, the Brahman and the Jackal (a Play)**

Minor use of capitals
Capitals are used only for the first word in the title, and words that would normally have a capital (proper nouns and proper adjectives).
> **Letters to Leah**
> **The first lunar landing**

Full use of capitals
Every letter in the main title is capitalised. Sometimes a mix of full capitals and the other methods is used when there is a sub-heading.
> *PILAWUK: When I Was Young*

Full capitals may be used on the covers of books, CD-ROMs, videos, magazines, or on the title screen of a movie. However, if the same title were written in an index, or quoted in a text, then either the major or the minor method of using capitals would be used.

Sometimes a chapter heading is written in full capitals and a subheading (apart from the first letter) in lower case.
> WHAT ARE THE PROBLEMS?
> Household waste

This makes it easy for the reader to distinguish between a main heading and a subheading.

See also **articles**; **conjunctions**; **nouns**: **Proper nouns**; **prepositions**.

Trends and rules for using capitals
The main rule for using capitals is to choose a style and be consistent with it in a piece of writing. When different styles, such as *major use*, *minor use* and *full use* of capitals, are acceptable, choose the style that you prefer.

The use of capitals for emphasis has become more popular, especially in children's books, although some people find this use unnecessary.
> The giant was so **BIG** that everyone trembled.

Email

Full capitals are often used in email when someone is replying to an email. Some writers write answers or comments in full capitals within the original email.

> <rod@footyco.com>
> Hi Charles
> Thank you for your report. I have given my comments to your points below in capitals.
> Rod
>
> >Hi Rod
> >Here is my report on things that happened yesterday.
> >1. The footballers arrived for practice but we couldn't find the equipment in the clubroom. They will return tomorrow for a practice session.
> THE EQUIPMENT WAS SENT OUT FOR REPAIRS. THAT IS WHY IT WAS NOT IN THE CLUBROOM. YOU WILL FIND IT AT PETE'S SPORTS STORE.
>
> >2. We can't find the new uniforms for the team playing this weekend.
> THE NEW UNIFORMS ARE SUPPOSED TO BE DELIVERED ON THURSDAY IN TIME FOR THE GAME ON SATURDAY.

The style shown in this example is becoming less popular because:

* Full capitals are more difficult to read.
* The reply is cut up into sections and some text is easily missed by the reader.
* Coloured text (especially blue) is becoming a more popular way of showing replies.

It is common for writers to use capitals less often in emails, especially in informal writing between people who know each other well.

> <jenny@horses.co.uk>
> hi cathy
> i will be arriving by train at 10 am on sunday looking forward to seeing you at the station
> love jenny

In this email example, the writer ignores capitals and punctuation altogether. This is usually because, in informal writing like this, people find it quicker to communicate without capitals and punctuation. We will have to wait for some years to discover whether this trend becomes well-established.

Emphasis

The use of capitals for emphasis has become popular, especially in children's books.

> Dear Diary
> I saw Richard today. He is **SO BOSSY** I think I will avoid him.

This example is written in the style of a personal diary. The use of capitals for emphasis is suitable here because diaries are usually an informal writing style. Many people prefer not to use capitals in this way for formal writing.

Using full capitals in emails is used by some writers as a form of emphasis. Often this is considered as 'shouting' and is regarded as impolite. It can be quite acceptable among friends, as shown in the following example.

> <cathy@stablemate.com>
> Jenny
> I can't understand the homework we are supposed to do this weekend. HELP! CAN I COME OVER TO YOUR PLACE?
> Cathy

In this example, the email is an informal letter to a friend. The 'shouting' in capitals shows that the writer is excited or shouting for help.

> <smith.r@warehouse.com>
> Subject: Wrong delivery
> Today our warehouse received damaged goods from your office. We are returning the goods for replacement. PLEASE ENSURE THAT THE NEXT SHIPMENT IS WELL PACKED.
> A Jones
> Manager

In this example, the email is a formal business letter. The capital letters would be considered ill-mannered. In business correspondence, people do not appreciate being 'shouted' at. See also **correspondence: Appointment by informal email**.

For information about other uses of capitals see under:
abbreviations
acronyms
addresses
captions and legends
colon (:)
compass points
direct speech
emphasis
eponyms
headwords
measures
small capitals

captions and legends

Captions

A caption is a group of words that explains a picture, diagram or chart. Captions begin with a capital letter. If a caption is a full sentence, then it can end with a full stop — but this is not always done. Captions are usually placed under or alongside the picture, diagram or chart they describe.

In the following example from a newspaper style text, the caption is a very short sentence that adds humour. The author has used alliteration (*wears winter woollies*) to make the language interesting and hold the reader's attention. The informal word 'woollies' suggests to the reader that this is a funny story.

Hello Cocky!

Cocky wears winter 'woollies'

Rescues, p.14

Legends

Captions with more than one full sentence are sometimes called *legends*. The following example is a legend — it has two complete sentences. Each sentence begins with a capital letter.

This equipment collects methane gas from a landfill site. The gas is used as energy for homes.

A legend can also be colour codes used in an illustration or chart. The following example is from a book that reports on four types of climate. The legend helps readers to understand the information on the map.

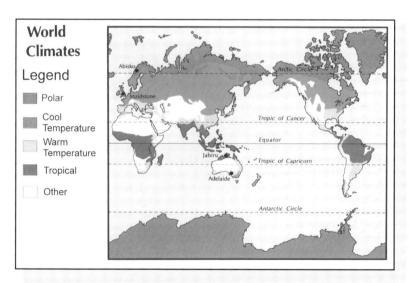

World Climates

Legend

Polar

Cool Temperature

Warm Temperature

Tropical

Other

The following example is a legend with a list of symbols that show the reader details about journeys made by people in Antarctica.

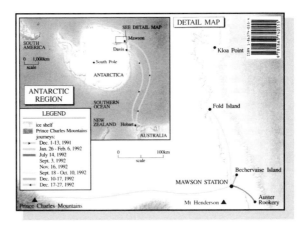

See also **symbols**.

case

In English, nouns and pronouns can have different uses in a sentence. These different uses are called *cases*. Nouns and pronouns have three cases — *subjective, objective* and *possessive*.

Further information on case is under the following headings:
Case of nouns
Case of pronouns
Pronouns and prepositions

Case of nouns
The case of a noun is usually shown by its position in a sentence.
> The child held the dog's collar.

In this sentence, *dog* owns or possesses the collar. So the word *dog* has changed to *dog's*. It is in the possessive case.

> The **child** chased the **dog**.

In this sentence, the noun *child* is in the *subjective* case.

> The **dog** chased the **child**.

Here, the noun *child* is in the *objective* case, but the noun looks exactly the same in both cases. Nouns do not change their form if they are a subject or an object in a sentence.

Nouns *do* change their form in the possessive case.
> The child fetched the **dog's** ball.

In this sentence *dog* owns the ball, so the word *dog* has changed to *dog's*. It is now in the *possessive case*.

See also **apostrophe**: **Apostrophe of possession**; **nouns**; **pronouns**; WORD HISTORIES: **apostrophe of possession (')**.

Case of pronouns

Like nouns, pronouns have three cases (*subjective, objective* and *possessive*). However, unlike nouns, many pronouns change their form for all three cases. This table shows the three cases for each singular pronoun.

Subjective	Objective	Possessive
I	me	my
you	you	your
he/she/it	him/her/it	his/her/hers/its

I gave a friend a gift. (*I* is the subject of *gave*.)
A friend gave **me** a gift. (*me* is the object of *gave*.)
My friend gave me a gift. (*My* 'owns' the friend, so it is possessive.)
In these examples, the pronouns *I*, *me* and *my* are used to suit the case needed to make sense in each sentence. If the wrong case is used, then the sentence would not be correct in formal writing.
Me friend gave me a gift. (X)
In this example, the writer has used the objective *me* when it should be the possessive *my*.
My friend gave me a gift. (✓)

Most pronouns also have different forms for singular and plural in each case. This table shows the three cases for each plural pronoun. Notice how *you* has the same word for two cases. All the other pronouns have different words.

Subjective	Objective	Possessive
we	us	our/ours
you	you	your/yours
they	them	their/theirs

We invited friends for dinner. (*We* is the subject of *invited*.)
Friends invited **us** for dinner. (*us* is the object of *invited*.)
We went to dinner with **our** friends. (*our* 'owns' the friends, so it is possessive.)

My friend and me (or I)?

Sometimes the subject or object in a sentence can be a noun plus a pronoun. When this happens, many writers are confused about which pronoun to use (me or I). The trick is to work out whether the noun and the pronoun is the subject or the object in the sentence.

My friend and I (me?) gave him a gift.

A simple way to work this out is to leave out the other person and see which pronoun makes sense.

Me gave him a gift. (X)

I gave him a gift. (✓)

Therefore the correct sentence is My friend and I gave him a gift.

He gave my friend and I (me?) a gift.

He gave I a gift. (X)

He gave me a gift. (✓)

Therefore the correct sentence is He gave my friend and me a gift.

Pronouns and prepositions
When a pronoun follows a preposition (*for, between, to, by, over, around, on* etc), it is in the *objective* case.

You had to feel sorry **for him**.
We went to the city **with him**.
It is hard to choose **between you and him**.

In these sentences, the pronoun *him* is in the objective case because it follows the preposition *for*. It would not make sense to write *You had to feel sorry for he* or *You had to feel sorry for his*. In the last example, both pronouns *you* and *him* follow the preposition *between*.

See also **agreement**; **between you and me**; **plural**; **prepositions**; **singular**.

case study

A case study is a report on one thing or person as an example of a larger group of things or people. Case studies are used when a book, magazine or video is not large enough to hold all the information known about a topic. So the writer gives information about enough examples within a topic to give the reader a general understanding of the subject.

In her book *Investigating fungi*, the author, Gwen Pascoe, did not have enough room to write everything there is to know about fungi. So she began her book with a general description of what fungi are, then presented the reader with a number of case studies on certain examples of fungi. These case studies give the reader enough detail to make the topic interesting and informative. The following example shows the case study *Puffballs* from this book.

See also **report**: **Case studies**.

Puffballs

Puffballs are like pouches of spores. If you step on a ripe puffball, it sends up a cloud of spores. Some puffballs are very large, up to about 1.8 metres (5.9 ft) in circumference!

◁
Common puffballs, *Lycoperdon sp.* Usually found in grasslands and forests.

Earthstar, *Geastrum indicum*
∨

Puffballs called *Earthstars* can be used as weather forecasters. If wet weather is coming, the points open so that spores can spread, but if the weather is very dry, they close.

Investigating fungi, p. 10

cause and effect

Cause and effect is a way to present information in a text. It shows how one thing leads to another. Conjunctions and connectives can be used to link the ideas in a cause and effect text. A cause and effect text has sections that are linked to explain how one thing has an effect on something else.

SMOKING KILLS!

Nicotine and tar are substances that are found in tobacco. When tobacco burns, these substances are carried in the smoke. Smokers inhale the smoke into their lungs. A child in a car in which others are smoking, inhales the smoke created by others. This is called *passive smoking*.

Tobacco smoke is known to be a cause of cancer, asthma and many other illnesses. People who do not smoke can still inhale nicotine and tar through passive smoking, and can be affected as if they are smokers.

In this example, the first sentence in each paragraph is a summary of what that paragraph is about. The first paragraph describes tobacco (the *cause*) as a substance, and how it gets into the human body. The second paragraph describes the *effects* of tobacco on humans. The writer links the ideas by having the *effect* paragraph immediately follow the *cause* paragraph. The first sentence of the second paragraph begins with the words *Tobacco smoke*, which was the topic of the first paragraph.

Tobacco smoke is **known to be** a cause of cancer …

The connective phrase, *known to be*, then connects that idea to the effect.

A flood may happen **if** more rain than usual falls during a rainy season.

The *cause* in this sentence is *more rain than usual falls during a rainy season*. The *effect* is *a flood may happen*. The conjunction *if* links the ideas.

Other conjunctions used to link ideas in *cause and effect* sentences include: as, when, because, which, for, so, since, if … then

When a cow is milked, the milk runs into a space called a cistern and finally passes out through the teat.

The conjunction *when* links the cause *a cow is milked* with the effect *the milk runs into a space*.

The bird had an incurable disease, **which** stops new feathers from growing.

The conjunction *which* links the cause *incurable disease* with the effect *stops new feathers from growing*.

Some snake bites are more deadly than others **because** their venom is more toxic.

The conjunction *because* links the cause *their venom is more toxic* with the effect *some snake bites are more deadly than others*.

See also **conjunctions**; **connectives**; **explanation**.

cereal / serial

Cereal is a seed or grain (*wheat, barley, oats, rye* etc).

Many people eat **cereal** for breakfast.

A *serial* is a tale that is written, presented or performed in several parts at different times. Serials can be books, plays, movies or television programs. *Serial* is related to the word *series*.

The children insisted on seeing their favourite TV **serial** every Tuesday night.
I read the first book in the **series** and then had to buy the next one.

See also WORD HISTORIES: **cereal**, **serial**.

certain / curtain

Certain means 'for sure'. It is pronounced /**sir**-tun/.

One thing was **certain**: the stranger was not to be trusted.
The pupils were no longer **certain** that they were glad to be back.

Curtain means 'a window covering' or 'hanging cloth'. It is pronounced /**kir**-tun/.

A thin **curtain** gave little privacy between decks of the old ship.
The **curtain** was drawn across the window.

chant

The noun *chant* means 'a verse or short text that is sung, read or spoken in a sing-song way'. Chants can be performed by groups or individuals.

The verb *to chant* means 'to sing in a rhythmic, repeated way'. In the following example, three characters in the play *Macbeth* chant these words to cast a spell.

> Double, double toil and trouble;
> Fire burn and cauldron bubble.
> Fillet of a fenny snake,
> In the cauldron boil and bake;
> Eye of newt and toe of frog;
> Wool of bat and tongue of dog,
> Adder's fork and blind-worm's sting,
> Lizard's leg and howlet's wing,
> For a charm of powerful trouble,
> Like a hell-broth boil and bubble.

Macbeth: IV. i. 10-19; 35-38, William Shakespeare

The following example is a favourite children's chant:

> Miss Mary Mac, Mac, Mac
> All dressed in black, black, black,
> With silver buttons, buttons, buttons,
> All down her back, back, back.

Traditional

See also WORD HISTORIES: **chant**.

character

A character in a story is a person, animal or thing that the writer invents. Characters act out the events in a story, like actors on a stage. Main characters in a story can be heroes or villains. It is important for characters to have interesting personalities so the reader will care about them and want to keep reading the story to the end.

See also **narrative**.

check / cheque

Check can be used as a verb. It means:

* to inspect, review or examine
  Nurses would pop their heads around the door and **check** what was going on.
* to stop
  The driver used the handbrake to **check** the car from rolling.
  They managed to **check** their tempers even though they were angry.

Check can also be used as a noun.
  The mechanic gave the car a thorough **check**.

Check can be part of compound words.
  checkup, spellcheck, checkmate, checkpoint

Cheque is a noun. It means 'a money order — a signed paper that can be used instead of coins or notes, to order a bank to pay money to someone'.
  Many people pay their bills by **cheque**.
In the United States of America, the word *check* is used for both the above meanings; *cheque* is not used as a US spelling.

See also **nouns**; **verbs**.

choose / chose

Choose is pronounced /chooze/ as in *snooze*. It means 'to select'.

  May I look through your books and **choose** one to read?

Chose is pronounced /choze/ as in doze. It is the past tense of *choose*.
  Yesterday I **chose** to read one of your books.

See **verbs**: **Tenses (time)**.

chronological

Chronological means 'in order of time'. Chronological writing is written in the order that events happened. Texts that recount events (*journals, diaries, biographies, autobiographies, narratives*) or explain a process, are usually written in chronological order.

Some chronological texts, for example *journals*, are organised according to dates and even hours of the day.

In the following example from a personal journal, the writer has dated the journal entry Wednesday, 5th February. The author then made notes at different hours of the evening and night.

Date: Wednesday, 5th February 2002

Temperature: -4°C

Weather: Cloudy with some wind

6 p.m. One of our vehicles has broken an axle. This is a problem, especially if a blizzard sets in. I radioed the base camp for assistance.

8 p.m. The team of mechanics arrived and began work on the disabled vehicle.

10 p.m. Still repairing the vehicle. Cold winds are hampering progress. We prepared hot drinks for the mechanics.

2 a.m. Job completed at last. We all settled in the sleeping compartments as it would be too dangerous to continue to travel in this weather at night.

Words and phrases such as *first, initially, in the beginning, then, after, afterwards, the following, next, finally* and *last*, are often used in chronological writing.

First I was taken to the hospital. **Then** a nurse wheeled me into a small room.

At first chicks stay very close to the hen for warmth and protection. She makes gentle noises to them. **Within** three to five hours of hatching, the chicks become dry. Their soft, fluffy coats are called *down*. **After** a few hours, they follow the mother around the yard.

Chapter headings sometimes show that the author is presenting information in the order of time that events happened. This can be seen in the following table of contents from a nonfiction text *The first lunar landing*. After doing the research for this text, the author planned the chapter headings in the order that things happened. He then did the first draft by grouping information from his notes under these headings.

Contents

	Page
Introduction	3
Apollo Spacecraft/Saturn V Rocket	4
The Astronauts	5
Training for the Journey	6
Journey to the Moon	8
At Work on the Moon	12
Returning to Earth	14
Lesson from Apollo 11	16
Apollo Lunar Landings	18
Index	19
Glossary	20

See also **explanation**; **recount**; WORD HISTORIES: **chronology**.

cinquain

A cinquain (pronounced /**sin**-kwain/) is a poem that has five lines. Each line has a particular purpose.

Line 1: names the topic or title of the poem.
Line 2: describes the topic, often with adjectives.
Line 3: focuses on an action — one or more verbs are often used.
Line 4: describes a feeling.
Line 5: returns to the topic. It may have a synonym.

> Children
> Eager and adventurous
> Splashing in a puddle
> Joyfully exploring the water —
> Tomorrow's pioneers

See also **adjectives**; **synonyms**; **verbs**.

clauses

A clause is a group of words that expresses a complete thought. It has a *subject* (something the clause is about) and a *predicate* (something that is said about the subject).

Celia's eyes shone.

This example is a clause because it has a subject (*Celia's eyes*) and a predicate with a complete verb (*shone*).

Celia's shining eyes.

This example is not a clause because, although it has a subject (*Celia's shining eyes*), it does not say anything about the subject.

See also **predicate**; **verbs**.

There are two main types of clauses:
Main clauses
Subordinate clauses

Main clauses

A main clause makes sense on its own. Main clauses are also called *independent* clauses. This is because they can be complete sentences without needing other parts.

> As usual, the team met before the game.

Main clauses can be joined to make a longer sentence. Each main clause in the sentence is equally important. They are joined by conjunctions such as *and, but, or, so* and *yet*.

> As usual, the team met before the game, **but** the players were not as confident as usual.

This sentence has two main clauses. Each clause could be a complete sentence by itself.

> As usual, the team met before the game. The players were not as confident as usual.

See also **conjunctions**.

Subordinate clauses

A subordinate clause does not make sense on its own. It always needs a main clause to complete the sentence.

> … which was the last match of the season.

This example is a subordinate clause; it does not make sense alone.

A subordinate clause and a main clause can be joined to make a sentence. The main clause is the most important part of the sentence. The subordinate clause adds meaning to the main clause.

> As usual, the team met before the game [*main clause*] which was the last match of the season [*subordinate clause*].

There are four kinds of subordinate clauses. For information on the four kinds, see **adjectival clauses**; **adverbial clauses**; **conditional clauses**; **noun clauses**.

clichés

Clichés are expressions that are used so often they make speech and writing sound boring and unoriginal. It is best to avoid clichés in your writing. Some examples include:

> keep your nose to the grindstone
> as slow as a snail
> as bright as a button
> put the cat among the pigeons
> living in the fast lane
> at the crack of dawn

See also WORD HISTORIES: **cliché**.

clipped words

Clipped words are shortened forms of other words. People create clipped words so they can say words and phrases more quickly. The clipped form sometimes becomes so common that the original, longer word is forgotten. For example, the clipped word *pram* is more common than the original word, *perambulator*.

Many clipped words are used in writing.

> Today **zoo** staff try to create more natural habitat exhibits.

The word *zoo* is a clipped form of *zoological gardens*.

> There's a **fax** from Dad and a **plane** ticket to visit him.

Fax is a clipped form of *facsimile*. *Plane* is short for *aeroplane* or *airplane* (US). Some clipped words, for example *bike* (bicycle), *ad* (advertisement), *croc* (crocodile), and *roo* (kangaroo), are slang and are not usually used in formal writing. They are used more in personal notes, letters or in speech.

See also writing sample under **correspondence**: **Informal business letter**; WORD HISTORIES: **goodbye**, **handicap**, **pram**.

clipped words

Here is a list of clipped words:
- ad (advertisement)
- Aussie (Australian)
- bike (bicycle)
- bra (brassiere)
- Brit (British person)
- budgie (budgerigar)
- burger (hamburger)
- bus (omnibus)
- bye (goodbye)
- cab (cabriolet)
- cello (violoncello)
- chimp (chimpanzee)
- chips (chipped potatoes)
- cinema (cinematograph)
- cox (coxswain, in a rowing team)
- croc (crocodile)
- curio (curiosity)
- deli (delicatessen)
- disco (discotheque)
- email (electronic mail)
- exam (examination)
- fan (fanatic)
- fax (facsimile)
- flu (influenza)
- fridge (refrigerator)
- fries (French fries)
- gas (gasoline)
- gent (gentleman)
- goodbye (God be with ye)
- gym (gymnasium)
- handicap (hand in cap)
- hanky (handkerchief)
- hippo (hippopotamus)
- knickers (knickerbockers)
- marge (margarine)
- maths/math (US) (mathematics)
- memo (memorandum)
- mike (microphone)
- Net (Internet)
- pants (pantaloons)
- perm (permanent wave — hairdressing)
- petrol (petroleum)
- plane (aeroplane/airplane (US))

- photo (photograph)
- piano (pianoforte)
- polio (poliomyelitis)
- pop (popular)
- pram (perambulator)
- pro (professional)
- prof (professor)
- pub (public house)
- quads (quadruplets)
- quins (quintuplets)
- rhino (rhinoceros)
- roo (kangaroo)
- scrum (scrummage — rugby)
- spec (speculation)
- specs (specifications, spectacles)
- sub (submarine, subscriptions, substitute)
- taxi (taximeter cab)
- TB (tuberculosis)
- telly (television)
- turps (turpentine)
- TV (television)
- typo (typographical error)
- undies (underpants or underwear)
- vet (veterinary surgeon)
- video (video tape)
- Web (World Wide Web)
- wellies (Wellington boots)
- yank (Yankee — US person)
- zoo (zoological gardens)

See also WORD HISTORIES: **goodbye**; **handicap**.

close

Close is pronounced and used in two different ways.

- It can be an adverb meaning 'near or nearby'. It is pronounced /cloas/ as in *dose* or *gross*.
    They kept a very **close** watch on everything at the zoo.
- It can be a verb meaning 'to shut'. It is pronounced /cloze/ as in *doze* or *those*.
    The jaws of the trap **closed** upon the bear's foot.

coarse / course

Coarse is an adjective. It means 'rough'.

>   The sandpaper felt very **coarse**.

Course is usually a noun. It can mean:
*   a program of study
    >   The class began lessons in an English **course**.
*   a direction or way
    >   They became lost because they took the wrong **course**.

Course is also used in the phrase *of course*. It means 'certainly, naturally, yes'.
>   I wanted to help but **of course** I couldn't with my broken arm.

See also **adjectives**; **nouns**.

collective nouns

Collective nouns are words that describe groups of people, animals or things. Some examples of collective nouns are:
*   people:
    >   family, team (of players), class (of pupils), committee, crowd, council, audience, group
*   animals:
    >   pride (of lions), school (of fish), herd (of cattle, horses, elephants), gaggle (of geese on the ground) but a skein (of geese flying), murder (of crows), flock (of sheep, birds)
*   things:
    >   pack (of biscuits), bunch (of grapes), hand (of bananas), bundle (of sticks), pile (of logs)

It is important in writing to remember that collective nouns mean a single group even though there is more than one member in the group. Writers often make the mistake of using a plural verb with a singular collective noun in a sentence. This means the sentence does not have agreement.
>   The crowd **were cheering** the players. (X)
>   The crowd **was cheering** the players. (✓)

There is only one crowd. So the verb must be *was cheering*, not *were cheering*.

See also **agreement: Agreement for collective nouns**; **nouns: Collective nouns**.

colloquial language

Colloquial language is informal, everyday language. It includes words and phrases (*colloquialisms*) that are used and understood by a particular group of people (in a particular region or community), but not by people who are outside that group or region.

> "Go get some vittals. An' get yerself somewheres to sleep. Me friends can't watch out fer ya by the earth baths f'rever."

Hannah, p. 46

In this example, the character uses the words vittals to mean food and earth baths to mean graves. These are colloquialisms.

Further example:

> The other day, I met a bear,
> In groovy shoes, a smacking good pair.

Traditional

Writing tip

When to use colloquial language in writing

Colloquial language is useful if you are writing for a local audience that understands words and phrases commonly used within that region. Articles in local magazines and newsletters, or newspaper reports about topics of local community interest, can be successful if they have local words that make the audience feel the article was written especially for them. It is *not* a good idea to use colloquial language if your audience will not understand the words or phrases you are using.

See also **slang**.

colon (:)

A colon is a punctuation mark used to introduce more details about something that has been said in a sentence.

> There are two types of seadragons: weedy seadragons and leafy seadragons.

In this example, the author could have ended the sentence after the first clause *There are two types of seadragons*. The colon introduces or links the phrase *weedy seadragons and leafy seadragons* to this clause. The phrase adds more details to the main clause.

A dash can be used instead of a colon. Some people think the dash is more informal.

> There are two types of seadragons — weedy seadragons and leafy seadragons.

See also **dash (—)**; **report**: **Compare and contrast**.

Further information is under the following topics:
Lists
Captions
Play scripts and transcripts
Titles and subtitles
Headings, memos, journals and faxes
Newspaper articles
When to use with capitals

Lists

A colon is often used at the end of a clause or phrase that introduces a list of items.

> **For example, people can:**
> • buy non-toxic products and refuse to buy goods in unnecessary packaging;
> • persuade politicians to protect the environment;
> • recycle waste.

See also writing sample in **report**: **Classification**.

Captions

Colons are often used in picture captions, to introduce a list of items in the picture.

> **The astronauts (left to right):** Collins, Armstrong, and Aldrin

See also **captions and legends**.

Play scripts and transcripts

A colon is used after the name of a character speaking in a play.

> TIGER: (*Grabbing hunter*) Ha-haaaaa! Now I'm going to eat you!
> HUNTER: Oh, no! Please don't! I promise to leave the rainforest.
> TIGER: (*laughing wickedly*) It's a little late for that.

A colon is also used after the name of a person speaking in a transcript.

> Ground control: Thirty seconds
> Eagle: Contact light. OK engine stop …

colon (:)

Titles and subtitles
A colon is often used to separate the title and subtitle of a book or other work of art. A subtitle adds more detail to the title.

> Life in a rainforest: A tree-top walk
> Cousteau: An unauthorized biography

In these examples, the titles are *Life in a rainforest* and *Cousteau*; the subtitles are *A tree-top walk* and *An unauthorized biography*.

A colon is sometimes used in the title of a reference book to give details about the volume.

> A children's medical encyclopedia **Volume 1: a–i**

Headings, memos, journals and faxes
Colons are sometimes used after the headings in memos, journals and faxes.

> **Date:** 16 August 1990
> **Fax to:** Peta Luma 5158 2345
> **From:** Jason Winer

> **Date:** Saturday 20th April, 2002
> **Temperature:** 14°C
> **Weather:** Cool day with clear skies, no wind.

Newspaper articles
Newspaper articles about foreign places often begin with the name of the place, followed by a colon.

> **Nome, Alaska, 2001:** Three gray whales became trapped under thickening ice off the shores of Alaska.

When to use with capitals
When a colon introduces a series of sentences as dot points or bullets, each sentence in the list begins with a capital letter.

> A rainforest is a special kind of forest:
> • **It** is wetter than other sorts of forest.
> • **Tree** tops form a canopy which blocks out most of the sunlight.
> • **Trees** are usually evergreens with broad leaves.

Capitals are not used in dot points or bullets when a colon introduces single words or sentence fragments.

> Fungi have:
> • fruiting bodies
> • spores
> • a mycelium (my-**see**-lee-um)
> • no leaves or flowers.

See also **sentence fragments**; **sentences**; writing sample under **recount**: **Transcript**.

comma (,)

The comma is a punctuation mark that is used to separate words, phrases and clauses in sentences to make meaning clear.

> When Michael arrived at our school, I had a friend for life.
> Before long, Andrea could find nothing on TV to interest her.
> Her mate, the black stallion, was with her.

Amazing but true!

How important can a comma be?

Read these sentences and take special note of the commas.

> He ate ten pies, plus five cakes after dinner.
> He ate ten pies plus five cakes, after dinner.

The first sentence means that he ate five cakes after dinner. The second sentence means that he ate ten pies and five cakes after dinner!

See also **clauses**; **phrases**; WORD HISTORIES: **comma**.

Further information is under the following topics:
Correspondence
Direct speech
Numbers
Series

Correspondence

In correspondence, commas are sometimes used:
*   to separate the main parts of an address, when an address is written on a single line
    > 7 The Crescent St, Andrews
    > 7 The Crescent, St Andrews

In these examples, the position of the comma is important to avoid confusion. In the first address, the suburb is *Andrews*. In the second address, the suburb is *St Andrews*.

*   after greetings in letters and faxes
    > Dear Jim,
    > Dear Sir,
*   after signatures in letters
    > Yours faithfully,
    > Herman Wilson
    > Director

comma (,)

In email correspondence, there is a trend to use less punctuation. The comma in the greeting and signature is often left out.

See also **correspondence**.

Direct speech
A comma is often used to separate direct speech from the rest of the sentence.
> "The chick will grow fast now," she said.
> "But Allan," repeated my aunt, "I need that job done now."
> I said, "Please close the door as you leave."

See also **direct speech**.

Numbers
Commas can be used to separate numbers that have more than four numerals. The commas help the reader to read thousands and millions.
> Australian Aboriginal people lived for more than 40,000 years without a waste problem.
> The astronauts travelled at about 40,230 km/h (25,000 mph)
> Height: 8,848 m (29,028 ft)

It is becoming more common to leave out the comma at the thousands position in numerals. The trend is to use a space instead if there are five or more numerals.
> 1000
> 10 000
> 1 000 000

Some people prefer the commas to be kept in large numbers, especially in handwriting. This is because spaces are not even in many people's handwriting, so a number might be hard to understand. This is important in some professions. For example, air traffic controllers (people who direct planes at airports) often write notes for someone else who is taking over at the end of a work period. The notes must be clear. Mistakes could cost the lives of people in planes!

Series
When two or more items are listed in a sentence, commas are used to separate them. The listed items are called a *series*. The commas that separate them are called *serial commas*.
> It was empty, except for a chest — and in the chest they found a **dusty, dented, gold cup**.

A comma is often left out after the second-to-last item in a series, usually when words such as *and, or* etc are used after it.

What a magnificent, **studious and** patient pupil you are!
In this sentence there is no comma after the second-to-last adjective *studious*, because the word *and* is used after it.

A comma is used after the second-to-last item in a series, if it is necessary to make meaning clear.

> I'm serving it with Barry's fresh salad and **Ann's salad dressing,** and my chocolate fudge cake for dessert.

In this example, a comma is used after *Ann's salad dressing*, to make it clear that the salad dressing goes with *Barry's fresh salad* and not the *chocolate fudge cake*.

See also WORD HISTORIES: **serial**.

commands

See **sentences**: **Commands**; **exclamation mark**: **Commands**.

common nouns

Common nouns are the general words for people, places, things, feelings and ideas. Unless they begin a sentence, common nouns do not begin with a capital letter.

Examples of common nouns:
* people
      man, woman, child, teacher
* places
      town, city, river, galaxy
* things
      dog, building, pencil, computer
* feelings and ideas
      happiness, hunger, imagination, dream

See also **nouns**; WORD HISTORIES: **noun**.

comparative degree

The comparative degree is a form of some adjectives and adverbs when they are used to compare two things.

> The hare is a **faster** runner than the tortoise.

In this example, the word *faster* is an adjective in the comparative degree.

Going downhill the car ran **faster**.
In this example the word *faster* is an adverb in the comparative degree.

Further examples:
>This book is **more interesting** than the last book I read.
>The giraffe can reach **higher** than an elephant.
>The traffic moved **more slowly** at peak hour.

See **also adjectives: Adjectives of degree; adverbs: Adverb modifiers**.

compare and contrast

Compare and contrast is a way of presenting information in a text. An idea can be explained by comparing it with something similar, or by contrasting it to something different.

You can compare and contrast ideas with words in a simple sentence.

>**Small** friends can be a **big** help.

In this example, the word *small* is contrasted with the word *big*. They are opposites in meaning. This helps the reader to remember the message in the sentence. It is a moral or lesson from a fable.

Further examples:
>**Persuasion** is better than **force**.
>A **little** kindness goes a **long** way.
>**Help** — don't **hinder**!

You can compare and contrast ideas in clauses. One way of doing this is to link clauses with the conjunctions *but, whereas, however* or *while*.

>Monkeys often live in trees, **but** gorillas usually live on the ground.

In this example, the author gives information about monkeys and gorillas by comparing the two. The conjunction *but* links the two clauses.

Further examples:
>Rabbits nest underground, **whereas** hares nest on the ground.
>In summer the water runs freely; **however**, in winter it freezes.
>Richard collects stamps, **while** his brother prefers to play sports.

See also **clauses: Main clauses; conjunctions**; writing sample under **report: Compare and contrast; oxymoron**.

Information on other ways you can compare and contrast information is under the following headings:
>**Charts**
>**Lists**
>**Photographs**

Charts

Charts can be used to compare and contrast information. In the following chart, the author contrasts different types of fungi. This is done with photographs and captions under headings. Charts are a useful way to present a lot of information at a glance.

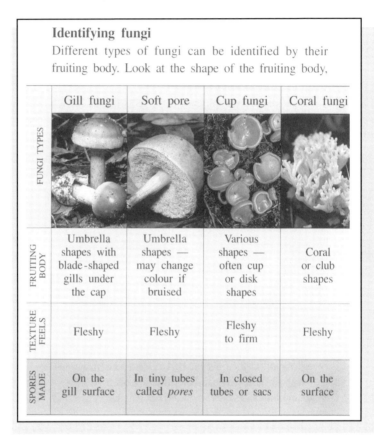

Identifying fungi

Different types of fungi can be identified by their fruiting body. Look at the shape of the fruiting body.

	Gill fungi	Soft pore	Cup fungi	Coral fungi
FUNGI TYPES				
FRUITING BODY	Umbrella shapes with blade-shaped gills under the cap	Umbrella shapes — may change colour if bruised	Various shapes — often cup or disk shapes	Coral or club shapes
TEXTURE FEELS	Fleshy	Fleshy	Fleshy to firm	Fleshy
SPORES MADE	On the gill surface	In tiny tubes called *pores*	In closed tubes or sacs	On the surface

Investigating fungi, p. 14

Lists

Lists can be used to compare and contrast information. In the following text the author compares two types of whales by listing facts alongside each other. In this way, the reader can more easily see how the two groups of whales differ. They are being compared with each other on certain topics — how they eat, how they use sonar, where they feed etc.

APPENDIX: Some facts about whales

All whales are mammals and so have warm blood. They mate and produce live young which drink milk from the mothers.

In place of arms, whales have flippers. All whales have a tail with two horizontal sections called *flukes*. Some whales have a back *(dorsal)* fin.

There are two main groups of whales - *baleen* whales and *toothed* whales. Today there are 11 known species of *baleen* whale and about 30 species of *toothed* whale. Toothed and baleen whales differ in several ways.

Baleen whales:
- have plates of baleen (whalebone) which hang down from the upper jaw - the baleen have small fibres which help to sieve food from the water;
- may use sonar; but if so, to a lesser degree than toothed whales;
- move from food-rich waters, which may mean going without food for many months;
- have no recorded live mass stranding;
- are usually born head first (not fully known);
- eat mainly krill;
- make sounds including moans, rumbles and chirps.

Toothed whales:
- have teeth which are usually all the same size and shape - they keep the one set throughout their life;
- use sonar to explore their surroundings - the sounds used are called clicks;
- tend to stay in food-rich waters throughout the year;
- (some species) are sometimes seen in live mass strandings;
- mostly seen to be born tail first;
- eat mainly squid, octopus, cuttlefish and fish;
- make sounds including whistles, clicks and groans.

Baleen, p. 39

Photographs

Photographs can be used to compare and contrast information. In the following text, the same scene is shown at different seasons so the reader can compare one season to another.

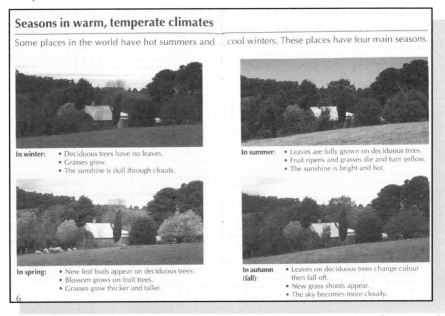

Seasons in warm, temperate climates

Some places in the world have hot summers and | cool winters. These places have four main seasons.

In winter: • Deciduous trees have no leaves.
• Grasses grow.
• The sunshine is dull through clouds.

In summer: • Leaves are fully grown on deciduous trees.
• Fruit ripens and grasses die and turn yellow.
• The sunshine is bright and hot.

In spring: • New leaf buds appear on deciduous trees.
• Blossom grows on fruit trees.
• Grasses grow thicker and taller.

In autumn (fall): • Leaves on deciduous trees change colour then fall off.
• New grass shoots appear.
• The sky becomes more cloudy.

Seasons, pp. 6-7

compass points

The words for the compass points (*north, west, north-west, south-east, north-north-west* etc) are often used in writing and on maps and charts. Information on their use is under the following headings.

Abbreviations
Capitals
Punctuation

Abbreviations

Compass points are abbreviated by using the first letter of each word in the compass point. This happens most often on maps, charts, street names, journal notes and scientific instruments.

N (north), **S** (south), **W** (west), **E** (east)

In the following map, the compass points are shown on a cross. This tells the reader the directions on a local map. The map also shows landmarks — things walkers might find along the way. (Maps of regions or the world usually have north at the top of the map.)

Tree Top Walk

(Not Drawn to Scale)
(Length of Walk: 900 metres)

Capitals

Compass points are written in full capitals when abbreviated — usually in maps, charts, tables and addresses.

NE (north-east), **SE** (south-east), **NW** (north-west), **SSW** (south-south-west)

Compass points are written in lower case if they are written in full, unless they are a proper noun or adjective.

Location: 300km **south** of Alice Springs.

The wagons headed **north**.

Compass points are often part of the name of a country, region or business. When this happens, they are given a capital letter.

Place: Sinai Desert, **Middle East** region

Places near the **North** and **South** Poles are always cold.

Punctuation

When compass points form a compound word, they are linked with a hyphen.

South-East Asia is a growth region.

A **south-easterly** breeze was blowing.

The plane flew **south-south-west** of the mountain.

See also **hyphen**: Directions.

complex sentences

See **sentences**: Sentence structures.

compound adjectives

See **adjectives**: **Compound adjectives**.

compound sentences

See **sentences**: **Sentence structures**.

compound verbs

See **verbs**: **Compound**.

compound words

Compound words are words made from two or more separate words.

The word parts can be joined with a hyphen.

> Apples become **tree-ripe** in autumn.
> The **newly-born** giraffe stayed by its mother.

The word parts can be joined without a hyphen.

> **Zookeepers** care for animals in zoos.
> Silk comes from the cocoons of **silkworms**.

The parts of compound words are sometimes proper nouns or adjectives. When this happens, the parts have a capital letter. The personal names of people and particular places are examples of this.

> The book *Rock and roll Clyde* was written by Telene **Clarke-Giles.**
> They travelled to **South-West** Africa.

See also compass points: **Punctuation**; **hyphen (-)**; **nouns**: **Proper nouns**.

concrete nouns

Concrete nouns are the names of things that can be seen or touched.

> rain, horse, house, hair

See also **nouns**: **Concrete nouns**.

conditional clauses

A conditional clause is a clause that tells what is necessary for an event to happen. It begins with *if, so, though*, or *unless*.

> **If she'd known the time**, she would have left earlier.
> You wouldn't have computers **if you didn't have electricity**.

See also **clauses**.

conjunctions

Conjunctions are words that join or link other words, phrases and clauses within a sentence. Examples of conjunctions include:

> and, but, yet, so, or, which, if, that, because, since, whether, whereas, while

> The storm water swells rivers **and** creeks.

In this example, the conjunction *and* links the words *rivers* and *creeks*.

> The spacesuits had oxygen tanks **so** the astronauts could breathe **while** they were on the moon.

In this example, the conjunctions *so* and *while* link the three clauses:
> The spacesuits had oxygen tanks.
> The astronauts could breathe.
> They were on the moon.

connectives

Connectives are words or phrases that are used to link ideas in clauses, sentences, paragraphs or chapters in a text. They give readers signals to show how ideas in a text are developing.

> Sometimes they did not enjoy the training. **One reason was that** they were often away from their families. **Another reason was that** some of the training was very uncomfortable. **For example**, they disliked being spun around in a huge machine like the gravitron at an amusement park.

If the author had not used connectives in the example above, the ideas in the text would not have made as much sense.
> Sometimes they did not enjoy the training.
> They were often away from their families.
> Some of the training was very uncomfortable.
> They disliked being spun around in a huge machine like the gravitron at an amusement park.

See also **conjunctions**; **explanation**.

consonants

The *consonant letters* in the alphabet are:
b, **c**, **d**, **f**, **g**, **h**, **j**, **k**, **l**, **m**, **n**, **p**, **q**, **r**, **s**, **t**, **v**, **w**, **x**, **y**, **z**

The only letters that are not consonants are **a**, **e**, **i**, **o**, **u**. They are called *vowels*.

Some consonant letters can have different sounds.

>In the word **catch**, the letter **c** has a /k/ sound as in 'kiss'.
>In the word **cereal**, the letter **c** has a /s/ sound as in 'send'.

Further examples:

>**g**: magic, regard
>**q**: quarter, queue
>**s**: desert, serious
>**x**: box, xylophone, anxious

The letter *y* is a *consonant letter*, but it is sometimes used as a *vowel sound*.

>In the word **yellow**, the letter **y** has a consonant sound.
>In the words **funny**, **sky** and **mystery**, the letter **y** has three different vowel sounds.

Consonants are often joined to represent other sounds.

>**ch**: church, machine, chemist
>**sh**: ship, dish, fashion
>**wh**: who, whole, where, wheel, what, why
>**sch**: schedule, schnitzel, school
>**th**: then, theory, thyme
>**tch**: wretched, catch, itch

Sometimes, vowels are given a consonant sound.

>In the word **union**, the letter **u** has a consonant sound /y/ as in 'yes'.
>In the word **once**, the letter **o** has a consonant sound /w/ as in 'won'.

See also **vowels**; WORD HISTORIES: **cereal**, **desert**, **who**.

continuous present tense

See **verbs**: **Present**.

contractions

A contraction is a shortened word or phrase. There are two types of contraction — *single words* and *phrases*.

Single words can become contractions when some middle letters are left out.

>**Mr** is a contraction of **Mister**.
>**Dr** is a contraction of **Doctor**.

contractions

Phrases can become contractions when letters are left out and the words become one word. An apostrophe is used to show that letters have been left out of a phrase.

> **Don't** is a contraction of the phrase **do not**.
> **I'll** is a contraction of the phrase **I will**.
> **Haven't** is a contraction of the phrase **have not**.

Did you know?

its and it's

A very common error in writing involves the words *its* and *it's*.
Do you know the difference between them and when to use each?

See **it's / its** for the answer.

Contractions are often used in personal letters, diaries, journals and other types of informal writing.

In stories, when characters are speaking, contractions make the dialogue sound more natural.

> "Living with my brother is really quite exhausting," Kirsten began. "**It's** a bit like being in a zoo except we **don't** have bars. **I've** seen zoo animals, and often I think their behaviour is better than the antics **we've** witnessed from my brother."

Many contractions are slang words.

> I don't **s'pose** you'd be able to help me with my horse would you?
> I've got to clean out the stable **'cos** it's become a mess.

Further examples:

> "I'm not a **flamin'** trapeze artist," yelled the electrician up the ladder.
> The whole family is coming to dinner. '**Course** you're invited too!

See also **apostrophe**: **Apostrophe for contractions**; **correspondence**: **Informal business letter**; **dates and time**; **dialogue (US: dialog)**; **recount**: **Fiction**, **Non-fiction Journal**, **Oral history**.

Hint

Contractions

Your writing sounds more serious and formal if you do not use contractions.

In her book *Baleen*, author Josephine Croser wanted her story to sound like an epic tale — a great and important story — because it explains something serious about nature. If you search the whole story, you will not find a single contraction! Josephine thought that contractions would make her story sound casual and less believable.

See also **formal / informal writing**.

correspondence

Correspondence (*letters* etc) is delivered in several ways — by mail or post (now often called *snail mail*), telegram (now almost a 'dinosaur'), facsimile (better known as *fax*) or email (*electronic mail*). As these different forms of delivery were invented, people's writing styles changed.

Letter writing became more common after Roland Hill invented the postage stamp in 1840. Letter writing was a popular activity and was considered by many people to be an art.

Greeting cards (eg Christmas cards) with very short informal notes became very popular in the 1870s.

When the fax was invented in the 1980s, correspondence became much more informal, even in many business letters. This may be because delivery and the speed of reply were so quick.

In the 1990s, email made correspondence quicker than fax — writers did not have to leave their desks to send a message! Correspondence became even more informal; the standard letter greeting 'Dear …' changed to words like 'Hi' — or was left out altogether. Letter signatures changed — writers now often just write their first name. Less punctuation is used in emails and messages are usually short.

Whether a letter is formal or informal depends on why it is being written and to whom it is being written. If the letter is for someone the writer knows well, or if the letter is written in fun, then it is usually written informally. A letter written for a serious purpose to someone whom the writer does not know, will probably be more formal.

See also **style**; **tone**.

The following topics give information about abbreviations used in correspondence and different types of letters, both formal and informal:

Appointments
Appointment by formal email
Appointment by informal email

Business letters
Formal business letter
Informal business letter

Capitals in correspondence

Invitations
Formal invitation (business)
Personal invitation

RSVP

Appointments

Business people plan meetings with other people. Part of the planning can be to write to someone asking for an appointment. This is sometimes done by 'snail mail', but is more often done by fax or email today.

Appointment by formal email
In this email the writer is trying to arrange a meeting with someone he has not met before, so the letter is formal.

To: hans.m@astor.com
Cc:
Subject: Meeting at Frankfurt

Dear Mr Maximus
I have heard about your company and the excellent work you do in education in Sweden. I would like to meet you at the Frankfurt Book Fair this year to show you our new children's picture books.

Would it be possible for you to meet me at my exhibit? I will be in Hall 8, Stand C936.

I suggest that we meet at 11.00 am on 7 October. If this time is not suitable, would you please suggest another time.

I look forward to meeting you.
Yours faithfully
Rodney Stuart
Editor

- The greeting begins with the word *Dear* and the person's title and family name — *Dear Mr Maximus.*
- The writer quickly explains the reason for the email.
- The writer does not use contractions (*I would* is used rather than *I'd*).
- Punctuation is not used for the greeting and the signature. There is a trend to use very little punctuation in email.
- The meeting details are given (*place, date* and *time*).
- A formal signature is used (*Yours faithfully*).

Appointment by informal email
In this email, the writer is trying to arrange a meeting with someone he knows well, so the letter is informal.

To: hans.m@astor.com
Cc:
Subject: Meeting at Frankfurt

Hi Hans
It's time to plan for the Frankfurt Book Fair again. Let's make a time to meet. How about 11 am 7 October at my exhibit? I'll be in Hall 8, Stand C936. If this time isn't suitable, please suggest another.

If you're free on the Thursday evening, why don't we go out and HAVE SOME FUN?

Hope you are well. See you soon my friend.
Rod

- The writer quickly explains the reason for the email.
- Punctuation is not used for the greeting and the signature. There is a trend to use very little punctuation in email.
- The writer uses contractions (*It's, Let's, isn't, don't*).
- The writer uses full capitals to emphasise a point of humour, as if he is shouting or cheering (*HAVE SOME FUN*). Care must be taken when using full capitals in email. They are sometimes regarded as rude in email if the reader feels the writer is 'shouting'.
- The writer concludes with incomplete sentences (*Hope you are well.*)
- The writer signs off informally with a short form of his name.

See also **capitals**: **Full use of capitals**; **Trends and rules for using capitals**.

Business letters

Business letters can be formal or informal depending on how well the writer knows the other person.

Formal business letter

In the following formal business letter, a publisher writes to an author to tell her that her manuscript has been accepted for publication. The letter is formal and businesslike, because the publisher and author do not know each other.

---

7 April 1991

Mrs Josephine Croser
15 Dukesbury Rd
GOLDEN GROVE SA 5125

Dear Mrs Croser

RE: Manuscript titled *Dear Sam Dear Ben*

Thank you for sending this manuscript to me. I enjoyed reading it and am delighted to tell you that I would like to publish this work. The correspondence style of the text is particularly interesting and effective.

Would you please telephone me so that we can arrange a time to discuss a contract and some editorial changes that I would like to suggest.

Congratulations on writing this engaging story.

Yours faithfully,

R Martin

Rodney Martin
Publisher

- Punctuation is not used in the address, greeting and signature. There is a trend to use less punctuation because it saves time.
- The writer addresses the envelope to *Mrs Josephine Croser*, but addresses the actual letter to *Mrs Croser*.
- The writer does not use contractions (*I am* is used rather than *I'm*).
- The writer uses more formal words (*Thank you* rather than *Thanks*).
- The signature *Yours faithfully* is formal.

Informal business letter

In the following informal business letter, a publisher writes to an author to tell her that her manuscript has been accepted for publication. The letter is businesslike, but less formal than the previous example, because the publisher and the author know each other well. They have probably worked together before.

---

7 April 1991

Mrs Josephine Croser
15 Dukesbury Rd
GOLDEN GROVE SA 5125

Dear Jo

RE: Manuscript titled *Dear Sam Dear Ben*

Thanks for sending this manuscript to me. I enjoyed reading it and I'm pleased to say that I'd like to publish it. The correspondence style of the text is particularly interesting and effective.

Would you please call me so that we can arrange a time to discuss a contract and some editorial changes that I would like to suggest.

Congratulations on writing another engaging story.

Best wishes

Rod

Rod Martin
Publisher

- The writer addresses the letter to *Mrs Josephine Croser*, but uses the more familiar name *Jo* in the actual letter.
- The writer uses more informal words (*Thanks* rather than *Thank you*).
- The writer uses contractions (*I'm, I'd*).
- The signature *Best wishes* is informal.
- The writer signs with the less formal name *Rod* instead of *Rodney*.

See also **clipped words**; **contractions**.

Capitals in correspondence

Capitals are used in greetings and the first word of signatures in correspondence.

> Dear Sam
> Dear Sir
> Dear Sue and Paul
> Yours faithfully
> Yours sincerely
> Your friend
> Cheers
> Bye for now
> Yours truly
> Kind regards
> Regards

See also **addresses**: **Business letters**; **Personal letters**.

Invitations

An invitation is sent by people holding an event, to the people they wish to attend the event. If a reply is needed, then an RSVP date (*date to reply*) is given with the name and details of the person to be contacted. Invitations are usually short — they just give the necessary information.

Formal invitation (business)

Businesses often invite customers and other business people to special business meetings or occasions. In this invitation, a publisher is inviting people to a book launch.

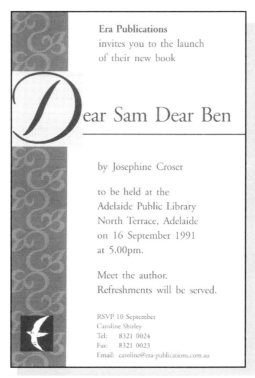

Era Publications
invites you to the launch
of their new book

*D*ear Sam Dear Ben

by Josephine Croser

to be held at the
Adelaide Public Library
North Terrace, Adelaide
on 16 September 1991
at 5.00pm.

Meet the author.
Refreshments will be served.

RSVP 10 September
Caroline Shirley
Tel: 8321 0024
Fax: 8321 0023
Email: caroline@era-publications.com.au

- The topic, time, place and date are all in one sentence. It doesn't have to be organised like this. This information could be presented under sub-headings. This is a matter of personal choice.
- There is other information about what will happen at the event (*Meet the author, refreshments will be served*).
- Information for the RSVP is given at the end.
- Each line has just one piece of information to make the writing easy to read and understand.
- Invitations are often designed in interesting ways to make the event seem special.

See also **correspondence**: **RSVP**; WORD HISTORIES: **RSVP**.

Personal invitation

People often send invitations for a party. Party invitations can be bought at a stationery shop or you can make them up yourself.

Let's Party!

Rebecca is absolutely excited that the school tests are over!

Ivan
you are invited to a "tests are over" party at 15 Hillman Drive, Brighton on Saturday, 16 March 2 pm to 5 pm.

RSVP 13 March
Rebecca
Tel: 9116 3456

- The invitation explains what is being celebrated.
- There is room to write the name and address of the invitee by hand (but on a word processor you can type in the name of the person).
- The time, date and place of the celebration are given.
- The personal name of each invitee is used.
- Information for a reply is given at the end.

RSVP

An RSVP is a reply to say that you accept or are unable to accept an invitation. An informal RSVP might be made by telephone or by fax with a simple 'yes' or 'sorry, I can't make it' written on the invitation.

In this example, the writer is *formally* accepting an invitation.

See also WORD HISTORIES: **RSVP**

March 12

Rebecca
15 Hillman Drive
Brighton

Dear Rebecca

Thank you for the invitation to your "tests are over" party. It sounds like great fun. I accept the invitation and will be there at 2 pm Saturday.

Kind regards,

Ivan

---

could have (of)

It is a common error to write *could of*. The correct form is *could have*.

> I **could of** done that better. (X)
> I **could have** done that better. (✓)

This error is common because when people say *could have* they often pronounce it as the shortened form — *could've*. Then when they write it, they think the ending *'ve* is the word *of* — which, of course, it is not! It is *have*.

The same error is made with *should have* (*should've*) and *would have* (*would've*).

> "He **should've** caught up by now, even if he's walking," said Kerry.
> I **would've** done it myself if I'd had time.

could / should / would

Could is a past tense form of *can*. It means 'to be able to'.

> Sometimes she wished she **could** avoid Mrs Spicer.
> This prize **could** have been awarded to two or three people.

Should is a past tense form of shall. It means 'ought to'.

> The money **should** be donated to a wildlife fund.
> He **should** have taken our advice.

Would is a past tense form of will.

> This child **would** have drowned had he not been rescued quickly.
> The young boy kept close to her, so he **would** be safe.

Could, should and *would* are all modal verbs.
See also **modal verbs**.

count nouns

Words that name things that can be counted are called *count nouns*. They have plurals.

> people, hills, rivers, trees, days, accidents, thoughts, meals

See also **mass nouns**; **nouns**: **Count nouns**; **plural**.

couplet

A couplet is two lines of verse that rhyme.

> Do you love me or do you not?
> You told me once … but I forgot.

> If this book should chance to roam,
> Box its ears and send it home.

course

See **coarse / course**.

critical review

See **review**.

cross-references

Cross-references tell a reader where more information on a topic is available in a text. Cross-references are often given in this guide. This is so that

readers have a better chance of finding useful information even if they are not sure where to look.

In the following example from a nonfiction book, the author uses a cross-reference to show where the reader can get more information from a photograph. The cross-reference is written inside brackets. The author also uses shortened words or abbreviations and numerals to save space and make it easy to read quickly.

Hatching

When the ducklings are ready to hatch, they chirp and tap from inside the egg. Each duckling has a sharp scale, called an *egg tooth*, at the end of its bill (see photo p11). The duckling uses the egg tooth to break a hole in the shell from inside. This can take one or two days. The egg is now called a *pipping egg*.

The life of a duck, p. 9

currant / current

A *currant* is a type of seedless grape.

> Some children do not like **currants** in buns or cakes.

Current can be:
- an adjective meaning 'present, fashionable, of this time, now'
  > By reading newspapers you learn about **current** events.

- a noun meaning 'the flow of water, air or electricity'.
  > The raft drifted wherever the **currents** took it on the sea.

See also **adjectives**; **nouns**.

curtain

See **certain / curtain**

dash (—)

The dash is a punctuation mark that is used to show a break in a sentence. Printers and editors often call it an *em dash* or *em rule* because it is the width of the letter *M*. It should not be confused with the *hyphen* (-).

The dash is sometimes written with a space before and after it.

> After lunch everyone did work duties — cleaning inside the buildings, taking waste outside.

The dash is also written with no space. It depends on what an editor or designer decides is best for a particular book.

> The blue whale—the largest animal known to have lived on earth— is found in all oceans but not usually near coastlines.

See also **hyphen (-)**.

The use of the dash is explained under the following headings:

To add or emphasise information
To bracket text
To show a pause
With other punctuation

To add or emphasise information

Dashes can be used to add information at the end of a sentence. Authors sometimes do this to make the text sound more dramatic.

> This was undoubtedly an open and shut case — the butler did it!
> There are two kinds of drivers — safe and dangerous.
> To go, or not to go — what would they do?

To bracket text

Dashes can be used like brackets and commas — to separate words, phrases or clauses that add extra detail to a sentence.

> The explorers set off on their long trek — far away across the ice towards the South Pole — hundreds of kilometres away.

See also **brackets ( )**; **comma (,)**.

To show a pause

Dashes can be used to show a pause in a sentence.

> Strangely, she didn't know where he was — home or away.

With other punctuation

A question mark or exclamation mark can be used before a dash, but not a comma or a full stop.

> Under the table there was a sleeping dog — should it be there? — and what looked like a long-haired kitten.

Hint

Don't over-use the dash

Writers need to be careful not to over-use the dash. In personal correspondence people often write loose ideas as they come into their head, and link them. This 'dash between friends' is OK, but it is less acceptable in formal writing.

In this example, a story character speaks informally to a friend. The author uses the dash to link a number of thoughts into one sentence.

> "I'm not going — not feeling well — would probably have to come home early anyway — if I went, that is," Kate mumbled to Jenny.

In a formal text, it would probably be written as two or three sentences without the dashes.

> "I am not going. I'm not feeling well. If I went, I would probably have to come home early anyway," Kate mumbled to Jenny.

---

dates and time

The following topics explain ways to write the date and time.

Abbreviations of the date
Abbreviations of time
AD, BC and BCE
Circa
Order
Writing the full date

Abbreviations of the date

Abbreviations of dates are used in the headings of letters, tables, notes and journals. The abbreviations save space and time.

16 Sept 1998
Mr R Smith
Smith Metals Inc
PO Box 64
NEW YORK NY 200649
USA

If the numerals in a date are placed together, a comma is placed between them so the reader will not be confused.

Sept 16, 1998

The months of the year are usually abbreviated as shown.

Jan Feb Mar Apr Aug Sept Oct Nov Dec

May, June and *July* are usually not abbreviated because they are already short words.

Abbreviations of time

The time is often abbreviated in writing. It can be abbreviated by using the contraction *o'clock,* which is short for 'of the clock'.

Dear Mr Smith
I would like to make an appointment to meet you at your office. Would 10 **o'clock** on the morning of Wednesday, 16 September 1998 be suitable?

The time is also abbreviated by using *am* and *pm.* This tells the reader whether it is morning or afternoon.

Dear Mr Smith,
I would like to make an appointment to meet you at your office. Would **10.00 am** on Wednesday, 16 September 1998 be suitable?

See also **contractions**.

AD, BC and BCE

The years in the Christian calendar are measured in western countries mainly by two time periods — before the birth of Christ and after the birth of Christ.

The acronym *BC* is used for the years before Christ.

Julius Caesar became leader of the Roman Empire in the year 49 **BC**.

dates and time

The acronym *AD* is used for the years after the birth of Christ.
> St Patrick of Ireland died in 461 **AD** (or **AD** 461).

BC and *AD* are often used in history books and sometimes on special places such as the foundation stones of buildings.
> This stone was laid by
> the Hon RM Speake, MP
> on 10 December 1935 **AD**.

The acronym *BCE* means 'before the common era'. It is a term some writers use if they don't want to use *BC*, which includes *Christ*. Some audiences are sensitive to the use of BC because of their religious or cultural beliefs. However, many people think of BCE as meaning 'before the Christian era', so it does not necessarily solve the problem!

See also **acronyms**; WORD HISTORIES: **AD**, **BC**, **BCE**, **circa**.

Circa

Circa is a Latin word that means 'about' or 'around'. The abbreviation of *circa* is *c*. Writers use *circa* or *c*. with numerals, when they do not know the exact date of an event.
> The photograph (**c**. 1932) was a rare picture of Max's grandparents.
> Max's grandparents were photographed **circa** 1932.

Note that *circa* and *c* are used only with numerals, not with words.

See also **Latin abbreviations**; WORD HISTORIES: **circa**.

Order

Dates are written in different orders in different parts of the world.
Day–month–year is the most common order in Australia, the United Kingdom, New Zealand, Singapore and South Africa.
> 31 December 2002

Month–day–year is the most common order in the United States and Canada.
> December 27, 1892

Year–month–day is the order and style recommended by the International Organisation for Standardisation. This style is mainly used in some banks and technical situations.
> 1992 December 27

Writing the full date

Dates are usually written in full when they are in the body of a letter or text.

> Dear Mr Smith
> I will be able to meet you on **16 September 2002**.

Note that the date would be spoken as 'on the 16th of September'. The words *the* and *of* are usually not written, but are understood.

If the numerals in a date are placed together, a comma is needed to separate them and avoid confusion.

> Sept 16, 2002

The abbreviations *st* (*1st*), *nd* (*2nd*), *rd* (*3rd*) and *th* (*4th*) are often used.

> Sept 16**th,** 2002

Commas are often used to separate the day and month.

> **Monday, 16th September,** 2002

debate

See **argument**: Discussion, Debate.

declarative sentences

See **sentences**: Statements.

definite articles

See **articles**: Definite article.

demonstrative pronouns

See **pronouns**: Demonstrative pronouns.

desert / dessert

Desert can be:

- a noun meaning 'a dry piece of land often covered with sand or ice'. It is pronounced /**dez**-zert/.
  > Antarctica is a frozen **desert**.
- a verb meaning 'to abandon or leave someone or something in trouble'. It is pronounced /dee-**zert**/.
  > The sailors decided to **desert** their ship when they reached the port.
- a noun meaning 'a reward or punishment that has been deserved'. It is pronounced /dee-**zert**/ and is always written together with the word *just*.
  > The team got its **just deserts** when it won the grand final.

Dessert is a noun. It means 'something sweet eaten at the end of a meal'. It is pronounced /dee-**zert**/.

> We prepared the **dessert** well before the meal.

See also WORD HISTORIES: **desert**, **dessert**.

determiners

Determiners is a word used in grammar. It means 'words that point to nouns'. Determiners begin noun phrases.

*   *Articles* are determiners.
        a, an, the

> As if in **a trance**, she wandered into **the crowded hallway** and stood before **an old woman.**

In this example, the words *a*, *an* and *the* begin the noun phrases *a trance*, *the crowded hallway* and *an old woman.*

*   Some *pronouns* are determiners. They are called *demonstrative pronouns*.
        that, these, this, those

> They couldn't decide whether to take **this road** or **that road**.

*   *Possessive pronouns* are determiners.
        his, my, your, her, our, their, its

> Leave **your books** on **your desk**.

*   Adjectives that describe *how many* are determiners.
        all, every, most, each, few, some, many, lots

> **All the big green apples** had **lots of wriggly worms** in them.

*   *Cardinal numbers* are determiners.
        one, two, three, four, five, six, sixteen, sixty

Many of the determiners listed above could replace the word *a* in this noun phrase.

> **a** newly-hatched silkworm

For example:

> I photographed **that** newly-hatched silkworm, not this one.
> I photographed **the** newly-hatched silkworm, not the older ones.

I photographed **our** newly-hatched silkworm, not theirs.
I photographed **one** newly-hatched silkworm, not more.

Each of these determiners gives the reader a different way of thinking about the phrase *newly-hatched silkworm*.

See also **a / an**; **adjectives**; **articles**; **noun phrases**; **nouns**; **pronouns**: **Demonstrative pronouns**, **Possessive pronouns**.

device / devise

Device is a noun. It means 'a gadget, a tool, or a method'. It is pronounced /dee-**vys**/ to rhyme with *nice*.

> The inventor created a **device** for peeling potatoes.

Devise is a verb. It means 'to invent, arrange, or plot'. It is pronounced /dee-**vyz**/ to rhyme with *wise*.

> The inventor **devised** a plan for selling the invention.

See **nouns**; **verbs**.

dialect

A dialect is a variation of a language. Dialects are used by people in a particular region or group. They differ from the standard language in their words (vocabulary), grammar and sounds, and have their own colloquialisms. There are many different dialects of English throughout the world, and even within England.

In fiction, writers use dialects to make their characters and story more interesting and believable.

> The woman handed her one of the dolls.
> "Like it?" she asked. "I could **learn ya** to make 'em. **Me** own 'ands are too old and **crabbit** now. But you make 'em, an' I'll **getcha** some oranges cheap to sell to **them theatre swells**. From yer pretty **baskit**."

Hannah, p. 46

In this example:
*   there are non-standard words. The character says *crabbit* instead of *crippled*; *swells* instead of *rich people*.
*   there are non-standard pronunciations. The character says *getcha* instead of *get you*; *baskit* instead of *basket*. Because dialects usually have particular sounds, writers may alter the spelling of characters' words to mimic the sounds of speech used in a dialect.

- the grammar is non-standard. The character says *learn* instead of *teach*; *me* instead of *my*; and *them theatre swells* instead of *those theatre swells*.

Dialect is different from *dialogue*. Dialogue is conversation between characters; dialect is the way the characters use the language in their conversation.

See also **colloquial language**; **dialogue (US: dialog)**; WORD HISTORIES: **dialect**.

dialogue (US: dialog)

Dialogue is words spoken between two or more people. Writers often use dialogue in narratives; it gives life to characters in stories. The way a character speaks can give the reader greater understanding of that character.

> "It's dead I tell you," said the first.
> "You're too hard on us," laughed the second.
> "I tell you, honesty is dead."
> "We'll put it to the test," said the second man, eyeing Hannah.
> "Child," he said, "take this penny and buy me an apple. I'll give you a half-farthing when you return."

Hannah, p. 18

In the above example, the editor used double quotation marks (" ") to surround the words actually spoken by the characters. Some editors use single quotation marks for dialogue.

> 'It's not fair,' I added. 'Verity didn't get teased when she got hers.'
> 'She did so too. Everyone called her exactly the same names as you.'
> 'How come I don't remember?' I asked.
> 'Because she just ignored them and they soon stopped.'

Seb & Sasha, p. 17

Dialogue can also be written as a *play script*, as *speech bubbles* (*callouts* or *balloons*), or in nonfiction as a *transcript*.

See also **callout**; **quotation marks (' ' and " ")**; **transcript**; WORD HISTORIES: **dialogue**.

diary

A diary is a recount text — the author records daily events. It is a type of journal, usually written just for the author and not to be read by others. Diaries are important to people who study history. Some famous diaries have described what life was like in earlier times. Famous diaries include *The Diary of Anne Frank* (written by a Jewish girl whose family hid from the Germans in Holland during World War 2), and the *Diary of Samuel Pepys* (a man who wrote about the Great Plague, the Great Fire of London and daily life in the 1600s).

Not all diaries are nonfiction. The diary can be used by fiction writers.

In the following example, the author used a diary style to tell the story of a girl who was trapped in a building after an earthquake. In the beginning of the story, her diary entries help us to get to know the character.

> Monday, April 14
> Today was awful. I was late for school and so it was embarrassing walking into class late. Then I discovered we were to have a test. I had forgotten all about it! My mind was swimming as the teacher handed me the paper. Susan said she did OK in her writing, but I'm sure mine was a disaster.

- Diaries are usually written from the point of view of the writer, so first person pronouns are used (*I, me, my, mine*).
- They are usually written in the past tense (*was, discovered, had forgotten, was swimming, handed, said, did*) because the writer is recalling things that have already happened that day.
- The writer often records personal thoughts or feelings.
- The writing style is often very informal because it is not intended to be read by others.

See also **person**; **personal writing**; **tense**.

direct speech

Direct speech is words spoken by someone. The author writes the words as if a character actually said them. Direct speech is usually surrounded by quotation marks. The first word in direct speech begins with a capital.

> "**What a great fuss!**" declared Uncle Henry.

The direct speech in this example is *What a great fuss!* The words *declared Uncle Henry* describe who is speaking and how that person spoke or acted.

The spoken words can be at the end of a sentence.

> The other players shouted together, "**Well done, Davo, well done!**"

Direct speech can also be within a sentence.

> Then she said, "**It's not true,**" but her voice was a whisper.

Direct speech can be interrupted by words that describe what is happening or who is speaking.

> "**There are ants everywhere**," said Giles. "**They're in the cupboard.**"

Direct speech is the opposite of indirect speech or reported speech.

See also **capitals**: **Direct speech**; **indirect speech**;
quotation marks (' ' and " ").

discreet / discrete

These words are easily confused because they sound the same, look similar and have the same grammar — but they have very different meanings.

Discreet is an adjective. It means 'wise, careful, sensible, able to keep a secret'.

> The mouse kept a **discreet** distance from the cat.
> She could have joined the others in gossiping about Alice, but she decided to be **discreet** and not say anything.

Discrete is also an adjective. It means 'single, separate, only, particular, distinct'.

> Each study group had a **discrete** work area in the classroom.
> The sounds made by the different animals in the zoo were quite **discrete**. You could easily tell them apart.

See also **adjectives**.

discussion

A discussion text is nonfiction writing that informs the reader by giving different viewpoints on a topic in a balanced way. It presents more than one way of thinking about a topic.

A common structure for a discussion text is an *introduction*, followed by *information and evidence*, and finally, a *conclusion*.

Introduction
The writer gives a short outline of the topic and explains the issues or questions that will be discussed. The introduction could also list the particular viewpoints that will be offered.

Information and evidence
Information (facts) and evidence that proves these facts is given from different viewpoints.

Conclusion
The writer sums up the different viewpoints. Often, a summary opinion on the discussion is given by the author. Sometimes, a discussion text will invite readers to come to their own decisions based on the evidence in the text.

The penicillin puzzle

Introduction
Scientists make discoveries that build on research already done by other scientists. Each piece of new knowledge builds on what is already known. If scientists do not publish their results, others cannot use them to build knowledge.

This book discusses the question Who discovered and developed penicillin? The first chapter reports on the people and events that were involved. The second chapter discusses who has been given the credit and recognition.

Early discoveries
The first pieces of the penicillin jigsaw were put together by scientists who recorded what they had noticed about *Penicillium* moulds. Some of their notes and papers provided clues that would help other scientists.

Penicillin's effect
The Oxford team was ready to begin tests on living animals and then humans. First they had to show that penicillin would stop infections in animals and humans. They had to find a way to make enough penicillin for these tests.

Public recognition
Reporters sought out both Fleming and Florey for news about penicillin. Florey refused to be interviewed because he knew he could not produce enough penicillin to help everyone who needed it. Fleming, however, did give interviews. So, many more stories were published about him. He was made a popular hero …

Conclusion
Given the information in this book, it is still not easy to answer the question Who discovered and developed penicillin? Considering the evidence, many people should have been given recognition for their parts in putting together the jigsaw puzzle. Why did Fleming get the main public credit and recognition? What role did the media play? How did personalities influence who got the credit? How did the war affect what happened?

History is full of puzzles. To understand what has happened in the past, people need to ask questions and seek answers from different sources. In the end, they must decide for themselves.

- In the introduction, the author uses the present tense to explain the background to the topic in a general way.

     Scientists **make** discoveries.

- When the author presents historical events as evidence about the topic, the text is in the past tense.

     So, many more stories **were published** about him. He **was made** a popular hero …

- The author says *what* topic is discussed in the text and *how* the text is organised in chapters.

- To explain events that are evidence about the topic, the author uses adverbs of time. This is so that the reader understands the order in which things happened.

     The Oxford team was ready to begin tests on living animals and **then** humans. **First** they had to show …

- To give evidence in a discussion, the author uses a cause and effect sentence using the conjunction *because* to connect ideas.

     Florey refused to be interviewed **because** he knew he could not produce enough penicillin …

- In the conclusion, the author uses the word *should* to express an opinion.

     … many people **should** have been given recognition …

- The conclusion has a series of interrogatives (*who*, *why*, *what*, *how*) to form questions on the information in the book. This helps readers to think about the topic in different ways and decide for themselves.

See also **adverbs**: **Adverbs of time (when)**; **cause and effect**; **conjunctions**; **connectives**; **interrogatives**; **modal verbs**; **verbs**: **Past, Present**.

dot points

See **bullet points (•)**.

double negative

When a writer uses two negatives in a sentence, it is called a *double negative*. In formal language, this is regarded as poor writing, unless it is a part of dialogue.

     "That **wasn't no** accident," said the old man. "That was done on purpose."

This example could be taken to mean that if it were *not no* accident, then it really *was* an accident. The above example is a double negative in a character's speech. It helps to give the character a particular personality. It shows that the character is emphasising a negative by saying it twice.

Writers sometimes have their characters use this kind of language when they are stressing a point.

"Me? The fittest person here? I **don't** need **no** exercise!"

In the following nonsense poem, the poet uses a *triple* negative to make the poem amusing. The poet is using parody — making fun of English grammar.

> What a wonderful bird the frog are.
> When he sit, he stand almost;
> When he hop, he fly almost
> He **ain't** got **no** sense **hardly**;
> He **ain't** got **no** tail **hardly** either.
> When he sit, he sit on what he ain't got — almost.

Anonymous

The words *ain't*, *no* and *hardly* are negative words. So the poet is really emphasising the point!

See also **negatives**; **parody**.

drafting

Drafting is one of the early stages of writing. It is important because it is when authors first write their ideas down, either on paper or on a computer.

For details on drafting and how it fits with other stages of writing, see **writing process**: **Drafting**.

drama

A *drama* is a story played out by actors on stage, television, film, video, radio, CD, cassette or any other method of reaching an audience. The drama unfolds as the characters in the story speak to each other.

The following example shows a drama written as a play script. It includes directions or instructions to the actors about moods, feelings and movements.

> ROBERT: Was that you I saw late last night leaving the warehouse? (Andy looks away to avoid his gaze.)
> ANDY: Ah… I don't think so. Why? What makes you ask?
> ROBERT: Well, this morning we discovered a large amount of goods missing from the warehouse.
> ANDY: (Nervously clearing his throat) Surely you don't think it was me!

See also WORD HISTORIES: **drama**.

drawers / draws

Drawers is a noun. It is the plural of *drawer*, meaning 'a pull-out section of a cabinet'.

> I decided to tidy the **drawers** in my bedroom.

Draws is the present tense of the verb *to draw*. It can mean:
- 'to paint or sketch a picture'
  > An illustrator **draws** pictures.
- 'to pull or drag'
  > When he **draws** on the string, the kite dives in the sky.

See **nouns**; **plural**; **verbs: Tenses (time)**.

e-

The prefix *e-* is often used to create words that mean something is 'electronic', for example *email* (electronic mail). This prefix became very popular in the 1990s when new technology introduced many new uses of computers and digital products. Many 'fad' words were created using the *e-* prefix.

- e-book (electronic book)
- e-tailing (retail activity done through the Internet)
- e-commerce / e-business
- e-zine (electronic magazine)
- e-home (home wired for electronic control systems)

Words like these may disappear when the technology producing them has been better understood and accepted. For example, when using computers becomes the standard way to do business, there will be no need to call it *e-business* — it may be just *business*. Some words, such as *email*, are so useful and grow so popular that they become standard English words. As words become standard, they usually lose their hyphen (*e-mail* becomes *email*).

-e

The letter *e* on the end of many English words is not sounded. However, the *-e* often affects the sound given to a vowel in the middle of a word. The rule is that the *e* placed after a consonant at the end of a word, gives vowels placed before the consonant a long sound.

> cap / cape

In this example, the *a* has a short sound in the word *cap*. In *cape*, the *e* is placed after the consonant *p*, so the *a* is given a long sound.

Further examples:

> mad / made, them / theme, win / wine
> late, concrete, site, remote, flute

Some words ending in *e* are exceptions to this rule. They have a short vowel sound even though the word ends with *e*.

> give, have, love, dove, shove

The letter *e* on the end of some words is sounded. This is usually because the words come from other languages such as Greek or French.

e pronounced /ee/ as in see

> anemone, apostrophe, catastrophe, epitome, finale, guacamole, hyperbole, recipe, simile

e pronounced /ay/ as in say

Words in this group are often spelt with an accent mark over the letter *e* *(é)*.

> blasé, café, canapé, cliché, exposé, fiancé, macramé, papîer maché, protegé, résumé

ee pronounced /ay/ as in say

Words in this group are also often spelt with an accent mark over one letter *e*.

> entree (entrée), fiancee (fiancée), negligee (negligée),
> soiree (soirée)

See also WORD HISTORIES: **anemone**, **cliché**, **entrée**, **hyperbole**.

-ed / -t

For information on words such as *spelled/spelt*, see **alternative spellings**: **-ed / -t (spelled, spelt)**.

editing

Editing is an important part of the writing process. During this process, an author's draft writing is improved so that it is ready for publication.

For details on editing, see **writing process**: **Editing**.

effect

See **affect / effect**.

-ei- / -ie-

When the letters *e* and *i* are linked to make an /ee/ sound in a word, the old spelling rule is:

> **i** before **e**, except after **c**.

Words with i before e, but not after c
These words obey this rule.

> achieve, belief, believe, besiege, brief, cashier, chief, field, fierce, grief, handkerchief, hygiene, niece, piece, pier, relief, relieve, retrieve, siege, thief, thieves

Words with e and i after the letter c
These words have the letters *-ei-* because they follow the letter *c*.

> ceiling, conceive, conceit, deceive, deceit, perceive, receipt, receive

Words that are exceptions to the 'i before e' rule
Some words that disobey this rule are:

> caffeine, geisha, heinous, protein, seize, sheila, species, weir, weird

Two of these can also be pronounced with an /i/ sound to rhyme with *eye*.

> either, neither

-el

For information on words such as *levelled/leveled*, see **alternative spellings: -eled / -elled (modeled, modelled)**.

elegy

An *elegy* is a poem written to mourn the death of a person, or in memory of a past event. An elegy is usually formal, and solemn or sad. English-speaking poets have always had a sense of humour, so many humorous elegies have been written on tombstones.

> This is the grave of Mike O'Day,
> Who died maintaining his right of way;
> His right was clear, his will was strong,
> But he's just as dead as if he'd been wrong.

Anonymous

See also **epitaph**; **obituary**; WORD HISTORIES: **elegy**.

ellipsis (…)

The ellipsis punctuation mark shows that something has been left out in a line of text. It is marked by a series of three dots (…). It is sometimes written with a space before and after each dot (. . .).

ellipsis (…)

The ellipsis is mostly used when writers quote from another person's writing or speech. When the writer leaves out some words, then the ellipsis shows the reader that the quotation is not exactly as the original person spoke or wrote it. An ellipsis can be used:

To show incomplete lines in text
To show interruption in speech
To show omissions in quotations
With other punctuation

To show incomplete lines in text
An ellipsis can suggest that there is more to come in a story.
> "Follow me," said the guide. "I have something to show you …"

To show interruption in speech
An ellipsis can show an interruption in dialogue, for example when one speaker interrupts another.
> Robert began, "I think I know who is responsible …"
> "Robert," interrupted the teacher. "I hope you have proof."

See also **dialogue (US: dialog)**.

To show omissions in quotations
It is important to know when words have been left out of a quotation, because the meaning of the original text can be changed by leaving out certain words.
> Armstrong said, "… Earth itself is … an odd kind of spacecraft … you've got to be pretty cautious about how you treat your spacecraft."

In this example, the ellipsis is used in three places to show where words have been left out of Armstrong's original sentence. Speech usually has extra words that are not useful in writing. We don't speak the way we would normally write. Writers often leave words out in a quotation so they can focus on the main point being made.

> "It has to be a shared responsibility … between the people we elect for government, the people who make decisions in factories … it has to be a responsibility for each of us."

In this example, the quotation is from an interview the author had with someone. The ellipses show two places in the sentence where words have been left out. So we do not know the interviewee's complete statement.

If we do not know an interviewee's complete statement, it is possible for a writer to take words out of context and change their meaning. In the following example, an interview is used as the basis for a newspaper article.

Interviewer: Mr Lee, if you are elected into government at the next elections, what will you do for schools?

Mr Lee: I will investigate the needs of schools. If it is found that schools need more teachers, then I will immediately act to see if I can get the government to solve the problem.

LEE TO HIRE MORE TEACHERS
An exclusive interview was held with Mr Lee, shadow Minister for Education, today. Mr Lee stated that "… schools need more teachers …" He declared that, if elected, he will "… immediately act … to solve the problem".

The ellipses show where words have been omitted from quotations in the newspaper article. However, the reader cannot see that Mr Lee did not actually mean that 'schools need more teachers' and that he will 'immediately act to solve the problem'. The journalist has used Mr Lee's words out of context.

With other punctuation

When the ellipsis is used with a question mark or an exclamation mark, it is placed *after* the other mark.

"Why? …" Robert began.

"Who? …" continued Beth.

"Not now," said the stranger. "All will be revealed later."

In this example, the ellipsis is used because the characters Robert and Beth were interrupted in their speech by the next speaker as they tried to ask questions.

See also **exclamation mark (!)**; **question mark (?)**.

email

Email is an abbreviation of the words *electronic mail*. People write letters or notes on computer and send them to their audience through the Internet. Email can have attachments — documents written on a word processor, photographs, charts, audio recording and other things that can be scanned or filed on a computer.

See also **correspondence**: **Appointments**.

emphasis

A writer often needs to show emphasis in writing — to express excitement, amazement or loudness. *Italics, bold, underline*, *exclamation marks* or *capital letters* can be used to show emphasis.

Italics

> It was *his* fault that the horse had escaped.

Bold type

> **evergreen** A tree or plant that has leaves all year.

Exclamation mark

> Warning! Smoking is a health hazard.

Capitals

Here, the author used capitals to emphasise just one word.
> The trip to the coral reef was **AMAZING**.

In this example, the author used capitals to emphasise a whole sentence.
> **SMOKING CAUSES LUNG CANCER**.

ensure

See **assure / ensure / insure**.

epi-

Epi- is a prefix. It comes from the Greek language. It means 'over' or 'something that happens afterwards or is added'.

Some English words that begin with this prefix are:

> episode, epicentre, epilogue, epicure, epitaph, epithet

> The program was broadcast over two **episodes**.

See also WORD HISTORIES: **epitaph**.

epilogue (US: epilog)

In books, an *epilogue* is the final or closing thought an author can add after the main story has been told. It often brings the different parts of a story together. In the following example, the epilogue presents a conclusion to the story *Perseus the Gorgon-slayer*. It takes the reader back to a prophecy that was explained at the beginning of the story. The last sentence gives a closing thought about the main characters.

EPILOGUE

King Acrisius heard of his grandson's great deed. Fearing Perseus would seek him out, Acrisius hid on the remote island of Larissa.

Athletic games were held annually on Larissa and that year Perseus competed in the discus event. He threw the discus and watched in amazement as it flew far into the rows of spectators, striking an old beggar on the head. The beggar was killed instantly. He was Acrisius, who had hidden in the crowd to watch his grandson. And so the prophecy was fulfilled.

Perseus and Andromeda claimed Acrisius' kingdom, where they lived happily and ruled wisely.

Perseus the gorgon-slayer, p. 32

epitaph

An *epitaph* is a message written on a tombstone, to commemorate a person's death. Most epitaphs give information — names, dates, and names of parents or children.

Some epitaphs have been written with a sense of humour. Some humorous verse is written as a parody (a 'send-up') of an epitaph.

See also **elegy**; WORD HISTORIES: **epitaph**.

Wise & wacky works, p. 31

In this example, the poet played on the word Knott which sounds like not. If you read *not* instead of *Knott* in the poem, it becomes funny. For example, *He lived Knott (not), He died Knott (not).*

See also **pun**.

epithet

An *epithet* is a word or phrase added to a person's name to describe that person.

Historical epithets:
> William the Conqueror
> Eric the Red
> Alexander the Great
> Billy the Kid
> Richard the Lion Heart

Modern epithets in literature:
> Hagar the Horrible (*comic strip*)
> Herbertia the vile (*book by Yvonne Winer*)
> Perseus the gorgon-slayer (title of a Greek myth retold *by Jane O'Loughlin*)

eponyms

Eponyms are words that come from people's names. Some people's names are made famous by becoming a common word for something associated with that person. Some eponyms become so common that we often forget these words were once people's names.

- The word *bloomers* (meaning long, baggy women's underwear/pants) was named after a New Yorker, Amelia Bloomer, in the 1950s.
- The word *biro* was named after Laszlo Biro, who invented the ballpoint pen.
- The *ferris wheel* was named after its inventor George Ferris.

Most eponyms do not begin with a capital letter. They are common nouns — even though they originally came from a proper noun (a person's name).

Some eponyms *do* have a capital — usually eponyms that are units of measure or names of places. The measures of temperature *Celsius* and *Fahrenheit* are both eponyms that have kept their capital letters.

See also **measures**.

For stories of the people behind eponyms, see WORD HISTORIES:
- **Achilles heel**
- **Adam's apple**
- **anemone**
- **arachnid**
- **atlas**
- **babble**
- **biro**
- **bloomers**
- **blurb**
- **Celsius**
- **cereal**
- **Fahrenheit**
- **Ferris wheel**
- **Friday**
- **Granny Smith apple**
- **guillotine**
- **January**
- **July**
- **OK**
- **Thursday**
- **Tuesday**
- **Wednesday**

-er / -re

For information on words like *centre/center*, see **alternative spellings**: **-er / -re (center, centre)**.

even

See **only**.

eulogy

A *eulogy* is speech or writing that praises someone or something. It is usually formal. It is pronounced /**yoo**-lo-jee/.

euphemism

Euphemism is the use of pleasant or polite expressions to describe something that is unpleasant, embarrassing or awkward.

euphemism

Direct meaning	Euphemisms
dead	resting in peace; gone to heaven; left this life; passed away
short (person)	slight; vertically challenged
people killed (war)	collateral damage
stink	unpleasant odour; on the nose
toilet	bathroom; WC (water closet); washroom; loo

Euphemisms are useful when writers need to avoid upsetting an audience or wish to be polite. However, they can also be used to mislead an audience into thinking a situation is better than it really is.

> **PUBLIC STATEMENT**
> Savoury Meat Company **has experienced some difficulties** recently **as a result of a rare mishap in the quality control** department. A **bacterial organism** found its way into a batch of sausages and resulted in a **medical condition** in a **few consumers. Enquiries by health authorities** are underway.

This 'statement to the public' might have been written to protect the reputation of the Savoury Meat Company. It has several euphemisms that make matters sound better than they might really be.

> **SAVOURY MEAT COMPANY HEALTH BLUNDER**
> Savoury Meat Company **is in trouble**. Sausages made by the Company are responsible for **at least ten consumers** being **rushed to hospital** with a **life-threatening disease**. **Poor quality control** at the factory allowed **rotten, infected meat** into their products. The Company is **under serious investigation by the health authorities**.

This 'newspaper article' makes the Savoury Meat Company look bad. Compare the expressions in bold type with the euphemisms in the first example. The facts might be correct, but they could also have been sensationalised to make matters sound worse than they might really be.

In formal writing it is generally better to communicate in plain or direct language, as long as you are sensitive to the position of your audience.

See also WORD HISTORIES: **euphemism**.

except

See **accept / except / expect**.

excess

See **access / excess**.

exclamation mark (!)

The *exclamation mark* is used to show strong feelings in writing, such as surprise, excitement or amazement. It affects the way a reader understands or reads a sentence out loud.

In dialogue, the exclamation mark tells the reader in which tone to read the words. Compare these two lines — how would you read them?

> I don't believe it.
> I don't believe it!

The exclamation mark is sometimes repeated to show *extra* urgency, surprise or loudness. Writers should be careful not to overdo this; it may be acceptable in personal letters, notes or journals, but not in formal writing.

> **Guess what!!!** We won for the first time!
> **Help!!!** I hate snakes!

See also WORD HISTORIES: **exclamation mark (!)**.

The following topics show how exclamation marks are used:
Exclamations
Commands
Greetings
Humour
Interjections
With other punctuation

Exclamations

Exclamation marks are used to mark exclamations.

> Then he stared at the person in the grey coat. "**That's who it was!**"

In this example, the exclamation mark shows that the speaker is saying something very strongly.

See also **exclamations**.

exclamation mark (!)

Commands

Exclamation marks are used after some commands to show the reader that the command should be read with emphasis or force.

Run! Take cover!

See also **sentences**: **Commands**.

Greetings

Exclamation marks are often used after greetings in speech.

Hello! I'm your new coach.

"**Good morning, everyone!**" The teacher's voice came clearly over the radio.

Humour

Exclamation marks are sometimes used to show something is in fun — as a joke, or mischievous comment.

Let's see — you could go dressed as a gorilla or a crocodile or disguised as yourself! (Just joking.)

Interjections

Exclamation marks are often used in interjections.

The hero fought off the robbers. **Pow! Zap! Kapow!**

See also **interjections**.

With other punctuation

Brackets

Exclamation marks are often used together with brackets. If the exclamation is the complete sentence inside the brackets, then the mark is also placed inside the end bracket.

I said you could borrow my bike. (But I didn't say you could wreck it**!**)

If the whole exclamation is not within the brackets, then the exclamation mark is placed outside the end bracket

I said you could borrow my bike (but I didn't say you could wreck it)**!**

Quotation marks

Exclamation marks are often used in dialogue or direct speech to show feelings. The exclamation mark is always placed inside the quotation marks.

"Oh, no!" yelled her brother. "She's destroyed my room**!**"

See also **ellipsis (…): With other punctuation**; **question mark** (?): **With other punctuation**.

exclamations

Exclamations are words, phrases or sentences that express a strong emotion such as fear, surprise, excitement, or happiness. They are usually followed by an exclamation mark.

> "You are so funny!"
> "What a fabulous ride!"
> "Come back here, immediately!"

See also **exclamation mark (!)**: **Exclamations**; **O**; **sentences**: **Exclamations**.

expect

See **accept / except / expect**.

explanation

An *explanation text* is nonfiction writing that explains how something works or happens. It might explain how machines like bicycles or computers work, how and why weather patterns happen, how a library operates or how and why diseases happen in the human body.

There are two main parts to an explanation.
* *the title and general description*
The writer describes the topic of the explanation.
* *a detailed explanation*
The writer explains the topic, usually in *chronological order* — beginning with what happens first and ending with what happens last. The following example is a section from a book that explains how milk is produced.

exposition

> ### How cows make milk
>
> Cells in the udder change the nutrients into milk parts and store them in tiny spaces like a sponge. When the cow is milked, the milk runs into a bigger space called a cistern and finally passes out through the teat. The udder has four cisterns and four teats.
>
> The place where the cows are milked is called a dairy. The cows are herded into the yard where they wait to be milked. The dairy farmer milks a small group of cows at a time. Each group takes about ten minutes. The cows are milked every morning and every night.
>
> The farmer connects the cows' teats to a milking machine. The suction cups on their teats draw out the milk. The milk passes through stainless steel pipes to a refrigerated tank where it is stored.
>
> A bulk tanker normally comes every day to the farm to collect the milk from the tank in the dairy. It visits several farms on the same day and takes the milk to the milk factory. When the milk arrives at the milk factory it is tested to make sure it is good quality. It is then pumped into big holding silos ready for processing. All milk is pasteurised, which means it is heated to kill germs.

How cows make milk, pp. 8-13

- Adverbs of time and ordinals (*then, after, before, first, last*) are often used in explanations.
- The verbs are usually in the simple present tense. (*is, are, has, have, works, makes* etc)
- The sentences are usually statements. (*The udder has four cisterns and four teats.*)
- The sentences often have a cause and effect structure. (*If ... then*; *This happens because ...*; *It does this so that ...* etc)

See also **adverbs**: **Adverbs of time (when)**; **chronological**; **abbreviations**: **Ordinals**; **sentences**: **Statements**; **verbs**: **Tenses (time)**.

exposition

An *exposition* (or *expository writing*) is text in which the writer gives an argument to support a point of view.

See also **argument**.

fable

A fable is a very short story that has a moral or a lesson. Fables usually have only two characters — often animals that act like humans. The moral is usually stated at the end of the story.

An allegory is also a story that presents lessons about life — often with animal characters — but it is usually much longer than a fable. The lesson in an allegory is woven throughout the story. A fable is a very simple type of allegory.

See also **allegory**; **narrative**: **Fable**.

fewer / less

Fewer and *less* both mean 'smaller' but they are used in slightly different ways. Writers need to be careful about how they use each word.

Fewer means 'not as many, a smaller number'. *Fewer* should be used when describing things you can count.
> There were **fewer** people swimming when the weather turned cool.
In this example, the author used the word *fewer* because it describes how many *people*. You can count people (two people, three people etc) so the word *fewer* is correct.

Less means 'not as much, a smaller quantity'. *Less* should be used when describing things you can't count.
> One solution to the pollution problem is to create **less** waste.
In this example, the author used the word *less* because it describes how much waste. You can't count waste (one waste? two wastes?) so the word *less* is correct.

See also **nouns**: **Count nouns**, **Mass nouns**.

fiction

Fiction is writing that is created from the writer's imagination. Characters, plots and settings in stories and poems are things the author invents.

There are many ways to write fiction, including novels, poems and plays.

For details on different forms of fiction, see under the following:
* **allegory**
* **ballad**
* **chant**
* **cinquain**
* **drama**
* **fable**
* **free verse**
* **haiku**
* **limerick**
* **narrative**
* **parody**
* **play script**
* **poetry**
* **recount**: Fiction
* **rhyming couplet**

finite verbs

See **verbs**: Finite and non-finite verbs

flour / flower

Flour is ground grain (wheat, rye, corn) used in cooking.

> **Flour** is used to make bread.

A *flower* is a part of a plant.

> The brilliant colours of the **flower** attracted the bee.

footnotes

See **notes**.

foreword

A *foreword* is a short section of text that follows the title page of a book. In a foreword the author of the book explains the aims of the book and gives some background information about how the book was created.

> **FOREWORD**
>
> An oral history is a record of a person's memories of their life. It tells us much about their family, schooling and interests.
>
> This book records some of the important things Pilawuk remembers about her childhood.
>
> I taped an interview with Pilawuk. This recorded information was typed and edited. Pilawuk then read the edited text. She checked to make sure that it was an accurate record of her memories and of her viewpoint of events at the time.
>
> *Janeen Brian*

Pilawuk: When I was young, p.2

- The first two paragraphs are in the third person (the author uses the pronouns *their*, *it* and *her*) because she is writing/explaining about something and someone else.
- The author uses the plural pronoun *their* in the first paragraph instead of writing *he or she*. This does not agree in number with the singular *a person*, but it avoids the clumsiness of writing *he or she*. This is a modern trend which worries some people.
- The last paragraph begins in the first person (the author uses the personal pronoun *I*) because she is writing about herself.
- The first two paragraphs are in the present tense (the author uses the verbs *is*, *tells*, *records* and *remembers*). This is because the author is presenting an explanation.
- The third paragraph is in the past tense (the author uses the verbs *taped*, *was typed*, *edited* and so on). This is because the author is recounting events that have already happened.

See also **agreement**: **Agreement and gender**; **person**; **recount**; **verbs**: **Past**, **Present**; WORD HISTORIES: **foreword**.

foreword / forward

These two words sound similar. They are easily confused, but they shouldn't be. They have quite different meanings.

A *foreword* is a section in a book.

> The author, Janeen Brian, wrote a **foreword** in her book *Pilawuk: When I was young*.

Forward means 'ahead, in front, confident'.

> She played a **forward** position in the soccer team.
> The car moved **forward**.

The post office did not **forward** the letter to the correct address.
Because he was a very **forward** person, they asked him to speak on their behalf.

See also **foreword**.

formal / informal writing

Formal writing is the careful use of language to make a message sound more important, proper, professional or official. If writers want an audience to take their message seriously, they usually use formal language.

Informal writing is the relaxed use of language to make a message sound more casual, personal, familiar, friendly or direct. Informal writing often includes colloquialisms and slang. It may also have capital letters and punctuation marks used in ways that are not serious or formal.

If an audience expects writing or speech to be *formal*, and writers or speakers use *informal* language, the audience could lose confidence in the writers or speakers or think they are unprofessional or cheeky.

If an audience is expecting *informal* writing or speaking and the writer or speaker uses *formal* language, then the audience might find the writer or speaker pompous, arrogant or uncaring about the audience. The following examples show the difference between formal and informal writing.

Formal letter

Mr S Marron
14 Count St
Lowcester

Dear Mr Marron,
Congratulations. You have won a consolation prize in our TV Quiz competition. Your prize will be delivered shortly. We hope you enjoy it.
Thank you for entering our competition.

Yours faithfully,
Herman Spring
Director

Informal letter

Sam Marron
14 Count St
Lowcester

Hi Sam,
Congratulations! You've won a prize in our TV Quiz competition
you lucky thing. It's on its way in the mail. ENJOY BUDDY!
Thanks for taking part — you've got to be in it to win it!!!
Cheers,
Herman

See also **colloquial language**; **slang**.

fort / fought

Fort is a noun. It means 'a place, such as a castle, that is protected from attackers'.

The soldiers stood on the walls of the **fort**, ready for the enemy.

Fought is a verb. It is the past tense of the verb *to fight*.
The soldiers **fought** their way out of the ambush.

See also **nouns**; **verbs**: **Tenses (time)**.

free verse

Free verse is poetry that does not rhyme or have a regular rhythm.

You ask me, what did I dream?
I dreamt I became a bird.
You ask me, why did I want to become a bird?
I really wanted to have wings.
You ask me, why did I want wings?
These wings would help me fly back to my country.
You ask me, why did I want to go back there?
Because I wanted to find something I missed.

Extract from 'Dream of a bird', Nga Bach Thi Tran, *Poems not to be missed*, p. 28

-fs / -ves

For information on words such as *hoofs*/*hooves*, see **alternative spellings**:
-fs / -ves (hoofs, hooves)

full stop (.)

The *full stop* is one of the oldest punctuation marks in English writing, and is the mark most often used. In the United States it is called a *period*. The following topics explain some uses of the full stop:

In abbreviations
To mark the end of a sentence
With numerals

In abbreviations

Full stops are used in some abbreviations to show that the word has been shortened. There is a trend to use the full stop less in abbreviations.

> 4 p.m. We all returned safely to the base camp in the helicopters.

In this example, full stops are used in the abbreviation *p.m.* which is a shortened form of the Latin words *post meridiem*.

> **mollusc (mollusk)** A group of animals that have a soft body, often with a shell, but no backbone. e.g. snails, slugs, clams.

In this example, full stops are used in the abbreviation *e.g.* which stands for *exempli gratia (for example)*.

> **louse** (pl. **lice**) Tiny, wingless insect that lives on mammals; a parasite.

In the example above, a full stop is used in the abbreviation *pl.* which stands for *plural* (*lice* is the plural of *louse*).

See also **abbreviations**: **Full stops**; WORD HISTORIES: **eg, pm**.

To mark the end of a sentence

A full stop marks the end of a sentence (unless an exclamation mark, question mark or ellipsis is used in its place).

> I had my first day in high school today. It was OK.
> It was a day for bushwalking, swimming and picnicking.
> 10 a.m. We had a late breakfast. I cooked. The others talked.

See also **ellipsis (...)**; **exclamation mark (!)**; **question mark (?)**.

With numerals

The full stop is used with numerals in measures, times and dates. When it is used with numerals it is called a *point*, or *decimal point*.

> The daily maximum reached 37.6°C.
>
> 3.15 p.m. The helicopter landed too hard on a slope and rolled over.

Did you know?

Period can mean 'the end'.

Have you ever heard anyone end a sentence with the word *period*?

> You'll get nothing more out of me — *period*.
>
> It's the best product in the world, *period*.
>
> That's my last word on the subject. *Period*.

This use of the word *period* really makes no sense in writing. In these examples, the speaker ends the sentence by naming the punctuation mark (the *period* or *full stop*). What the speaker is saying is:

> You'll get nothing more out of me — *end of sentence* (*or end of argument*).

Usually *period* is used in speech to emphasise a point, meaning there is nothing more to be said on a subject.

This is not used in formal writing. It might be used in dialogue, a story or in a play.

---

future tense

Tense in grammar is about when events or actions happen. Verbs in the *future tense* tell about actions that have not yet happened.

> Tomorrow morning I **will read** my story to an audience.

The verb *will read* is in the future tense.

For more details about verbs and future tense, see **verbs**: **Future**.

gender

Gender is about whether something is male, female or neither. The pronouns *he*, *him*, *his*, *she*, *her*, *hers*, *it* or *its* can be used to show the gender of a topic in English.

Some suffixes in English show whether something is male or female (eg *lion*, *lioness*; *tiger*, *tigress*). These suffixes tend not to be used nowadays for words to do with people, because such words are regarded by many people as sexist.

> waiter / waitress, actor / actress, host / hostess,
> typist / typiste, hero / heroine, aviator / aviatrix

Today the words that tend to be used for both male and female in these examples are *waiter*, *actor*, *host*, *typist*, *hero* and *aviator*.

See also **agreement**: **Agreement and gender**; **he / she**; **sexist language**.

genre

Genre means 'text type'. It is a name given to the different forms of writing. Writers use different genres or text types to suit the audience and purpose of their writing. Each genre has its own structure and grammar.

For information on the main genres or text types, see **argument**; **discussion**; **explanation**; **narrative**; **poetry**; **procedure**; **recount**; **report**.

See also **audience**.

gerund

A *gerund* is a present participle (*-ing* word) used as a noun.

> **Smoking** is forbidden in this room.
> The contestants were ready for the **beginning** of the race.

See also **nouns**: **Verbal nouns**; **participles**.

glossary

A *glossary* is a list of technical words and their meanings. Glossaries are usually used in nonfiction texts to explain words that are not explained within the text. The glossary is placed at the end of a book.

Features of a glossary:
- Glossaries are organised with headwords placed in alphabetical order.
- The headwords in a glossary are usually not capitalised unless they are proper nouns.
- The headwords are usually in bold or italics so they are easy to find.

• The explanations in a glossary are usually very brief, but must give full and accurate explanations of the headwords. Sometimes they are 'dictionary style' sentences or sentence fragments.

GLOSSARY
camouflage To use colour and shape to look like the surroundings.
crustacean A group of animals that have external skeletons. It includes crabs, shrimps, prawns and lobsters.
evergreen A tree or plant that has leaves all year.
germinate To sprout (seeds and spores); to grow.

good / well

Good is an adjective. It means 'excellent, well-behaved, enjoyable'.

Charles had always been **good** at everything.
The children were **good** for the baby-sitter.
Everyone had a **good** time at the party.

This word is commonly mis-used in conversation.

Teacher: How are you, Sam?
Sam: **Good**, thanks.

The dialogue in the example is common today, but usually does not mean what the speaker says. Sam probably should have said, "*Well*, thanks."

Well can be used as:

• an adverb meaning 'properly, carefully'
They washed the dog **well**.

• an adjective meaning 'healthy'
The patient was not a **well** person.
I'm feeling **well**, thank you.

• a noun meaning 'a hole which holds water'.
A pump drew water from the **well**.

When words have more than one meaning, writers can often create jokes with them. In this verse, the poet's last line is a pun on the word *well*.

> Doctor Bell fell down a **well**
> And broke his collar-bone.
> Doctors should attend the sick
> And leave the **well** alone.

Anonymous

See also **adjectives**; **adverbs**; **pun**.

grammar

Grammar is the set of rules people use to make sense with words, phrases and sentences in their speech and writing. Words like *adverb* and *adjective* are used to talk about language. Writers and editors use grammar to know how they can combine words in various ways to communicate with their readers.

People who study the language and how it works are called *linguists*. The grammar explained in this guide is not a study of linguistics. It just makes it easier to talk about and improve your writing.

Writing tip

Understanding grammar

You *know* English grammar if you can read and understand this sentence, or speak so that others can understand you.

You *understand* English grammar if you can discuss the ways the language works and check whether your writing can be made clearer by rearranging words, phrases and clauses.

English grammar works at two main levels:
Word forms
Word order and links

Word forms
Most words in English have different forms.

> true, untrue, truly, truth, truths, truthful, truthfully, truthfulness, untruthfully

The examples above are all forms of the word *true*, but they are used differently. Each affix (*un-*, *-ly*, *-th*, *-s*, *-ful,* and *-ness*) gives the word *true* a different use and meaning in English grammar.

> It was a **true** story.
> The story was **truly** interesting.
> The author wrote the **truth**.
> There were many **truths** in the author's story.
> The author was **truthful**.
> The author acted **truthfully**.
> The author acted **untruthfully** in claiming that the story was **true**, when, in fact, it was **untrue**.

See also **affixes**.

grammar

Word order and links

Meaning in English can be changed by changing the order of words in a sentence.

>The dog bit the child.
>The child bit the dog.

These two sentences have exactly the same words, but the words are in a different order. This gives the sentences different meanings. The link between the subject and the verb has changed. In the first sentence, *the dog* is the subject. In the second sentence *the child* is the subject.

Often, word order in English can be changed *without* changing the meaning of a sentence. This happens when the link between a subject and its verb is not changed.

>**Yesterday**, the dog bit the child.
>The dog bit the child **yesterday**.
>The dog, **yesterday**, bit the child.

In all of these sentences, *the dog* is the subject of the verb *bit*. Changing the order of the word *yesterday* did not change this link.

Sometimes whole phrases or clauses can be moved without changing the meaning of a sentence.

>**Without any warning**, the dog bit the child.
>The dog, **without any warning,** bit the child.
>The dog bit the child, **without any warning**.

Writers need to take special care with some words in English, because they can change the meaning of a sentence whenever their position changes. The word *only* is one of these words.

>Nigel ate **only** five pies. (Nigel did not eat more than five pies.)
>**Only** Nigel ate five pies. (No one else ate five pies.)
>Nigel ate five pies **only**. (Nigel did not eat anything else.)

See also **clauses**; **only**; **phrases**; **sentences**: **Word order in sentences**; **subject**.

Writing tip

Changing word order to improve your writing

The main words in a sentence are the *subject* (topic) and its *verb* (action or event). They are what the whole sentence is about. The order of the words will usually not change the meaning of a sentence unless it changes the subject that is linked to the verb.

> The child bit the dog. (*The child* is the subject of the verb *bit*.)

> The dog bit the child. (*The dog* is the subject of the verb *bit*.)

The meaning of these sentences is different because they have different subjects linked to the verb *bit*.

Adverbs and adverbial phrases can often be moved around in a sentence without changing the meaning.

> Yesterday, the child bit the dog.

The adverb *yesterday* can be moved to different places in the sentence without changing the meaning — because it does not change the subject *child* and its link to the verb *bit*. It simply tells *when* the child bit the dog.

If you understand these simple rules, then you can move words, phrases and clauses around in your sentences to see if there are better ways to say things, without changing the meaning of your sentences.

See also **adverbial phrases**; **clauses**; **subject**; **verbs**.

grateful

Grateful is often spelt incorrectly as *greatful*. This word has nothing to do with being *great*. It means 'thankful'. The spelling *grate* comes from a Latin word *gratus* meaning 'pleasing or thankful'.

See also WORD HISTORIES: **grateful**.

groan / grown

Groan means 'to make a sound that expresses pain, boredom or disapproval'.

> "We lost the game!" **groaned** the coach.

Grown is the past participle of the verb *grow*.
> The chick had **grown** inside the egg.
> The Penicillium mould was **grown** in a 'mould broth'.

-gue / -g

See **alternative spellings**: -log / -logue (dialog, dialogue).

guessed / guest

Guessed is the past tense of the verb *to guess*. It means 'to estimate something'.
> Patrick **guessed** there were over fifty people in the audience.

Guest is a noun. It means 'a person or character invited to a place or event'.
> The mystery **guest** arrived on time for dinner.

haiku

Haiku is a Japanese form of poetry. Each poem has seventeen syllables. The topics of haiku poems are usually images or feelings.
> Sun beats down on the beach
> Children play excitedly
> Pale skin turns red

See also **syllable**.

hair / hare

Hair is a noun. It means 'the growth on people's heads'.
> Her red **hair** stood out in the crowd.
> She brushed her curly **hair**.

Hare is a noun. It means 'a four-legged mammal that looks like a rabbit'.
> **Hares** have longer hind legs than rabbits.

hardly

The word *hardly* is a negative word. Therefore, it should not be used together with another negative word (*no*, *not*, *n't*, *nothing*, *none*). This would be called a 'double negative'.
> He ain't got no sense **hardly**.

In formal writing this sentence would be written as:
> He has **hardly** any sense.
> or
> He has almost no sense.

Further example:
> The children were **hardly** in bed when the alarm sounded.

See also **double negative**; **negatives**.

hash symbol (#)

See **addresses**: Ampersand (&) and hash (#); **symbols**: Hash (#).

he / she

Authors sometimes need to write *he or she* and *him or her* in a text when they are writing about a topic.

> When an author begins to write a story, **he or she** must first think of an idea or topic to write about.

In this example, if the writer needed to use the phrase *he or she* often, then it would sound clumsy.

If the writer used either *he* or *she*, then the text could be seen as being sexist.

> When an author begins to write a story, **he** must first think of an idea or topic to write about.

This sentence would be regarded as sexist because it suggests that only males are authors.

One way of avoiding this problem is to use the plural. The pronouns *they*, *them* and *their* can mean either male or female.

> When **authors** begin to write a story, **they** must first think of an idea or topic to write about.

See also **agreement**: Agreement and gender; **plural**; **pronouns**; **sexist language**.

headwords

The key words in reference books such as dictionaries, encyclopedias, thesauruses, style guides and glossaries, are called *headwords*. In some reference books, the headwords are capitalised. Many editors believe that only headwords that are proper nouns or proper adjectives should be capitalised. This tells the reader whether a word is a proper word or a common word.

>**German measles**: (See RUBELLA)

In the headword *German measles*, *German* is a proper adjective (it is the name of a particular nationality). Therefore it has a capital letter.

>**jugular vein** A large vein in the neck.

There is no proper noun or proper adjective in the headword *jugular vein*, so it does not have a capital letter.

Headwords in this guide have a capital only when they are proper words.

See also **glossary**; **proper nouns**; **report**: **Reference texts**.

hiccough / hiccup

These words mean the same thing. Both are correct spellings. *Hiccough* is an old spelling which some people still use. *Hiccup* is also an old spelling. It shows how the word is pronounced and it has become the more popular spelling.

>Full of lemonade, he **hiccupped** loudly and the whole room heard.

See also WORD HISTORIES: **hiccough / hiccup**.

high frequency words

Although there are over 600,000 words in the English language, most people use only a few thousand words regularly. Among these few thousand, some words are used much more often than others. These are called *high frequency words*. It is important for writers to know how to spell and use these words because they are used so often. Here are fifty of the most commonly used words in English.

>I, up, look, we, like, and, on, at, for, he, is, said,
>go, you, are, this, going, they, away, play, a, am, cat, to,
>come, day, the, dog, big, my, mum, no, dad, all, get, in,
>went, was, of, me, she, see, it, yes, can, about,
>after, again, an, another

higher / hire

Higher means 'above, taller, greater than'. It is the comparative degree of the adjective *high*.

>They planned to score a **higher** number of goals than last year.
>This building is **higher** than the other.

Hire means 'to pay for the use of something or someone'.

> Today we **hired** a boat and went fishing.
> The business needed to **hire** more workers.

See also **adjectives**: **Adjectives of degree**.

hoarse / horse

Hoarse means 'having a husky or rough voice', sometimes caused by too much shouting.

> Jennifer was **hoarse** from yelling at the football.

A *horse* is a four-legged animal.

> The **horse** cantered across the field.

homographs

Homographs are words that have the same spelling but different sounds and meanings. For example, the word *tear* can be pronounced in two different ways.

> There was a **tear** in his eye. (*tear* rhymes with *hear*)
> There was a **tear** in his shirt. (*tear* rhymes with *bear*)

Homographs are a type of homonym.

Further examples of homographs:
- wind
  > The **wind** blew the candle out. (rhymes with *sinned*)
  > **Wind** the clock. (rhymes with *kind*)
- bow
  > He wore a **bow** tie. (rhymes with *show*)
  > The actors took a **bow** at the end of the play. (rhymes with *cow*)
- resume
  > A **resume** is useful if you are going for a job. (rhymes with *you may*)
  > After a week in hospital, the worker was fit to **resume** work duties. (rhymes with *presume*)

Careful or formal writers would spell the first example for *resume* with an accent mark over the letter *e*. (résumé)

See also **-e**; **homonyms**.

homonyms

Homonyms are words with the same sound or spelling, but different meanings.

Bear / bare
These words sound the same but have different spellings and meanings.
> The **bear** lived in the woods.
> He caught a fish with his **bare** hands.

Row
This word can have two different sounds and meanings.
> **Row** the boat. (rhymes with *toe*)
> The cheats cause a **row**. (rhymes with *now*)

Writers use homonyms to create jokes.
> The forest ranger carries **bear** essentials.
> The tailor **seams** to like his work.

There are two types of homonyms — *homophones* and *homographs*.

See **homographs**; **homophones**; **pun**.

homophones

Homophones are words that have the same sound, but different meanings. They are a type of homonym.
> to, too, two

Homophones often cause a problem for writers because sometimes they cannot remember which spelling is correct. This is a time when writers use references (a dictionary or a style guide) to solve problems.

Further examples of homophones:
> paw, poor, pore, pour
> awe, oar, or, ore
> for, four, fore
> seem, seam
> discreet, discrete

See also **homonyms**.

hyperbole

Hyperbole (pronounced /hi-**per**-boh-lee/) means 'deliberate exaggeration'. Writers sometimes use hyperbole to create humour or to emphasise a point.

In narrative, this may take the form of characters 'over-acting' or 'hamming it up'.

> "Not that way!" **gasped** Gerald at the bottom of the stairs.
> "Well do I go up or down?" replied Frank quietly.
> "Neither. Just stop confusing me!" **spluttered** Gerald.
> "Well life could get boring very quickly just standing on a landing," Frank added with a hint of sarcasm.

In this example, Gerald 'gasps' and 'splutters'. The author created a character who dramatically overacts, to make the story humorous or entertaining.

Further example:

> She was caught last week with two speeding fines! At this rate she'll lose her driver's licence **for three lifetimes**!

See also WORD HISTORIES: **hyperbole**.

hyphen (-)

The hyphen is a small dash that links or separates words or word parts. Its main use is to show that two words should be read as a single word.

> The cars collided on a **one-way** road.

Some words begin as two separate words (*book keeper*). As they become better known they are usually joined with a hyphen (*book-keeper*). When words like this become very popular, they are eventually accepted as one word, and are set solid (*bookkeeper*).

Hint

Hyphenated words

Writers and editors around the world often argue about the use of hyphens. Hyphens are used more in the United Kingdom than the United States. For many words it is a matter of personal taste and style.

If you are unsure whether or not to hyphenate a word, check a good dictionary.

Further information is under the following topics:
Compound words
Directions
Family names
Job titles
Numbers

hyphen (-)

Compound words

Hyphens link the parts in compound words that describe a noun. Compound words like this are adjectives.

A **six-year-old** boy was reported missing from school.

In this example, the compound word *six-year-old* describes the noun *boy*.

Hint

Hyphens and ages

Take care when using hyphens in compound words that describe ages. The two sentences below do not mean the same thing, even though the words are the same.

Six-year-old pet dogs were saved from a burning house.

(This example means 'some pet dogs that were six years old'.)

Six **year-old** pet dogs were saved from a burning house.

(This example means 'six pet dogs that were one year old'.)

See also **compound words**.

Hyphens are also used in the following types of compound words:

Directions
Directions using more than one compass point are compound words linked with hyphens.

south-east, north-north-west, south-western, north-easterly, South-East Asia

See also **compass points**.

Family names
Family names that have more than one part often have a hyphen to link the parts.

Anthony **Lindford-Smythe**

hyphen (-)

Job titles
Some job titles have more than one word; the words are sometimes joined with a hyphen.

>Editor-in-chief
>Secretary-general
>Vice-president
>Deputy-sheriff

Numbers
Hyphens link the compound number words from twenty-one to ninety-nine.

>Grandma turned **fifty-two** last week.

See also **adjectives**; **compound words**.

Dialogue and nonfiction
Hyphens are used in dialogue and nonfiction to show:

Extended words
Hyphens are used to show words that are spoken in a drawn-out way.

>"Come **he-e-re**!" she screamed.

Pronunciation guide
Hyphens are used to show the syllables of a word in a pronunciation guide.

>Mycelium (my-**see**-lee-um)

Spelling guide
Hyphens are used to show when a word should be read letter by letter.

>"My name is spelled **S-a-r-a-h**," Sarah said, "not **S-a-r-a**."

Stammering or sobbing
Hyphens can be used to show stammering or sobbing in dialogue.

>"David…" she sobbed, but it came out, "**Da-avid**."

See also **dialogue (US: dialog)**; **syllable**.

Prefixes
Hyphens are used with some prefixes. It is difficult to remember which words with prefixes are hyphenated. Some guidelines are given below, but if you are unsure about a particular word, use a good dictionary.

The following prefixes sometimes need a hyphen when linked to a root word, except when the word is long-established and the meaning is not likely to be confused:

>*anti-* (anti-aircraft, anti-hero — but not antiseptic)
>*ex-* (meaning 'no longer' or 'former': ex-member, ex-president)
>*non-* (non-member, non-toxic — but not nonfiction)
>*re-* (re-invent, re-sent — but not reprint)

A few words with prefixes need hyphens so they will not be confused with other words that have the same letters but different meanings. This is very important with words beginning with the prefix *re-*.

>The teacher **re-marked** the papers. (*marked them again*)
>The teacher **remarked** on the papers. (*commented on the papers*)

A hyphen is also used when a prefix is added to a word with a capital letter.

>The **non-Aboriginal** family had a lot to learn about the desert.
>The behaviour of the sporting fans was said to be very **un-British**.
>The protesters were **anti-American**.

See also **prefixes**.

Word breaks

Hyphens are used to break a word when it will not fit into the end of a line of text. This is sometimes called *syllabification* because word breaks are made between syllables in a word. Each part of a word in a word break should sound as it does in the whole word.

>*thickening* could have a word break as *thick-ening* or *thicken-ing*.
>It would not have a word break as *thicke-ning* or *thi-ckening*.

Word breaks often happen in newspapers because the columns are usually narrow.

>Antarctica, 2001: Three
>ships became trapped
>by the plates of **thicken-**
>**ing** sea ice.

Some rules for word breaks:

- Always break a word at the end of a syllable.
- Do not break a one syllable word.
- Try not to break the names of people or places.
- Always place the hyphen at the end of the line — not at the beginning of the next line.

See also **syllable**.

iambic foot

When people speak in English, there is often a natural pattern of weak-strong beats or stresses in its sound, especially in poetry and song. This pattern is called the *iambic foot*. It is also called a *metric foot*. The pattern of weak-strong-weak-strong beats can make the language skip along.

Read the following verse by emphasising the syllables in bold type.

> I **said**, "This **horse** sir, **will** you **shoe**?"
> And **so** the **horse** he **shod**.
> I **said**, "This **deed** sir, **will** you **do**?"
> And **so** the **deed** he **dod**.

Anonymous

The iambic foot is also used in narrative writing.

With **just** one **snip** he **trimmed** the **rose** then **smelled** its **soft** per**fume**.

See also **ballad**; **blank verse**; **narrative**.

iambic pentameter

Iambic pentameter means a line of text (usually verse) that has a rhythmic pattern of five weak-strong beats or metric feet.

See also **iambic foot**; **blank verse**.

-ic

A *k* is added to words ending with *-ic* when adding *-ed*, *-er* and *-ing*.

frolic — frolicking, frolicked
mimic — mimicking, mimicked
picnic — picnicking, picnicked, picnicker

See also **suffixes**.

idioms

Idioms are sayings that have a different meaning from the dictionary definitions of the separate words. Some English idioms are:

You're **on thin ice** with that plan.

The idiom *on thin ice* means 'unsafe, uncertain, risky'.

My father likes to **cook up a storm** on the barbecue.

The idiom *cook up a storm* means 'to do a lot of cooking'.

-ie-

See **-ei- / -ie-**.

-ie / -y

For words such as *auntie/aunty*, see **alternative spellings**: **-ie / -y (auntie, aunty)**.

imperative

See **mood; sentences**: **Commands**.

impersonal writing

Impersonal writing is writing that does not show the author's point of view. It is used when the personal views of the author are not wanted by the audience. Official government writing and many nonfiction texts (explanations and reports) are often like this.

Impersonal writing often has third person pronouns (*it*, *they*, *them*).

> **This chapter describes** important stages in the discovery and development of penicillin. **It** describes pieces in the penicillin 'jigsaw puzzle' — the times, the people, the places and the events — from the discovery of penicillin to **its** use as a medicine. **It** is important to understand these events when thinking about who should be given the credit for penicillin.

• This writing sounds as if the text gives the view rather than the author. So the writing is impersonal.

> **This chapter describes** important stages …

If the author wrote from a personal viewpoint, then the text would have been something like this:

> In this chapter, **I describe** important stages …

• The author uses the pronoun *it* instead of *I* throughout the text.

> **It** is important …

If the author had used the pronoun *I*, it would have become a personal viewpoint.

> **I** think it is important ...

See also **person**; **personal writing**.

indefinite articles

The words *a* and *an* are called 'indefinite articles', because they do not point to particular things.

> **A** broken windmill.
> **An** old, broken windmill.

The writer is not being definite in these phrases — they could mean *any* windmill.

> **The** old windmill is broken. (This means a particular windmill so *the* is the definite article.)

See also **a / an**; **articles**; **determiners**; **noun phrases**.

independent clauses

See **clauses**: Main clauses.

indicative

See **mood**.

indirect questions

See **question mark**: Indirect questions.

indirect speech

When a writer reports what someone said, but does not write their words as if the person were saying them, it is called *indirect speech*. Indirect speech is also called *reported speech*.

> The man asked if **he liked fruit**. The boy said that **he did**.

In this example, the author is reporting what the man and the boy said. The author used indirect speech. Indirect speech often follows the words *if* (if he liked fruit) or *that* (that he did).

If the author wrote the words as if they were being spoken by a character, it would be called *direct speech*.

> "**Do you like fruit?**" the man asked.
> "**I do**," said the boy.

In this example, the author is quoting *exactly* what the man and the boy said. It is direct speech.

See also **direct speech**; **quotation marks** (' ' and " "); **split infinitives**.

infinitives

The infinitive is a verb form that does not have a subject. So it does not act as a complete verb. The word *to* usually comes before an infinitive verb.

> to run, to walk, to speak, to write

> What a challenge it would be **to win** the final match.

In this example, *to win* is an infinitive verb. The subject of the sentence (*it*) is linked to the verb *would be*. *To win* does not have a subject.

> The children snuggled up in bed **to read**.

In this example, *to read* is an infinitive verb.

Medicine was given **to prevent** pain.
In this example, *to prevent* is an infinitive verb.

See also **split infinitives**.

informal writing
See **formal / informal writing**.

information text
Information text is writing that gives a reader information on a topic. There are many forms of information text. It is also called *nonfiction*.

For details on the different forms of information text, see **argument**, **discussion**; **explanation**; **non-fiction**; **procedure**; **recount**; **report**.

initials
Initials are the shortened forms of people's names. Many writers use full stops after people's initials, but the modern trend is to leave out full stops.

A B Smith

Initials are used in lists such as telephone directories and bibliographies. In lists like a telephone directory, the family name is usually placed before the initials.

Smith A B
Smith A C

Initials are also used in addresses on letters.

Mrs A B Smith
20 Honeysuckle Lane
Andelooke SA 5357

See also **bibliography**.

instruction text
See **procedure**.

insure
See **assure / ensure / insure**.

intensifiers

Intensifiers are words that emphasise or boost the effect of other words. The most commonly used intensifier is *very*. Intensifiers are usually placed before the word or phrase they emphasise.

Some other intensifiers are:
        really, actually, absolutely, extremely, most, much, even

        They were **really** scared.
In this example, the intensifier *really* emphasises the adjective scared.

        'She's **actually** going to put the fire out.'
The intensifier *actually* emphasises the verb phrase *going to put*.

        Mum says that lemon sauce is delicious. I **absolutely** agree.
The intensifier *absolutely* emphasises the verb *agree*.

        Having a bonfire party is **definitely** out.
The intensifier *definitely* emphasises the word *out*.

Intensifiers are the opposite of *modifiers*

See also **modifiers**.

interjections

Interjections are words or short phrases that express strong emotion. They are usually followed by an exclamation mark (!). Some people believe that interjections are really one-word sentences.

Here is a list of interjections used for different purposes:
- greetings and farewells
        Hi! Hello! Howdy! G'day! Hey!
        Cheers! Goodbye! Ciao! Oo-roo! Bye! Ta-ta!
- fillers (words that 'fill in' blank moments in speech), or expletives (oaths or swear words)
        Ah! Oh! Er! Uh-huh! Mm-hmm! Aha!
        Darn it! Pooh!
- acknowledgements in speech
        OK, Thanks, Yes, Maybe, No, Perhaps
- reactions to senses (feeling, taste etc) and emotions
        Yuk! Ugh! Encore! Mm! Wow! Yum! Ha-ha! Ouch! He-he! Ow!
        Ho-ho! Yipee! Eek! Hooray! Oops!

internal rhyme

- interjections with more than one word
  Of course! Oh no! Good heavens! Strike me lucky!

Further examples of interjections:
  "**Holy smoke**!" yelled the driver.
  Grandpa forgot to… **Tut! Tut!** I must be patient.
The interjections *Holy moly* and *Tut! Tut*! express surprise and an interruption.

  Gee! They're here already.
The interjection *Gee!* expresses surprise.

  JACK: The well on the hill is empty!
  JILL: **No!**
The interjection *No*! is an emotional reply by Jill to Jack's statement.

Hint

Interjections

Interjections are often used in dialogue to make it sound more realistic.

Note how Josephine Croser used interjections in this dialogue.

  "I want my father. Can you take me to him?"
  "**Not likely!**"
  "**Please!**"
  "Please, **eh**? What about thanks then?"

Hannah, p. 27

See also **dialogue (US: dialog)**.

---

internal rhyme

Internal rhyme is rhyme within a line of verse.

  A tutor who tooted her flute,
  Tried to **tutor** two **tooters** to toot.

Writers may also use internal rhyme within a sentence in a story.
  My uncle tells a **whale** of a **tale** about mum when she was young.

See also **rhyme**.

interrogatives

interrogatives

The word *interrogate* means 'to ask questions'. *Interrogatives* are words, phrases or sentences that ask a question.

> Why is it dangerous?

This example is an interrogative sentence.

One way to create an interrogative sentence is to place the subject after the verb.

> What **did the sign** mean?

The subject of this sentence is *the sign*. It comes after the verb *did*, to make the sentence a question.

> How much **have you** grown?

In this sentence, the subject is *you*; it is placed after the verb *have*. If this order were reversed, then the question would become a statement (*How much* **you** *have* grown.)

Interrogative sentences often begin with interrogative words like *who, what* and *why*. These words are divided into two groups:

> **Interrogative pronouns**
> **Interrogative adverbs**

Interrogative pronouns

Interrogative pronouns include the words *who, whom, which, whose* and *what*.

> **Who** took the king's robe?
> **What** did the thieves do with it?

Interrogative adverbs

Interrogative adverbs include the words *how, when, where* and *why*.

> **How** should these problems be solved?
> **Why** was it dangerous?

See also **argument: Interviews**; **mood**; **sentences: Questions**.

interrogative sentences

See **sentences: Questions**.

inverted commas (' ')

Inverted means 'upside-down'. Quotation marks are sometimes called 'inverted commas' because the first mark looks like an upside-down comma.

See **quotation marks (' ' and " ")**.

invitations

See **correspondence**: Invitations.

irregular verbs

Irregular verbs are verbs that do not form their past tense by adding -ed.

> fall/fell, buy/bought, go/went, have/had, see/saw, fight/fought

For more details, see **verbs**: Irregular.

-ise / -ize

For the spelling of words like *realise/realize*, see **alternative spellings**: -ise / -ize (organise, organize).

it's / its

It's is short for *it is*. The apostrophe shows that the letter *i* has been left out.

> I hope you enjoy this movie. **It's** about polar bears.

Its is the possessive form of the pronoun *it*. It shows that *it* owns something.

> The emperor penguin keeps **its** chick on **its** feet.

In this example, the word *it* (*the emperor penguin*) owns the *chick* and the *feet*.

See also **apostrophe**: Apostrophe for contractions; **case**: Case of pronouns; **contractions**; **pronouns**: Possessive pronouns.

Hint

The apostrophe and possessive pronouns

The apostrophe is not used with any possessive pronoun — *his, hers, its, your, ours, theirs*. So if the pronoun owns something, do not use an apostrophe.

See also **pronouns**: Personal pronouns; **apostrophe** (').

---

jargon

Jargon is language used by a particular group of people who might live, work or study together or have an interest in a special area of knowledge. Writers or speakers find jargon useful when communicating with people who share their special area of knowledge. However, if writers or speakers use jargon with people who do *not* share their knowledge, then they may sound as if they are using a foreign language.

> The product was programmed in SGML to allow pdf output of the data as print, digital stand-alone cross-platform software or online media. The online version will depend on high bandwidth and having an ISP in each major user base. Without this, the user front end will see little of the potential functionality provided by the back end.

This is an example of computer jargon. The acronyms *SGML, pdf* and *ISP*, and the terms *output, stand-alone, cross-platform, bandwidth, front end* and *back end* would only make sense to people who are interested in, or understand computers.

If you are writing to people who share your knowledge of a topic, then jargon helps to keep your writing brief and to the point. However, jargon should be avoided if you are writing to a general audience. Jargon can make people think you are just trying to be smarter than they are.

The following examples highlight the difference between writing for a *general audience* and a *specialist audience*.

Text for general audience	Text for specialist audience
The baby bird growing inside an egg is called an *embryo*. The albumen and yolk provide the food it needs to grow. The albumen also acts as a cushion which protects the embryo if the egg is bumped. The embryo uses air from the air space at the wider end of the egg.	The avian embryo feeds on the yolk and albumen. The albumen also protects the embryo from external shocks. The air sac provides the embryo with air.

In the text for the general audience, the word *embryo* is explained. The text for the specialist audience does not explain this word, because the writer knows the reader will understand it. The writer also uses the scientific word *avian* instead of the common word *bird*.

See also **acronyms**; WORD HISTORIES: **jargon**; **audience**.

journal

A *journal* is a type of recount text. It is a written record of daily events, usually meant for others to read. Travellers and scientists sometimes write journals to record details about the weather or other background information so the reader has a better understanding of events.

> *Date: Wednesday, 6th February, 2002*
> *Temperature: -4°C*
> *Weather: Windy*
> *Location: 40 km from the Pole*
> 4 p.m. One of the vehicles broke a track. This was a big problem as it was a difficult repair to make. I radioed the base for help.

- Each daily record in a journal is called an *entry*. The entries are usually dated, so they are in chronological order.
- Journal entries are usually written in the past tense (*broke*, *was*, *radioed*).
- The sentences in a journal entry are often short. Journal entries are usually brief notes about events.

See also **chronological**; **recount**: **Journal**; **verbs**: **Past**.

journalism

Journalism is a type of writing used in newspaper articles. The writers are called *journalists*. Journalists write in different styles for different parts of the newspaper.

In sections such as the 'editorial', they write their opinions about news topics. This writing is called *exposition* or *argument*, because the journalists argue their position on the topic.

In 'feature articles' they write facts about a topic. This writing is called a report because the writers organise information in a logical way. Reports might be in subjects such as science, travel, business, history or social issues.

In sections for general news, they write about things that have happened around the world or special interest areas such as sport. This writing is a type of recount text, because the writer is recalling events. Often journalists make these events sound very dramatic.

Newspaper articles are often written in a 'diamond structure'. They have:
- a headline to get attention
- banner text — in larger print — to give the main information (who, what, when, where, how, why)
- the main body text — less important details in smaller print
- sentences that can be trimmed off the end of the story without changing its sense or meaning. Final sentences are the least important.

The following example is a 'human interest' newspaper article written in the style of a recount.

See also **argument**; **recount**; **report**.

Rosedale, South Australia, 1992: When 'Cocky' a featherless, sulphur-crested cockatoo was found eight years ago, the vet said it would never survive.

Cocky had an incurable disease, which stops new feathers from growing. The bird's rescuer decided to knit it woollen coats to keep it warm. Winter coats are made of thicker wool and have higher necks than summer coats. All the coats have little leggings, a hole at the back and are shaped around Cocky's wings. One coat had a Superman emblem, but Cocky didn't like it and picked it off. The coats have to be stitched round the cockatoo while it lies on its stomach.

When first rescued, Cocky was spoon-fed baby cereal. It now eats almost anything, including nibbles from the dog's

A normal sulphur-crested cockatoo

plate. Its biggest treats are walnuts from the garden.

Cocky cannot fly, but plays with the family dog and cats. At night, it sleeps in an aviary, safe from foxes and other predators.

Rescues, p. 15

knew / new

Knew is the past tense of the verb *to know*.

> When the rope broke, I **knew** that I would need help.

New is an adjective. It means 'young, fresh, recent, not old'.

> I found it difficult to make friends at the **new** school.
> The **new**-born giraffe was wobbly on its legs.
> The grocer put the **new** apples on display.
> Her **new** shoes were very shiny.

See also **adjectives**; **verbs: Tenses (time)**.

laid / lain
See **lay / lie**.

Latin

Latin was the language of the ancient Romans. After the Roman Empire disappeared, the Christian church and scholars in many parts of the world still used the Latin language. It had affected many languages — German, French and Spanish, among others. English scholars often used Latin words when they wanted to create a new word in English. Many English abbreviations, such as *AD*, *PS*, *ie*, *etc*, *viz*, *eg,* are shortened forms of Latin words.

See also **Latin abbreviations**.

Latin abbreviations

Many English abbreviations come from Latin words. Full stops were traditionally used with Latin abbreviations (e.g., etc., i.e.) but the modern trend is to leave them out.

The following Latin word abbreviations are commonly used in English:
*   c. (circa)
*   eg (exempli gratia — *for example*)
*   et al (et alii — *and others*)
*   etc (et cetera — *and others*)
*   ie (id est — *that is*)
*   NB (nota bene — *note well; take note*)
    > **NB** 'epi-' means 'against, above, after, in addition' as in *epilogue* and *episode.*

In this example, the abbreviation *NB* is used to explain a word used in a text.
*   PS (postscriptum — *postscript*)
*   pro tem (pro tempore — *for the time; temporarily*)
*   RIP (requiescat in pace — *rest in peace*)
*   viz (videlicet — *namely*)
*   vs (versus — *against*)

See also **RIP**; WORD HISTORIES: **AD**, **am**, **eg**, **etc**, **ie**, **pm**, **PPS**, **PS**, **RIP**, **viz**.

lay / lie

These words can be very confusing because they each have more than one meaning. It is a good idea to remember them together with the various forms of the different verbs.

lay / lie

Lay (laid, laying)

Lay is usually used as a verb. It can mean 'to put down; to place on something'.

> Silkmoths **lay** their eggs and soon after, they die.
> We usually **lay** a cloth on the table before serving the food.
> They could not **lay** their hands on the missing books.

Laid is the past tense and the past participle of *lay*.

> The silkmoths **laid** their eggs and soon after, they died.
> The silkmoths have **laid** their eggs.
> We **laid** the table before dinner.
> The table has been **laid** ready for dinner.
> They **laid** their hands on the desk.

Laying is the present participle of *lay*.

> The silkmoths are **laying** their eggs.
> We were **laying** the table for dinner.

Lie (lay, lying, lain)

Lie can be a verb meaning 'to be in a flat position; to be spread out'. With this meaning, the verb *lie* never has an object in a sentence. This means you cannot *lie* something — but you can lie in a place.

> Right now, I feel ill so I will **lie** down.
> On weekends they like to **lie** in bed all morning.
> She **lies** in the sun only when she has suncream on.

Lay is the past tense of *lie*.

> Yesterday I felt ill so I **lay** down.
> Last weekend they **lay** in bed all morning.
> I **lay** in the sun, but I wore suncream.

Lying is the present participle of *lie*.

> I am **lying** down because I feel ill.
> They were **lying** in bed all morning.
> She is **lying** in the sun, but she is wearing suncream.

Lain is the past participle of *lie*.

> I have **lain** down all morning because I felt ill.
> They would have **lain** in bed all morning if they could.
> She has **lain** in the sun all day, but she wore suncream.

Lie (lied, lying)

Lie can be a verb meaning 'to tell an untruth'.

> Is it always wrong to **lie** to people?

Lied is the past tense of *lie*.
> They **lied** to their parents at first, but told the truth later.

Lying is the present participle of lie.
> They are **lying** to their parents.

Lie can also be a noun meaning 'an untruth'.
> Is it always wrong to tell a **lie**?

The following table gives a summary of all these confusing verbs:

Present tense	Past tense	Present participle	Past participle
lay (to put down)	laid	laying	has laid
lie (to rest)	lay	lying	has lain
lie (to tell untruths)	lied	lying	has lied

See also **nouns**; **object**; **participles**; **verbs**: **Past**.

legend

A legend is a detailed caption to a picture or chart. Usually a caption becomes a legend when it has two or more complete sentences.

See also **captions and legends**.

legend (story)

A *legend* is a story (or a person a story is about) handed down from the past. The story could be true or invented. Hero tales are legends. Robin Hood (England), Johnny Appleseed (USA), Ned Kelly (Australia) are all legendary characters and stories. Some sporting heroes are regarded as legends. Sometimes, sporting heroes become legends within their own lifetime. Sir Donald Bradman of Australia was a legend within his own lifetime in the sport of cricket.

lend

See **borrow / lend / loan**.

less

See **fewer / less**.

letter to the editor
See **argument: Letter to the editor**.

letters
See **correspondence**.

lie
See **lay / lie**.

like / as
See **as / like**.

limerick
A limerick is a special type of humorous verse. Here are three examples:

> There once was a student named Bessor,
> Whose knowledge grew lesser and lesser.
> It at last grew so small,
> He knew nothing at all,
> So they made him a college professor.

Anonymous

> There was a big fish in the sea,
> That ate swimmers and small fish for tea.
> He grew quite tremendous,
> But his end was horrendous …
> 'Twas another fish bigger than he (Tee-he!)

Rodney Martin

> A tutor who tooted her flute.
> Tried to tutor two tooters to toot.
> Said the two to the tutor,
> "Is it harder to toot or
> To tutor two tooters to toot?"

Anonymous

- The limerick has five lines.
- The rhyming pattern is A, A, B, B, A.
- Lines three and four are shorter than the other three lines.
- Nonsense verse writers sometimes use non-standard forms of words for humour. (The word *lesser* in the first example above is a non-standard form of the word *less*.)

See also WORD HISTORIES: **limerick**.

lists
See **bullet points (•)**; **capitals**: Lists; **colon**: Lists.

loan
See **borrow / lend / loan**.

-log / -logue
For information on words such as *catalog*/*catalogue*, see **alternative spellings**: **-log / -logue (dialog, dialogue)**.

loose / lose
Loose is an adjective. It means 'not tight.' It is pronounced /loos/ to rhyme with *juice*.

> My shoelace was *loose* so I tied it again.

Lose is a verb. It means 'to misplace, to be defeated, to be unable to find'. It is pronounced /looz/ to rhyme with *snooze*.

> If you don't keep your key somewhere safe, you might **lose** it.
> The team would **lose** the game if it didn't score another goal.
> It is easy to **lose** your way in a strange city.

loud
See **aloud / allowed / loud**.

lying / laying
See **lay / lie**.

main clauses
See **clauses**: Main clauses.

mass nouns

Mass nouns are names of things that cannot be counted. They are singular words, even though they sometimes refer to things with many parts.

> assistance, bravery, cement, concrete, corn, courage, cutlery, flour, gravel, help, pasta, rice, rye, sand, universe, wheat

> The farmers grew **wheat**. **Wheat** is a grain.
> **Corn** is eaten by humans and animals.
> A truckload of **gravel** was delivered to the building site.

See also **count nouns**; **nouns**: **Mass nouns**.

may

See **can / may**.

measures

To measure anything, we need something to compare quantities with. For example, if we want to know how hot or cold something is, we need to be able to measure it and compare it with a scale of temperatures. Scales for measuring and comparing things are called 'units of measure'. Further information is under the following topics:

> **Abbreviations**
> **Capitals**
> **Plural**

Abbreviations

Units of measure can be abbreviated, but only when they are used with numerals. These abbreviations are used in nonfiction texts — technical or scientific writing, tables, charts and journals, or procedures (such as *manuals, recipes, instructions*).

> Temperature: -140**°C**.
> Weather: Some wind (about 15 **km/h**) and clear skies.
> Avalanches happen suddenly and swiftly, and can move up to 200 **km/h**; 124 **mph**)

Here is a list of abbreviated units of measure:
- C (Celsius)
- cm (centimetre/s)
- F (Fahrenheit)
- ft (foot, feet)
- g (gram/s)
- h (hour/s)
- in (inch/es)
- kg (kilogram/s)
- km (kilometre/s)
- km/h (kilometres per hour)
- l (litre/s)
- lb (pound/s)
- m (metre/s)
- mi (mile/s)
- min (minute/s)
- mm (millimetre/s)
- mph (miles per hour)
- s (second/s)
- t (tonne/s, ton)
- yd (yard/s)

Capitals
Most units of measure are lower case in both their abbreviated and full forms. However, some measures of temperature are capitalised. This is because they are proper nouns.

> The spacecraft shield became very hot (about 2,800°**C**/5,070°**F**).
> The air around the unhatched eggs should be 37.6°**C**.
> Temperature: Av. Max. 55°**F**/13°**C**.

Plural
Abbreviations of units of measure are the same for both singular and plural. No -*s* is added.

> 1 **km**, 10 **km**

See also **eponyms**; WORD HISTORIES: **Celsius, Fahrenheit**.

media report
See **journalism; recount**: Media articles (journalism).

metaphor

When authors write as though something *is* something else, they are using a metaphor. Metaphors make comparisons without using the words *like* or *as*. Writers use metaphors to build pictures for the reader.

> The coach **blasted** the team with a **long stream of words**.

In this example, the author says that the coach *blasted* the team. The author used a metaphor by comparing the coach's speech with the power of a rocket or explosion, but did not use the words *like* or *as*.

The author also writes that the coach used *a long stream of words*, so the reader understands that the coach's speech ran on and on like a stream. Again the author uses a metaphor to compare the speech with something, without using *like* or *as*. If the author had said the coach spoke *like a long stream*, it would be a *simile*.

Metaphors are useful in both fiction and nonfiction writing.

Further examples of metaphors:

> To the chick, the egg **was a prison**.
> The Earth **is our spacecraft**.
> A full moon **hung in the sky**.
> The refugees lived in **a warren of shanty houses**.

See also **simile**.

modal verbs

Modal verbs combine with other verbs to form compound verbs. Some examples of modal verbs are:

> can, could, shall, should, will, would, may, might, must, need, ought

See also **verbs**: **Compound**.

Writers use modal verbs to say three things:
> **What might happen**
> **What can happen**
> **What must happen**

What might happen
> The swimmer **might have drowned** had she not been rescued quickly.
> It **might** only **be** a few hours before the storm arrives.

What can happen

> Scientists **could send** a laser beam to the moon and the mirror would reflect it back to Earth.
> Some fungi **can produce** up to one million spores an hour, for several days.

What must happen

> To understand what has happened in the past, people **need** to ask questions and seek answers from different sources. In the end, they **must** decide for themselves.

See also **could / should / would**.

modifiers

Modifiers are words or phrases that weaken or soften the meaning of other words or phrases. They are the opposite of *intensifiers*. Modifiers are usually placed before the word or phrase they weaken.

These words and phrases are modifiers:

> almost, fairly, hopefully, just, nearly, only, perhaps, possibly, quite, rather, seem to, somewhat, tend to

> Some children **seem** to understand the mathematics.

In this example, the modifier *seem* weakens the verb *to understand*.

> Could you **perhaps** lend me you wheelbarrow?

The modifier *perhaps* weakens the verb *lend*.

> I **just** want to be free.

The modifier *just* weakens the verb *want*, so it does not sound so demanding.

See also **intensifiers**, **only**.

Hint

Being polite, careful or gentle in writing

Modifiers are useful if you want to suggest ideas or put a point of view politely, carefully or gently.

I'd like to propose an idea that will **perhaps** improve your writing.

Writers can also use modifiers to allow them to shift their point of view later, to the level of avoidance or even deceit.

News reporter (to politician): Before the election you said you were certain you would not raise taxes.

Politician: That is not *quite* true. I said I was *almost* certain that I would not raise taxes.

mood

Mood is a word used in grammar when talking about verbs and the way writers use them to express the attitude of a speaker, character or writer towards the audience. Writers express mood through the sentence types they use — statements, questions, commands and doubts or wishes. They do this by the ways in which they use verb forms with their subjects.

The different moods are explained under the following headings:
> **Imperative**
> **Indicative**
> **Interrogative**
> **Subjunctive**

Imperative
Writers use the imperative mood to give a command or instruction.
> **Bring** the food in with you!
> **Send** in your entry form today.
> **Glue** the panels together.

Usually, in the imperative mood, the verb begins the main clause of the sentence. This is because the subject of the sentence (*you*) is often left out.

The imperative mood is frequently used in procedures, and advertisements when the writer wants the reader to take action.

See also **argument: Advertisements**; **procedure**; **sentences: Commands**.

Indicative

Writers use the indicative mood to state facts or declare something.

> They **brought** the food with them.
> You **send** in your entry form today.

Sentences in the indicative mood are often called statements. Some people who study grammar also call this the declarative mood.

See also **sentences**: **Statements**.

Interrogative

Writers use the interrogative mood to ask questions.

> **Did** they **bring** the food with them?
> **Will** you **send** in your entry form today?

In many questions, a part of the verb is placed before the subject (*Will you* send? *You will* send.)

Some people who study grammar think that the interrogative mood is part of the indicative mood.

See also **question mark (?)**; **sentences**: **Questions**.

Subjunctive

Writers use the subjunctive mood to express wishes, doubts or conditions. It is used to talk about what might, should or must happen. The verbs *be* and *were* are often used to form subjunctive verbs.

> **Should** they **bring** the food with them, we **could eat**.
> If I **were** you, I would send in your entry form today.

In modern English, subjunctive verb forms are used mainly in formal writing.

> If I **were** you, I'**d** think about it.
> **Should** that **be** the case, then I will quit.

See also **formal / informal writing**.

myth

Myths are stories that involve superhuman characters such as gods, heroes or things that are not part of the natural world. Myths are often ancient tales that were told to explain natural things. All cultures had such tales. Here are some examples:

> *How the echidna got its spines* (Australian Aboriginal tale)
> *Why there are scratches on the Devil's Tower* (Native American tale)
> *Who made the Giant's Causeway?* (Irish tale)

names

Myths are an important part of a people's culture and often in the past became the basis for religions. The ancient Greeks had many myths about their gods. One example is *Perseus the gorgon-slayer*.

The storytelling pattern of the ancient hero tales are still used today by modern writers. Many of the modern super-hero characters and stories follow the storyboard of the ancient myths. How many of your favourite story heroes began life alone, floating across water or space, being found, adopted and raised by someone kind, then growing into a powerful, fearless fighter of evil.

See also **legend (story)**; **storyboard**.

names

The name of a person or company is part of their identity. Careful writers make sure that they address a person or company by their correct name and title. One way of understanding the importance of this is to think how you feel when someone spells your name incorrectly or even calls you by the wrong name!

Most people have a family name and one or more given names.

Further information on names is given under these headings:

> **Alphabetical lists**
> **Asian / western names**
> **Initials**
> **Nicknames**
> **Titles**

Alphabetical lists
When names are listed in alphabetical order, for example, in directories, they are written with the family name first.
> Jones A B 14 EverlyAveBnkstwn 7234 0101
> Jones A C 20 GeorgeStDevondle 7889 4433

Asian / western names
The names of many Asian people are written with the family name first, followed by the person's given names.
> **Cheng** Min Khoo

In this example, *Cheng* is the person's family name.

The names of people in western cultures (Europe, America, Australia, New Zealand, South Africa) are usually written with the family name last.
> Susan Olivia **Smith**

In this example, *Smith* is the person's family name.

names

Initials

People's names are sometimes abbreviated to the first letter of each name. These are called initials. Initials can be used for part or all of a person's name, depending on the situation.

Addresses on envelopes
Addresses on envelopes often have initials for a person's given names.

> Ms E M Foster
> Mr T McBride

Formal lists of names
When people's names are written in formal lists for business or social occasions, often the person's middle name is replaced by its initial.

> Mrs Maria N Mammone
> Miss Cynthia A Braithewaite
> Mr Ahmed L Farrah

Nicknames

People often have special names, called *nicknames*, given to them by family or friends. These nicknames are often shortened forms of their proper name.

> Nick (Nicholas), Bob (Robert), Sue (Susan)

Sometimes nicknames are humorous names based on the person's appearance, personality or habits.

> Shorty, Jungle, Animal, Goldie, Stretch

It is wise to use nicknames in writing only if the writing is informal, personal and addressed to an audience who is very familiar to the writer.

Titles

People have titles, depending on their occupation, gender and position. In correspondence, the correct title should be used in formal writing.

> Mr R Lim, President
> Ms M Bosco, Chairperson
> Sir John Campbell
> Dr J Springett
> Dame Margot Bentley

See also **acronyms**; **abbreviations**: **Business names**; **capitals**: **Proper nouns**; **nouns**: **Proper nouns**; WORD HISTORIES: **name**.

narrative

Narrative is writing that tells a story in prose or verse, and has an ending. Narratives can be written as fiction, nonfiction or poetry.

Further information about narratives is under the following headings:
Five main elements
Point of view
Structure
Types
  Fable
  Play script

Five main elements

Writers consider five main elements when they plan and write a narrative. Editors also consider these things and use them to find the strengths and weaknesses in a manuscript.

- *characters* (who) — the people, animals or things that act out the story
- *setting* (when, where) — the time and place the story happens in
- *plot* (what) — the series of events that make up the story, create a problem for the characters and solve the problem
- *style* (how) — how language is used to tell the story
- *theme* (why) — the main idea in the story, or what the story is about

Point of view

Narratives are written from a point of view, that is, through the eyes of the character telling the story or giving the information. The point of view can be:

- *in the first person* (*I*, *me*, *my*) — A character or the author tells the story from their point of view. This means that you see the events through the eyes of that character or the author.
- *in the second person* (*you*, *your*) — An author puts the story into the reader's point of view, for example, in 'choose your own adventure' stories.
- *in the third person* (*he*, *she*, *it*, *they*) — An observer or the author tells the story, but is not part of the story.

See also **viewpoint**; **point of view**

Structure

Most narratives have a particular structure or plan that writers follow. This structure is important for making a story appeal to the audience. It is used to gather the attention of readers and to lead them through a satisfying, entertaining experience.

In narratives, writers record events in the order that they happened. So narratives are usually written with the plot in chronological order, and in the past tense. The main parts of a story structure are:

- *introduction* — Who are the main characters and where is the story taking place?
- *the problem* — The characters have a problem they must solve. This is often in the form of a conflict between characters.
- *complication* — New characters enter the story. The problem becomes more complicated.
- *crisis* — The plot becomes dramatic. The main character(s) don't seem to be able to solve the problem.
- *resolution* — The 'hero' finds a way to solve the problem.
- *conclusion* — The characters have changed in some way because of their experiences and they continue life knowing more than they knew before.

Types

There are various types of narrative in both fiction and nonfiction. Writers choose the type of narrative to suit their audience and purpose. Some of these narrative types are:

- fiction — *allegory, ballad, fable, fairytale, fantasy, folk tale, legend, mystery, myth, parable* and *play script.* Some of these narrative forms have different styles within them; for example folk tale (tall tale, beast tale, trickster tale, pourquoi tale and simpleton tale).
- nonfiction — *recount* (anecdote, autobiography, biography, journal and oral history).

See also **allegory**; **audience**; **autobiography**; **ballad**; **biography**; **fable**; **journal**; **legend (story)**; **myth**; **parable**; **recount**.

The following examples are two different fiction narratives — fable and play script:

Fable

A fable is a short story with a moral or lesson. Many storytellers and writers have created fables. Two well-known writers of fables were Sir Roger L'Estrange (1616–1704) and Jean de la Fontaine (1621–1695). The most famous teller of fables is Aesop (c. 600BC) who was supposedly a Greek slave.

The following example is a traditional fable.

THE - Lion & the Mouse

Once a lion trapped a mouse under its large paw. The mouse pleaded for its life, so the lion let it go. Later the lion became tangled in a hunter's net and roared in distress. The mouse rushed to help. "You're too small to help," said the lion. But the mouse nibbled at the net until the lion was free.

Small friends can be powerful allies.

Fables: A short anthology, p. 22

- The title of a fable often comes from the names of the main characters in the story.
- There are usually only two main characters.
- The characters are usually animals that act like humans. Sometimes plants or other things (such as trees, the wind or the sun) are used as characters. This is called *personification*.
- The plot has three simple parts. First, the characters and the problem are introduced. Then the character(s) try to solve the problem. Finally, something goes wrong (or right) for one (or both) of the characters.
- The verbs in the plot (*trapped*, *pleaded*, *became* etc) are in the past tense because they are about events that have already happened.
- The moral of the fable does not mention the characters; it is about ideas.
- The moral is usually written in one short sentence.
- The verbs in the moral (*can be*) are usually in the simple or continuous present tense because morals are about ideas or thoughts that exist always.

See also **personification**; **sentences**: **Short sentences**; **verbs**: **Present, Past**.

Play script

A play script is a story that can be performed for an audience. It is a form of drama.

Cast • TIGER • BRAHMAN • TREE • BUFFALO • ROAD • JACKAL **Scene** TIGER *is trapped in a cage, roaring and pacing about.* BRAHMAN *comes walking by.*	BRAHMAN: Then how *would* you repay my kindness? TIGER: *(Thinking hard)* I'd . . . I'd . . . BRAHMAN: You'd eat me, that's what. Now, goodbye, Sir Tiger. I'm on my way.

The tiger, the Brahman & the jackal (a play), pp. 5, 9

- The characters in a play are listed at the beginning of the play script. They are called the *cast*.
- The setting of a play is often described at the beginning of a play script. The setting is called the *scene.*
- The text of a play script is dialogue — characters speaking.
- The name of the character who is supposed to speak is written at the beginning of each speech part, followed by a colon.
- The writer gives the actors instructions (prompts) on how they should act or express their lines. These prompts are enclosed in brackets.

See also **brackets ( )**; **colon (:)**; **dialogue (US: dialog)**; **drama**.

negatives

The English language has a few words that form negative sentences. These words are:

> hardly, never, no, nobody, none, nothing, no one, not, n't

> The words were **hardly** out of his mouth when the door flew open.
> When Jo stopped running there was **no** sign of the thugs.

Writers need to be careful not to use more negatives than necessary in a sentence. Two negatives (not, never, no, none, nobody, no one, nothing), or words that suggest negatives (hardly, without, barely, only), make a positive.

> When Jo stopped running there **wasn't no** sign of the thugs.

In this example, *wasn't no* is a double negative. This means that the sentence is no longer making a negative statement (if there *wasn't no sign of the thugs*, then there must have been a sign!)

See also **double negative**; **hardly**.

new

See **knew / new**.

non-fiction

Non-fiction is usually factual writing. Its purpose is to give information or points of view. There are many forms of non-fiction writing. These forms are sometimes called *genre*. Each genre has a different style and grammar.

Writers choose to write in a certain genre to suit the audience and purpose of their writing. For example, a procedural (instruction) text shows you how to do or make something.

See also **audience**.

You can find details about different forms of non-fiction under the following headings and topics: **abstract**; **anecdote**; **argument**; **autobiography**; **correspondence**; **discussion**; **explanation**; **journalism**; **narrative**; **obituary**; **procedure**; **recount**; **report**; **slogan**.

non-finite verbs

See **verbs: Non-finite**.

no one / no-one

The word *no one* can be written with a hyphen:

> When she explained the problem **no-one** felt embarrassed.

or without a hyphen:

> **No one** is supposed to come here after working hours.

Whether you use *no one* or *no-one* is a personal decision. The most important thing is to be consistent — don't change from one form to the other within a single piece of writing.

notes

Writers sometimes use notes in a text to give extra information about what they have written, or to show where they got their information. Notes that appear at the bottom of the page are called *footnotes*.

Symbols such as the *asterisk* (*) and the *cross* (†) can be used to show footnotes. The symbol is placed at the end of the sentence the writer wants to comment about, and also at the bottom of the text with the footnote.

(*Sentence within the text*)
Fill the aquarium with the fresh water and add the water weed.*

(*Footnote at bottom of page*)
*To stock an aquarium, you could check your local pet shop.

If there is more than one footnote on a page, symbols may be repeated. In this example, the author used the asterisk (*) as the footnote symbol. For a second footnote, two asterisks were used.

(Sentence within the text.)
WORLD WIDE FUND FOR NATURE**

(Footnotes at bottom of page.)
* Formerly *United Nations International Children's Emergency Fund*.
** Formerly *World Wildlife Fund*.

If there is more than one footnote on a page, a different symbol may be used for each footnote.

(*Sentence within the text.*)
WORLD WIDE FUND FOR NATURE †

(*Footnotes at bottom of page.*)
* Formerly *United Nations International Children's Emergency Fund*.
†Formerly *World Wildlife Fund*.

Numbers may also be used if there is more than one footnote on a page.
WORLD WIDE FUND FOR NATURE^2

(Footnotes at bottom of page.)
[1] Formerly *United Nations International Children's Emergency Fund*.
[2] Formerly *World Wildlife Fund*.

noun clauses

Noun clauses act like nouns — and they usually tell what someone is *thinking, feeling* or *saying*. They are usually placed next to a verb in a sentence.

My mum says **you should treat elderly people with respect**.
The clause *you should treat elderly people with respect* tells *what* mum says.

I wish **that I could find my lost dog**.
The clause *that I could find my lost dog* tells what *I wish*.

See also **clauses**; **nouns**; **verbs**.

noun phrases

A noun phrase is a noun plus any words that add meaning to it. It is sometimes called a *participant*.

the piano
the black piano
the big, black piano
the big, black and white piano

In these examples, the noun *piano* is in every phrase. The words that add meaning to the noun are articles (*the*), adjectives (*big, black, white*) and a conjunction (*and*).

Participant is a word used in grammar. It means 'nouns or noun phrases'. It is also called the *nominal group* (from the Latin word *nomen*, meaning 'name').

See also **articles**; **adjectives**; **conjunctions**; writing sample under **report**: **Compare and contrast**; WORD HISTORIES: **name**.

nouns

Nouns are the names of people, places, things and ideas. There are different types of nouns.

See also WORD HISTORIES: **noun**.

The different types of nouns are described under the following headings:
Abstract nouns
Collective nouns
Common nouns
Concrete nouns
Count nouns
Mass nouns
Proper nouns
Verbal nouns

nouns

Abstract nouns

Abstract nouns are the names of ideas — things we can think about, feel or imagine, but not touch. These words are abstract nouns:

anger, beauty, laziness, doubt, eagerness, friendship, greed

Abstract nouns do not have a capital letter, unless they begin a sentence.

Authors use abstract nouns to express ideas and thoughts behind their stories — the theme.

> He rested, breathing painfully, silently weeping with **shame**. Alone at last, Baleen began to sing. No more would he sing a **song** of **pride**, boasting of **victories** won. A new **song** formed in Baleen's throat, echoing the **pain** of his **thoughts**.

Baleen, p. 36

This example is at the end of the story *Baleen*. Notice the abstract nouns the author used. The author concentrated on the ideas behind the story. If this part of the story did not communicate the ideas well, then the audience would feel disappointed that the story seemed to have no meaning.

Did you know?

Suffixes and abstract nouns

There are several suffixes that form abstract nouns.

-ness (boldness, craziness, eagerness, haziness, helpfulness, laziness, sadness)

-ship (friendship, leadership, membership, ownership)

-ism (chauvinism, feminism, idealism, impressionism, multiculturalism, racism, realism)

-th (breadth, depth, health, length, stealth, strength, wealth, width)

-y (anonymity, beauty, calamity, certainty, enmity, pity, victory)

The suffix that forms more abstract nouns than any other in English is *-ness*.

See also **suffixes**.

Collective nouns

Collective nouns are the names of groups of animals, people or things. They are a kind of common noun.

Animals — colony (of ants), flock (of sheep, birds), gaggle (of geese), herd (of cattle), murder (of crows), pride (of lions), school (of fish)

People — class, choir, committee, crew, crowd, council, family, mob, staff, team

Things — bunch (of grapes), fleet (of ships), hand (of bananas), pile (of stones)

For information about how to use collective nouns in a sentence, see **agreement**: **Agreement for collective nouns**.

Common nouns

Common nouns are the general names of people, places, things, feelings and ideas. They do not have a capital letter, unless they begin a sentence.

People — boy, child, girl, man, teacher, woman
Places — city, river, galaxy, town, village
Things — building, computer, dog, pencil
Feelings and ideas — dream, happiness, hunger, imagination

Concrete nouns

Concrete nouns are the names of things that can be seen or touched. They are the opposite to abstract nouns. These words are concrete nouns:

building, doctor, dog, river

Count nouns

Count nouns are things that can be counted — they have plural forms.

one child — two children
one doctor — two doctors
one fungus — two fungi
one house — two houses
one mouse — two mice

See also **plural**.

Mass nouns

Mass nouns are the names of things that cannot be counted. They usually have a singular form only.

evidence, furniture, information, mud, rice, sand, spaghetti, water

Mass nouns may be given a plural form in unusual circumstances. For example, the mass noun *spaghetti* might be made plural when a waiter takes orders for a group at dinner. Or *sand* might be plural when we speak of time.

"That's three soups, two chickens and two **spaghettis**!"
The secret of the mystery valley was lost in the **sands** of time.

However, we would not normally say *spaghettis, sands, evidences, furnitures*, or *informations*.

See also **singular**; **singular words**.

Proper nouns
Proper nouns are the names of particular animals, people, places and things. They always begin with a capital letter.

> *Animals* — Fido the dog, Phar Lap the horse
> *People* — Dr Clark, Gurmit Singh, Mrs Browning, Peter, President Sheares, Professor McDonald, Susan
> *Places* — Adelaide, Australia, Europe, Jupiter, London, Mount Etna, River Thames, Sentosa, Singapore
> *Things* — Empire State Building, The Merlion Hotel, The Straits Times

See also **capitals**: **Proper nouns**.

Verbal nouns
Verbal nouns (also called *gerunds*) are present participles (*-ing* words) used as nouns.

> **Flying** is her hobby.

In this example, *flying* is an activity (noun). The verb in the sentence is the word *is* (part of the verb *to be*).

> He enjoys **fishing**.

In this example, *fishing* is an activity (noun). *Enjoys* is the verb.

See also **participles**.

numbers
See **abbreviations**: **Number(s)**; **brackets ()**: **Numbers and letters**; **hyphen (-)**: **Numbers**; **ordinals**.

O
The word *O* is a dramatic exclamation.

It is occasionally used before a name in dramatic exclamations, usually in play scripts or classic literature; it is less common in modern writing. When *O* is used in exclamations, it is an appeal to a person. It expresses surprise, respect or longing. It is always capitalised.

> DRAGON: (*Weeping*) The problem, **O** knight, is that I am no longer a fierce dragon, but a lonely coward.

oar

See **awe / oar / or / ore**.

obituary

An obituary is a short biography about someone who has died. It often has the heading RIP meaning 'may he/she rest in peace'.

RIP Daniel

Daniel was born on a farm, and spent his life in the country. From his youngest days, Daniel was special. Always eager to please those around him; always full of energy; always pleasant company. Daniel made people feel good about themselves and brought out the best in anyone. The world will be a sadder place without Daniel. He was the best dog I have ever had.

Obituaries are usually published in newspapers, newsletters or regular publications by special interest groups.

- An obituary includes facts about the background or life history of the subject. (*Daniel was born on ... and spent his life ...*)
- An obituary usually expresses positive thoughts about how the subject affected or influenced others. (*Daniel was special ...*)
- The writer usually concludes an obituary with a brief summary. (*The world will be ...*)
- The writer uses the past tense to recall facts about the subject. (Daniel *made ...* and *brought* out ...)
- The future tense is sometimes used when talking about life without the deceased subject. (*The world will be a sadder place ...*)
- An obituary is usually written in the third person (*he*, *she*) because the writer is writing about someone else.
- The writer sometimes includes the first person (*I*) because obituaries are frequently written from the personal experience of the writer.

See also **biography**; **elegy**; **epitaph**; **person**; **RIP**; **tense**.

object

A basic sentence needs a *subject* (something that does an action or exists) and a *verb* (the action or event). However, if the sentence has something that is acted upon by the subject and the action of the verb, it is called the *object* of the sentence.

Some bats [*subject*] eat [*verb*] **fruit** [*object*].

Fruit is what is acted upon by the subject *bat* when it eats.

An object can be a phrase.

> He [*subject*] snatched [*verb*] **a big, green apple** [*object*] from the bowl.

The object is the person or thing being acted upon.

> They [*subject*] awarded [*verb*] **him** [*object*] the prize.
> They [*subject*] awarded [*verb*] **the prize** [*object*] to him.

In grammar, the object in a sentence is said to be in the *objective case*.

See also **case**; **predicate**; **subject**.

-oes / -os

See **alternative spellings**: -oes / -os (haloes, halos); **plurals**: Nouns ending with -o.

of / off

Many writers confuse these two words, especially in draft writing. This should not be a problem because they sound different and mean different things.

Of is a preposition. It is pronounced /ov/.

> "**Of** course I can do it," boasted the giant.
> The rainforest is a community **of** many kinds **of** flora and fauna.

Off can be a preposition, an adjective or an adverb. It is pronounced /off/ to rhyme with *cough*.

> The bird nearly fell **off** its perch! (preposition)
> They couldn't eat the chicken because it was **off**. (adjective)
> When touched, the spines break **off** and release venom. (adverb)

See also **adjectives**; **adverbs**; **could have (of)**; **prepositions**.

Writing tip

Avoid mixing *off* with *from* and *of*

There are two common errors to avoid with these little words.

The words *from* and *of* should not be written after the word *off*.

You nearly fell **off of** the branch. (X)

You nearly fell **off** the branch. (✓)

You nearly fell **off from** the branch. (X)

You nearly fell **from** the branch. (✓)

OK / okay

See **alternative spellings**; WORD HISTORIES: **OK**.

only

The word *only* should be placed as near as possible to the word or phrase it is related to. This is because the word *only* draws attention to any word or phrase that follows it. In grammar, it is called a *modifier*.

> She was **only a baby**.

In this example, the word *only* draws attention to the phrase *a baby*. It suggests that *she* is very young. If the word *only* is moved to another place in this sentence, the meaning can change.

> **Only she** was a baby.

In this example, the word *only* draws attention to the word *she*. This means only one person was a baby.

Writers need to take care when using words like *only* or the meaning of the writing could be ambiguous (it could have more than one meaning or not mean what the author meant to say).

Here are some other words that draw attention to words and phrases:

> even, exactly, just, nearly, simply

> **Even** Emilio could play tennis tomorrow.
> Emilio could **even** play tennis tomorrow.
> Emilio could play tennis **even** tomorrow.

See also **ambiguity**; **grammar**: **Word order and links**; **modifiers**.

onomatopoeia

Onomatopoeia (pronounced ***on**-uh-mat-uh-**pee**-yuh*) means 'words that imitate sounds'. Writers use onomatopoeia to make their writing sound interesting or dramatic.

> With just one **whack** of his tail he could whip the water into foam.

Further examples:

> bang, boom, buzz, crash, hiss, roar, snap, snarl, snore, splash, whoosh

or

See **awe / oar / or / ore**.

-or / -our

For information on words such as *color/colour*, see **alternative spellings**: -or / -our (color, colour).

oral history

An oral history is a record of someone's memories of their life. The information is usually recorded in an interview. Oral histories are a way of preserving local history through the experiences of people who have lived in that area.

For details on how to write an oral history, see **recount**: **Oral history**.

ordinals

See **abbreviations**: **Ordinals**.

ore

See **awe / oar / or / ore**.

oxymoron

An oxymoron is the use of two words with opposite or contrasting meanings together in a sentence or phrase.

> They had **bitter sweet** memories of school.

In this example, the words *bitter sweet* form an oxymoron. Writers use oxymorons as a way of emphasising a point. It is a compare and contrast technique.

Further examples:
> He was a **lovable rogue**.
> You really are a **sad clown**.
> At the movies, I **enjoy** being **scared**.
> She ordered **sweet** and **sour** chicken.
> In the desert, the **silence** was **deafening**.

See also **compare and contrast**.

pain / pane

Pain is an abstract noun. It means 'suffering, ache, sting, agony, worry'.

> She still remembered the **pain** she felt when she broke her leg.

Pane is a common noun meaning 'a sheet of glass'.

> The cleaner washed the window **pane**.
> The builder broke a **pane** of glass accidentally.

See also **nouns**: **Abstract nouns**, **Common nouns**.

pair / pear

Pair means 'a set of two'.

> There, on the shelf, was a **pair** of sandals and a **pair** of sneakers.

A *pear* is a fruit.

> They sang the song 'A partridge in a **pear** tree'.

palindromes

Palindromes are words, phrases or sentences that can be read forwards or backwards with the same meaning.

> Dad
> Madam I'm Adam
> Pup
> A man, a plan, a canal — Panama
> redivider

parable

A parable is a short story that teaches a lesson. There are many parables told by Christ in the Bible. For example, the story of the prodigal son offers the lesson about the importance of family relationships.

Parables are like fables and cautionary tales.

See also **allegory**; **fable**.

paragraphs

A paragraph is a block of writing that presents details on a particular idea within a text. Writers use paragraphs as a means of structuring the ideas in their writing, and presenting the ideas one at a time. This makes a text easier for a reader to understand.

In dialogue, a new paragraph usually begins each time another person or character begins to speak.

paragraphs

Further information on paragraphs is under these headings:
Paragraph parts
Paragraph layout
Line spacing
Indenting the first line
Paragraph length

Paragraph parts

A paragraph often has up to three parts:

1. Topic sentence

The topic sentence is usually the first sentence in a paragraph. It tells the reader what the paragraph is about.

2. Detail

The topic sentence is followed by sentences that give details about the topic.

3. Summary sentence

Sometimes a paragraph ends with a sentence that summarises the point being made in the paragraph.

> The blue whale is a magnificent animal. The female can grow to a length of thirty-three metres. They can weigh as much as fifteen small motor vehicles, yet they feed on tiny plankton. The blue whale is the largest animal known to have existed on earth.

- The topic of this paragraph is *the greatness of the blue whale*.
- The author gives details of its length, weight and what it eats.
- The final sentence summarises the topic by comparing the blue whale to all other animals on earth.

Paragraph layout

There are two ways that paragraphs can be made to stand out in a text:

Line spacing

Paragraphs can be shown by separating blocks of text with a line space.

> There are two main types of whale. One type, called toothed whales, have teeth. The other type, called baleen whales, have plates of fine bone hanging from the upper jaw.
>
> Toothed whales feed mainly on fish, octopus and squid. Baleen whales feed mainly on krill, which they sieve from the water through their baleen plates.
>
> There are eleven species of Baleen whale. They range in size from the huge blue whale to the tiny pygmy right whale.

- This layout for paragraphing has become more common since the invention of the word processor.
- One disadvantage of this method is that it takes up extra space on a page.

paragraphs

Indenting the first line
In many texts, the first line of a paragraph is set in slightly from the left-hand margin. This is called an indent. The other lines in the paragraph are set against the left margin.

> There are two main types of whale. One type,
> called toothed whales, have teeth. The other type,
> called baleen whales, have plates of fine bone hanging
> from the upper jaw.
> Toothed whales feed mainly on fish, octopus and squid.
> Baleen whales feed mainly on krill, which they sieve from
> the water through their baleen plates.
> There are eleven species of Baleen whale. The range in size from
> the huge blue whale to the tiny pygmy right whale.

- The indented lines make it easy for the reader to see where each paragraph begins.
- This method is usually used in newspapers.
- In dialogue with quotation marks, the text is indented each time another person or character begins to speak. If the speech is short, then several lines might be indented one after the other.

> "I don't feel well. I want to go to
> the doctor."
> "Not likely!"
> "Why not?"
> "It's too late. You'll have to wait
> until tomorrow."

See also **dialogue (US: dialog)**.

Paragraph length
There is no rule about how many sentences should be in a paragraph, except that there should be enough text to properly explore the paragraph topic. If the paragraphs are too short, then it can seem to the reader that there is too little information on each idea. If paragraphs are too long, then readers can lose concentration, or the writer might be covering more than one topic in the paragraph.

As a general guideline, paragraphs in stories, correspondence, reports and other types of nonfiction, generally have not less than two sentences, but not more than ten. Of course, writers often go outside this range.

Journalists usually structure their writing with one sentence per paragraph. This is so the editor can easily shorten an article, if necessary, by trimming paragraphs off the end of the text, without altering the meaning of the whole text.

parentheses

Fiction writers sometimes use one sentence paragraphs for special effect. It can add a sense of drama to a story, but it should not be over-used, or the writing becomes jerky.

parentheses

Parentheses are punctuation marks that bracket or enclose text. There are several punctuation marks that can be used to do this.

See **brackets ( )**.

parody

A *parody* is a funny piece of writing, created by taking something serious or famous and changing it to the opposite — something ridiculous.

> Twinkle, twinkle little bat,
> How I wonder what you're at!
> Up above the world you fly,
> Like a tea tray in the sky.

Lewis Carroll

This example is a parody of the well-known nursery rhyme *Twinkle twinkle little star*. Lewis Carroll did not change the original style of the verse. He just changed some of the nouns (*star — bat*; *diamond — tea tray*) so the verse became nonsense.

Further examples:

> Little Miss Muffet sat on her tuffet
> Eating her Irish stew.
> Along came a spider
> And sat down beside her,
> So she ate the spider up too.

Anonymous

This example is a parody of the nursery rhyme *Little Miss Muffet*. The author changed the personalities of the characters — Miss Muffet becomes very bold and the spider becomes the victim instead of the scary character. The author did not change the style of the poem.

> Alex was the kitchenhand at *The Flinders' Cellar* restaurant. He was a hard and honest worker and it was not long before the chefs, Manuel and Russell Flinders, took advantage of this. Instead of just peeling vegetables and washing dishes, Alex was made to do the shopping, wash and press the two chefs' uniforms and clean the restaurant from top to bottom every day.

Alex and the glass slipper, p. 3

This example is a parody of the fairytale *Cinderella*. The author, Amanda Graham, made the hero a boy instead of a girl, and gave the story a modern setting. The original Cinderella was meant to be a serious story. Amanda Graham's story is fun because she places her modern characters in a very unlikely fairytale setting. She also jokes with the word *Cinderella* when she names the restaurant *The Flinders' Cellar*.

participant

Participant is a word used in grammar. It is sometimes called the *nominal group* (from the Latin word *nomen*, meaning 'name'). It means 'words or word groups that name persons, places or things'. Nouns and noun phrases are participants.

See also **nouns**; **noun phrases**; WORD HISTORIES: **noun**.

participles

Participles are forms of verbs. Verbs have two participles — a *present participle* and a *past participle*. They are described under the following headings.

> **Present participles**
> **Past participles**
> **Non-finite verbs**

Present participles
Present participles end with the letters -*ing*.

> jumping, laughing, diving, running, hiding, giving, having, writing

Past participles
The past participles of many verbs end with the letters -*ed*.

> jumped, dived, laughed

Many past participles do not end with the letters *-ed*. Many verbs have their own special form of past participle. They are sometimes called 'irregular verbs'. The following table shows some examples:,

verb	past participle
hide	hidden
give	given
have	had
write	written
keep	kept
run	run
fall	fallen
sing	sung

Participles join with parts of the verbs *to be* and *to have* to make other verb forms.

> has been keeping, was kept
> is giving, will be given
> will be jumping, could have jumped

Present participles and irregular past participles are *non-finite* (incomplete) *verbs*. This means they cannot have a subject by themselves. They need auxiliary verbs such as *is*, *was*, *have*, *had*, *be*, *will* or *been* to become a complete verb in a sentence.

> They **keeping** bees on their farm. (Not a complete sentence.)
> They **are keeping** bees on their farm. (A complete sentence.)
>
> She **written** an excellent story. (Not a complete sentence.)
> She **has written** an excellent story. (A complete sentence.)

See also **auxiliary verbs**; **verbs**: **Finite and non-finite verbs**, **Regular and irregular verbs**, **Simple and compound verbs**; WORD HISTORIES: **auxiliary**.

passed / past

Passed is the past tense of the verb *to pass*.

> As we **passed** the hospital, we heard an ambulance siren.

Further examples:

> More than a month had **passed** since they had left.
> A man **passed** a package to the child, then disappeared.
> Lice are easily **passed** from one head to another.

Past can be:
* an adverb. It tells *where*.
> I stood to one side as a lady rushed **past**.
* a preposition. It means 'beyond'.
> It was **past** their bedtime.
* a noun. It means 'a time before now'.
> The old man kept talking about the **past**.

Further examples:

> The crowd pushed **past** the gate and into the oval.
> **Past** the church, you will find a small shop.

See also **adverbs**; **verbs**: **Past**.

past or passed

Passed is always a verb. Look for the verb *pass* in ***passed***.

Past is never a verb. It is always about *where* or *when*.

passive verbs

A verb is passive in a sentence if its subject is *not* doing the action.

> The whale **was hunted**.

The whale is the subject of the sentence. The whale is not doing the hunting, so the verb *was hunted* is passive.

A passive verb usually has two parts — some form of the verb *to be* (*am*, *is*, *are*, *was*, *were*, *will be*) and a past participle. In the example above, *was hunted* has these two parts — *was* (part of the verb *to be*) + *hunted* (past participle of the verb *to hunt*).

See also **participles**; **passive voice**.

passive voice

In grammar, the word *voice* describes two forms of verbs — *active* and *passive*. Writing that is in the passive voice has passive verbs.

Writers use the passive voice so they can affect their audience in certain ways. Three uses for the passive voice are given under the following headings.

Being vague
Choosing a focus
Positioning the reader

Being vague

The passive voice is useful when you want to avoid saying who was responsible for an action. It makes it possible for you to be purposely vague.

The kitchen **was left** in a mess. (passive)

John **left** the kitchen in a mess. (active)

In the first example, the writer is vague about who left the kitchen in a mess. In the second example, there is no doubt about who is accused of leaving the kitchen in a mess. The passive voice allowed the writer to avoid pointing the finger at anyone in particular.

Further examples:
The passive voice is useful when you want to say something very politely, tactfully or not be exact about who or what is doing something.

It **is forbidden** to eat food in the library.

In this example, the author does not wish to say exactly *who* forbids people to eat food in the library, so the passive verb *is forbidden* together with the subject *It* is used.

Students **are not allowed** to use the library today. (passive)

The librarian **will not allow** students to use the library today. (active)

The first sentence says *what* the students are not allowed to do, but it does not say *who* will not allow them to use the library. The second sentence is more direct. It says *who* is responsible for not allowing students in the library.

Choosing a focus

Passive voice is useful when you want to give attention to a particular subject.

The injured people **were rushed** by the rescuers to the hospital.

In this example from a newspaper story, the writer wanted to make the *injured people* the subject or focus of the story. It was a story about 'victims' because the subject of the sentence is not doing the action, but instead is passive and helpless.

The rescuers **rushed** the injured people to the hospital.

In this example, the writer makes the *rescuers* the focus of the story. It was a story about 'heroes' because the subject of the sentence is doing the action and seems active and strong.

Imagine you are a journalist writing about injured people and rescuers. You could choose the focus of your story by using active or passive voice.

Positioning the reader
In stories, the reader usually identifies with the main characters, and can experience whatever emotion the character feels.

> The hideous creature landed on the front of the car and peered through the windscreen at Mai Ling. It clawed at the glass.
> "**I'm being attacked**," Mai Ling screamed into her phone.

In this example, the passive verb *am being attacked* means the creature is in control and the character Mai Ling is in a weak position (she is being acted upon). The readers would also feel 'under attack' because they identify with the main character. The author is 'positioning' the readers by making them feel the same fear as the character.

See also **active voice**; **passive verbs**.

past tense

Tense in grammar is about when events or actions happen. Past tense verbs tell about actions that have already happened.

> Yesterday I **told** my story to an audience.

The verb *told* is in the past tense.

See also **verbs**: **Tenses (time)**.

peace / piece

Peace is a noun. It means 'restfulness; calm; a time without war or violence'.

> I just want to find some **peace** and quiet.

Piece is a noun. It means 'a part or section of something'.

> The dog gnawed on the **piece** of bone for hours.

Piece can mean a 'topic, something to talk about'.

> The strange statue in the lounge made a good conversation **piece**.

Hint

piece / peace

Remember a **pie**ce of **pie**.

pear
See **pair / pear**.

person
Person is a word used in grammar to describe 'the three different forms of pronouns'. The three different forms are:
First person pronouns
I, me, mine, we, us, our, ours
Second person pronouns
you, your, yours
Third person pronouns
he, him, his, she, her, hers, it, its, they, them, their, theirs

First person pronouns
Writers use *first person pronouns* when the writer, an interviewee or a character in a story, is speaking from their own point of view.
I thoroughly enjoyed **my** stay at the ski resort.
Our problem is **we** are a throw-away society.

Second person pronouns
Writers use *second person pronouns* when a person or thing is spoken *to*. This can happen if one character is speaking to another in a story.
The mechanic said, "**You** have a problem. **Your** car needs attention or it will break down when **you** most need it."

It can also happen if an author is speaking directly to the reader, for example, in a procedure.
Look after **your** teeth. Make sure **you** clean them regularly.

Third person pronouns
Writers use *third person pronouns* when people or things are spoken *about.*
Fungi are living things. **They** belong to a kingdom of **their** own.
It is expensive for the government to collect garbage. **It**'s a long-term problem and **it**'s not going to go away.

See also **argument: Advertisements; impersonal writing; point of view; procedure; personal writing; recount: Biography; report: Question and answer — interviews.**

personal pronouns
See **pronouns: Personal pronouns.**

personal writing

Personal writing is text written from the writer's point of view. It is usually about personal thoughts, experiences, opinions and beliefs.

Typical examples of personal writing are journals, diaries, autobiography and some forms of argument such as letters to the editor.

Personal writing is often written in the first person, with the pronouns *I*, *me*, *my*, *mine*.

See also **impersonal writing**.

For examples and explanations of different types of personal writing, see: **anecdote**; **argument: Letter to the editor**; **autobiography**; **diary**; **journal**; **recount: Autobiography, Fiction Journal, Non-fiction Journal, Oral history**.

personification

Personification is a method that writers use to make animals or things seem human to the reader. This can make the reader have feelings for a character and become more involved with a story.

To do this, a writer can:
- use the pronouns *he* or *she* instead of *it*, to make the reader think of an animal character as a male or female person
- use human names (proper nouns) for an animal or thing to make the reader think of the character as a person
- use verbs such as *laugh*, *grumble*, *betray* or *rescue* to give the character human actions
- use adjectives such as *proud*, *angry*, *clever* or *evil* to give the character human feelings
- use adverbs such as *happily*, *eagerly*, *sneakily* or *impatiently* to give the character human feelings.

> **Waldo** the whippet was the **funniest clown in the street**. With **his** wagging tail and **his cheeky grin he** could beg a bone from any house.

In this example, the author gave a dog character a personal name *Waldo*, described the character as if it acted as humans do (*funniest clown in the street; cheeky grin*) and used the pronouns *his* and *he*.

Personification — be consistent

Personification is successful only if you use it throughout a piece of writing. Once you begin to say a character is *he* or *she*, then you must do it with all other words about that character.

For example, the example of Waldo the whippet would not have been effective personification if it had been written like this:

Waldo the whippet was the **funniest clown in the street**. With **its** wagging tail and **its cheeky grin it** could beg a bone from any house.

Something called *it* would not be *the funniest clown in the street*. Only humans are clowns.

persuasive text

See **argument**.

phrases

A *phrase* is a group of words that has meaning within a sentence, but does not make a complete sentence because it does not have a complete verb. Some examples are:

> to the shop
> near the lake
> the five pupils
> without wearing their shoes

The phrases above would have meaning within a sentence, but cannot stand alone as complete sentences.

> **The five pupils** walked **to the shop near the lake without wearing their shoes**.

All the phrases are now in a sentence. The sentence has the verb *walked*. Each phrase could not be a complete sentence by itself because it did not have a verb.

Writers use phrases to add meaning to their sentences. Without the phrases, the sentence in the example above would not give the reader much information.

> The five pupils walked.

There are different kinds of phrases.
See also **adjectival phrases**; **adverbial phrases**; **noun phrases**; **prepositional phrases**.

piece

See **peace / piece**.

plagiarism

Plagiarism happens when writers copy the work of another writer, then claim the work is theirs. If another writer's work is used within a piece of writing, then the original author must be stated. Plagiarism is regarded as stealing ideas.

planning

Writers usually plan their writing. They do not just sit down and write. The planning process helps a writer to organise the structure and order of the writing.

For details on planning writing, see **writing process**: **Planning**.

play script

A play script is a text written for performance — to be acted before an audience. The play script might be read or acted on stage, radio, television, a movie or a recording.

See also **colon**: **Play scripts and transcripts**; **narrative**: **Play script**; **quotation marks**: **Play scripts**.

plural

Plural means 'more than one'. Nouns, pronouns and verbs have plural forms. There are many ways to form plurals in English. Most plurals are formed by changing the ends of words.

The different forms of plurals are explained under the following headings:
> **Plurals of nouns**
>> *Adding -s*
>> *Adding -es*
>> *Nouns ending with o*
>> *Nouns ending with y*
>> *Nouns ending with -f or -fe*
>> *Nouns ending with -ful*
>> *Exceptions*
>> *Foreign words*
> **Plurals of pronouns**
> **Plurals of shortened words**
> **Plurals of verbs**
> **Words without plurals**

Plurals of nouns
Most nouns have word endings (*suffixes*) added to make the plural.

Adding -s
The most common suffix added to make plural nouns is -*s*.
    The **clouds** soon produced **raindrops** on the **windows**.
Further examples:
        one cup — a set of cups
        one shoe — a pair of shoes
        one storm — many storms
        one book — three books
        one table — two tables
        one horse — several horses

Adding -es
Nouns that end with the letters *s, x* or *z*, or with the letter strings *ch* or *sh*, have -*es* added to make them plural.
    They broke two **glasses** while washing the **dishes**.

s	x	z
dresses	boxes	waltzes
buses	taxes	quizzes
gases	prefixes	
lenses	suffixes	
viruses	climaxes	
walruses	indexes	
classes	foxes	
octopuses	appendixes	

ch	sh
bunches	lashes
beaches	bushes
leeches	brushes
peaches	rashes
benches	wishes
lunches	dishes

Nouns ending with -o

Most nouns that end with the letter *o* have *-s* added to make them plural. However, there are a few *-o* ending words that have *-es* added to make them plural.

-s	-es
pianos	heroes
solos	tomatoes
memos	potatoes
radios	tornadoes
biros	echoes
studios	
kangaroos	
cuckoos	

See also **alternative spellings**.

Nouns ending with -y

If a noun ending with *-y* has a consonant before the *-y*, then the *y* is changed to *i* and *-es* is added to make the plural.

Babies bring happiness to **families**.

Further examples:

lady/ladies, sky/skies, butterfly/butterflies, dairy/dairies, bully/bullies, gully/gullies

If a noun has a vowel before the *-y* ending, then *-s* is added to make the plural.

essays, trays, plays, keys, monkeys, valleys, donkeys, journeys, boys, toys, guys

See also **consonants**; **vowels**.

Nouns ending with -f or -fe

Most nouns ending with *-f* or *-fe* have the *f* changed to *v*, and *-es* added to make the plural.

Most caterpillars eat **leaves**.

Further examples:

knife/knives, calf/calves, wolf/wolves, wife/wives, life/lives, elf/elves, self/selves, shelf/shelves

If the /f/ sound is spoken in the plural form, just *-s* is added.

chief/chiefs, belief/beliefs, giraffe/giraffes, roof/roofs

Some words can be spelled either way.
>hoof (hooves or hoofs)

Nouns ending with -ful
Nouns that end with *-ful* have *-s* added to make them plural.
>All the **hopefuls** lined up for the audition.

Further examples:
>cupfuls, handfuls, mouthfuls, spoonfuls

Exceptions
Some nouns have vowels and consonants within the word changed to make them plural.
>goose/geese, foot/feet, tooth/teeth, mouse/mice, louse/lice

Some nouns end with *-en* in the plural.
>ox/oxen, child/children, man/men, woman/women

Foreign words
Many English nouns came from foreign languages. Their plurals are often made the same way they would be formed in those languages.
>**Bacteria**, **fungi** and **viruses** are all germs.

Further examples:
* Words ending with *-um*

Singular	Plural
bacterium	bacteria
maximum	maxima
minimum	minima
medium	media
datum	data

* Words ending with *-on*

Singular	Plural
criterion	criteria
phenomenon	phenomena

- Words ending with *-us*

Singular	Plural
fungus	fungi
radius	radii
locus	loci
terminus	termini

Some words ending with *-us* have *-es* added to make them plural. (The rule used to be to end these words with the letter *-i*, but this has changed in modern times.)

Singular	Plural
octopus	octopuses
platypus	platypuses
syllabus	syllabuses

- Words ending with *-is*
Words ending with *-is* have these letters changed to *-es* to form the plural.

Singular	Plural
axis	axes
basis	bases
crisis	crises
thesis	theses
oasis	oases

- Words ending with *-a*
Words ending with the letter *-a* have the letter *-e* added to form the plural.
At one stage in their lives, insects are **larvae**.

Singular	Plural
alga	algae
larva	larvae
persona	personae

- Words ending with *-ix* or *-ex*

The spelling of some of these plurals is changing.

Singular	Plural
appendix	appendices (now *appendixes* is also used)
index	indices (now *indexes* is also used)

See also **suffixes**.

Plurals of pronouns
Most pronouns have plural forms.

Singular	Plural
I	we
me	us
my	our
mine	ours
he, she, it	they
him, her	them
his, her, its	their
his, hers	theirs

The pronouns *you, your* and *yours* are the same in both singular and plural forms.

See also **pronouns**.

Plurals of shortened words
The letter *s* is added to many abbreviations, contractions and acronyms to make them plural.

> **Drs** Smith and Anderson performed the operation.
> **Capts** Jessop and Blandy entered the paddle steamer race.
> They played **CDs** at the party.
> The **VIPs** arrived in a limousine.
> **CFCs** attack the ozone layer.

Doubling a letter makes some abbreviations plural.

> p (*page*) — pp (*pages*)
> MS (*manuscript*) — MSS (*manuscripts*)

Plurals of verbs

Many verbs have singular and plural forms.

> She **eats** toast for breakfast. (singular)
> They **eat** toast for breakfast. (plural)

In the simple present tense, many singular verbs end in *s* and the plural is without an *s*. (This is opposite to singular and plural nouns.)

Further examples:

> He **likes** to swim. They **like** to swim.
> That dog **runs** fast. Those dogs **run** fast.

Some verbs have different words for singular and plural forms.

> (to be)
> I **am**. She **is**. It **was**. (singular) We **are**. They **are**. They **were**. (plural)
> (to have)
> He **has**. She **has**. It **has**. (singular) They **have**. (plural).

Plural verbs need to have a plural subject in a sentence.

> Throughout the town **it was** business as usual.

In this example the subject *it* is singular, so the author used the singular verb *was*.

> The **hunters were** closing in.

In this example the subject *The hunters* is plural, so the author used the plural verb *were*.

Further examples:

> **It has** to be a shared responsibility. (singular subject and verb)
> The female **moths have** large bodies. (plural subject and verb)

See also **agreement**: **Agreement in number**.

Words without plurals

Mass nouns (things that cannot be counted) and *singular words* do not normally have a plural. It is important to be careful with these words. They are often responsible for lack of agreement in a sentence.

See also **agreement**; **mass nouns**; **singular words**.

234

poetry

Poetry is a very personal form of writing. Poetry can be sung as well as read. The words to songs are called *lyrics*. People have written poetry and songs for thousands of years.

There are different techniques poets can use to focus on the sounds and rhythm of the English language. They also choose words carefully to keep their verse short. For details, see **alliteration**; **assonance**; **iambic foot**; **onomatopoeia**; **rhyme**; **syllable**.

Poets use special techniques to create word pictures. To find details about these techniques, see **compare and contrast**; **metaphor**; **simile**.

There are many forms of poetry. Some poems rhyme at the end of lines; some do not. Some poems are short; some can be long. For details about different forms of poetry, see **ballad**; **chant**; **cinquain**; **couplet**; **epitaph**; **free verse**; **haiku**; **limerick**; **quatrain**.

point of view

All narrative writing is written from a point of view. The point of view influences how the writer affects the reader. A writer does this by writing in the first person (*I* or *we*), second person (*you*) or third person (*he*, *she*, *it* or *they*).

Arguments are also written from a point of view. It is usually the point of view of the writer. In arguments, the writer can be personal and use the first person (*I*).

> **I** think that guns should be banned in homes.

However, the writer might also be *impersonal* and write in the third person using the pronoun *it*, so the text does not show the writer's point of view.

> **It** is thought that guns should be banned in homes.

The following examples show how a piece of writing changes, depending on whether it is written from the first, second or third person point of view.

First person

Text in the first person is written from the point of view of the writer or a particular character in a narrative.

> **I**, Eva Pappas, was born on a very isolated farm. It took a five-hour drive to reach **our** nearest neighbours. Throughout **my** childhood, **I** learned through 'School of the Air'. **My** family has lived on the farm since **my** grandparents first settled in the area as pioneers. It was the only life **we** knew.

This example shows how a writer might begin a nonfiction autobiography. It might also be the beginning of a fictional narrative as told by a character in the story. The information is given from the point of view of the writer or storyteller, using the first person pronouns *I*, *me*, *my*, *we* and *our*.

Second person
Text in the second person speaks directly to the audience.

> Eva Pappas, this is **your** life. **You** were born on a very isolated farm, five hours drive from **your** nearest neighbours. Throughout **your** childhood **you** learned through 'School of the Air'. **Your** family had lived on the farm since **your** grandparents first settled the area as pioneers. It was the only life **you** knew.

This example shows how a writer might create a script for a television or stage performance in which the subject, Eva Pappas, is spoken to by a presenter. The information is given from the point of view of the subject, Eva Pappas. The second person pronouns *you* and *your* are used.

Third person
If an author writes from the point of view of an observer telling a story about characters, then third person pronouns are used. The following text shows the two earlier examples written from the point of view of an observer or storyteller.

> Eva Pappas was born on a very isolated farm. It took a five-hour drive to reach **her** nearest neighbours. Throughout **her** childhood, **she** learned through 'School of the Air'. **Her** family had lived on the farm since **her** grandparents first settled in the area as pioneers. It was the only life **they** knew.

The writer used the third person pronouns *she*, *her* and *they*.

See also **argument**; **impersonal writing**; **narrative**: **Point of view**; **person**; **personal writing**.

portmanteau words

Portmanteau (/**port**-man-**toe**/) words are those formed by blending a part of one word with a part of another. This is one way new English words are created.

> breakfast + lunch = *brunch*

Further examples:

> binary + digit = *bit* (computing term)
> breath + analyser = *breathalyser* or *breathalyzer*
> guess + estimate = *guestimate* or *guesstimate*
> motor + hotel = *motel*
> Net + etiquette = *netiquette*
> news + broadcast = *newscast*

parachute + troop = *paratroop*
peach + nectarine = *peacharine*
quasi- + stellar = *quasar*
smoke + fog = *smog*
television + broadcast = *telecast*

See also WORD HISTORIES: **bit**, **portmanteau words**.

positive degree

See **adjectives**: **Adjectives of degree**; **Adverb modifiers**.

possessive

In grammar, the word *possessive* describes one of the forms or cases of nouns and pronouns. It means 'ownership' or 'belonging to'.

Possessive nouns have an apostrophe mark.
   The **fox's** eye was as cold as a stone.
The apostrophe in *fox's* shows that the *eye* belongs to the *fox*.

Pronouns have possessive forms, but they do not have an apostrophe.

Pronouns	Possessive forms
I, me	my, mine
you	your, yours
we, us	our, ours
he, him	his
she, her	her, hers
it	its
they, them	their, theirs

Examples:
   That is **my** bike. That bike is **mine**.
   Is this **your** home? Is this home **yours**?
   Let's pitch **our** tent. This tent is **ours**.
   She finished reading **her** book. That book is **hers**.
   They cleaned **their** rooms. The cleaned rooms are **theirs**.

See also **apostrophe**: **Apostrophe of possession**; **case**; **it's / its**; **pronouns**: **Possessive pronouns**.

possessive pronouns

See **pronouns: Possessive pronouns**.

practice / practise

These words are often confused. The secret lies in knowing their grammar.

Practice is a noun. It means 'a rehearsal'.
>All that **practice** on the piano had paid off at the concert.

Practise is a verb. It means 'to rehearse, to do something over and over'.
>The pianist had to **practise** a lot. He **practised** for hours each day.

In the USA, the word *practise* is used as both the noun and the verb. Americans do not use the spelling *practice*.

predicate

The *predicate* is the part of a sentence that says something about the *subject*. It is made up of the verb in a sentence, plus any object.
>Hannah's eyes **were shining**.

In this sentence, the subject is *Hannah's eyes*; the predicate is *were shining*. The predicate *were shining* says something about the subject *Hannah's eyes*.

The predicate can also include phrases that give further information about the subject.
>Hannah's eyes **were shining with great delight and excitement**.

See also **object**; **subject**; **verbs**.

predicative adjectives

See **adjectives: Predicative adjectives (after the noun)**.

prefixes

Prefixes are word parts (*affixes*) that are joined to the beginning of a root word. They change the meanings of root words.
>**a**moral
>**ab**normal, **ab**ominable
>**anti**venom
>**des**sert
>**dis**agree

illegal
impossible
inhumane
irresponsible
misunderstanding
nonsmoking
unhealthy

In these examples, *a-, ab-, anti-, des-, dis-, il-, im-, in-, ir-, mis-, non-* and *un-* are prefixes. They all mean 'not' or 'against'. So each of these prefixes changes the root word to an antonym (opposite meaning).

Here are some other examples of prefixes used in English words.

Prefix	Meaning	Examples
al-	every, all	already, alright, altogether, always
bi-	two	bicycle, bi-partisan, bi-plane
by-	beside	bystander, byway
co-	with	coincidence, cooperate, coordinate, co-pilot
con-	with	conform, connect, conspire, contact
contra-	against	contraband, contradict, contravene
hyper-	over	hyperactive, hyperbole, hyperspace, hypertext
mono-	single	monocycle, monopoly, monorail, monotone
multi-	many	multicoloured, multicultural, multiply
post-	after	postdated, post-mortem, postpone, postscript
pro-	forward, for	proceed, progress, pronoun, provoke
re-	again	repay, replace, research, reshuffle, return, revolve
sub-	under	subheading, submarine, submerge, subordinate, sub-standard
super-	above, beyond, over	superannuation, superhuman, supernatural

See also **affixes**; **antonyms**; WORD HISTORIES: **abominable**, **dessert**.

prepositional phrases

Prepositional phrases are phrases that begin with a preposition. They usually give information about the position of something or someone.

> Juanita made her way **up the hill to the cave entrance**.

Up the hill and *to the cave entrance* are prepositional phrases. They begin with the prepositions *up* and *to*.

It is possible to build very long sentences using prepositional phrases.

> The farmer searched for the eggs in the barn, around the haystack, in front of the gate, behind the shed, under the woodpile, over the fence, on top of the bench, among the hens, along the path, through the vegetable garden, up the ladder and down the chimney. He finally found them — in the fridge, inside a carton, beside the butter.

See also **prepositions**.

prepositions

Prepositions are words like *to, from, with, for, into* and *between*. They give information about the position of something. They are usually placed before (pre-) nouns, noun phrases and pronouns in a sentence.

> I brought a book **from** the library so I could read it aloud **to** you.

In this example, the preposition *from* is placed before the noun phrase *the library*. The preposition *to* is placed before the pronoun *you.*

> They waited **for** him to walk **by** the large window.

In this example, the preposition *for* is placed before the pronoun *him*. The preposition *by* is placed before the noun phrase *the large window*.

If a pronoun follows a preposition, then the pronoun is always in the objective case.

> To **whom** does this pen belong?
> This pen belongs **to whom**?

Whom is the objective case of the pronoun *who*. Even though the words are in a different order in the examples, the meaning is the same. However, in modern English this example would be more often spoken or written as:

> **Who** does this pen belong **to**?

Many formal grammarians would consider this incorrect. However, it seems that English language users naturally prefer to use the word *who* rather than *whom* at the beginning of a question, and that the word *whom* is becoming less popular in English as years go by. (See **Did you know?** below.)

See also **case**: **Case of pronouns**; **nouns**; **noun phrases**; **prepositional phrases**; **pronouns**.

present tense

Did you know?

Should you end a sentence with a preposition?

In the 1700s, grammar scholars said that in English you should never end a sentence with a preposition. Teachers taught this rule very well in schools — so well, that many people still believe it to be true. Even some grammar checkers on computers still use this rule!

To not have a preposition at the end of a sentence means that some sentences can sound very awkward.

They wondered which computer they would be working **on**.

They wondered **on** which computer they would be working.

Both these sentences make sense. The first example disobeys the old rule because it ends with the preposition *on*. The second example obeys the old rule, but sounds very awkward or unnatural when spoken.

The old scholars based their rule on the grammar of Latin, not English. In Latin, sentences did not end with a preposition because Latin did not use prepositions in the way English does!

Sometimes, sentences ending with a preposition sound as though they finish weakly. But this does not make them incorrect. Prepositions, like adverbs, can certainly sit at the end of a sentence — as long as the writer's meaning is clear.

present tense

Tense in grammar is about when events or actions happen. Present tense verbs tell about actions that are happening now, or all the time.

Right now I **am reading** my story to an audience.
She **reads** every day.
The earth **spins**.

The verbs *am reading*, *reads* and *spins* are in the present tense.
See also **verbs: Tenses (time)**.

procedure

Procedures, sometimes called *procedural texts* or *instructions*, show readers how to do or make something. Recipes, computer manuals, 'how to make it' activities, sewing patterns, knitting books and rules to games are all procedures.

Procedures usually include:
- an introduction or heading that names and describes the activity
- a list of things needed to do the activity
- numbered instructions that show the reader what to do, and what order to do it in. The instructions are usually written as commands — the sentences and clauses usually begin with a verb.

Making pancakes

Mix the ingredients in a bowl then **pour** small portions into a hot pan. In this example, the sentence has two clauses. Each clause is a command or instruction telling the reader what to do. Each clause begins with a verb (*Mix, pour*).

First Aid Treatment
1. **Wash** the area around the wound.
2. **Clean** the wound with antiseptic.
3. **Cover** the wound with a bandage.

In this example, the instructions are numbered, so the reader knows the order in which they should be done. Each command begins with a verb (*Wash, Clean, Cover*).

Examples of procedures are under the following headings:
Directions in a letter
First aid procedure
Recipe

procedure

Directions in a letter

The following example of a procedure is a letter from an editor's assistant to an author. It tells the author how to send a manuscript to the publisher.

To: g.spry@wave.com
Cc:
Subject: RE: Your query on how to submit a manuscript

Dear Mr Spry
The procedure for submitting a manuscript to Alpha Publications is as follows:

1. Check our web site for information on our publishing program. Make sure that your manuscript fits the style of book we are looking for.
2. Type your manuscript within the body of an email. Do not send attachments.
3. Address the email to "editor@Alpha.com".

Angela Morcombe
Editor's Assistant

- The body of the letter begins with a heading that explains the subject. This heading is introduced by the word *re. Re* means 'concerning' or 'on the subject of'.
- A sentence introduces the list of instructions. Such a sentence often ends with words like *as follows*.
- The sentence introducing the list of instructions ends with a colon.
- The instructions are numbered.
- The instructions are commands — the main part of each sentence begins with a verb (*Check our web site …, Type your manuscript …,* etc).

See also **colon (:)**; **sentences**: **Commands**; **verbs**; WORD HISTORIES: **re**.

First aid procedure

The following example gives instructions for first aid treatment for a snake bite.

Every snake should be treated as though it is venomous. NEVER ATTEMPT TO CATCH OR KILL A SNAKE. When you are in known snake habitats, be careful where you put your hands and feet.

1.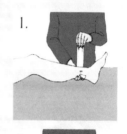

FIRST AID TREATMENT FOR SNAKE BITE:

1. Apply a wide pressure bandage over the bite site.

2.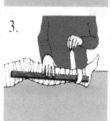

2. The bandage should be as tight as you would apply to a sprained ankle. Extend the bandage as high as possible.

3.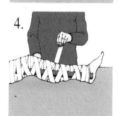

3. Apply a splint to the limb.

4. Bind it firmly to as much of the limb as possible.

4.

5. Get medical help.

Deadly & dangerous snakes, back cover

- The text has an introduction and title that explains what the procedure is about.
- Each instruction has an accompanying diagram.
- Most of the sentences are commands (they begin with a verb).
- The sentences are usually short so they are easy to read and understand.
- In instruction 2 the author uses the word *should*, telling the reader what ought to be done.

See also **could / should / would**.

Recipe

The following example is a recipe for making a 'Fruit energy drink'. It describes the project, lists the ingredients, then gives the method in numbered steps.

FRUITY ENERGY DRINK

This is a handy drink for after school snacks or times when you need to get some energy quickly to do something like cooking or playing sport.

Ingredients

- 1 cup very cold milk
- 1 small or ½ big banana (peeled)
- 8 strawberries (washed and without green bits) Save 1 strawberry for decoration
- 1 egg
- 1 teaspoon honey or sugar

Method

1. Put milk in a food processor or vitamiser for 30 seconds.
2. Chop bananas and add.
3. Halve strawberries and add, remembering to keep one over.
4. Break egg. Put shell in rubbish bin and egg in milk mixture.
5. Add 1 teaspoon honey or sugar.
6. Mix all together.
7. Pour into glass.
8. Decorate with the remaining strawberry.

One week with my grandmother, pp. 25, 27

- The introduction describes the project so the reader knows why it is useful or worth making.
- The list of ingredients includes measures so the reader knows the correct amounts of ingredients to use.
- Some of the instructions are sentence fragments (*Break egg … Pour into glass.*) This is to save space and make it possible for the reader to read quickly.

See also **measures**; **sentence fragments**.

prologue (US: prolog)

A *prologue* is an introduction to a poem, a play or a story. The prologue allows the writer to give the audience background information to a story, so the audience will better understand the tale.

See also WORD HISTORIES: **dialogue**.

pronouns

Pronouns are words that replace nouns or noun phrases that have already been mentioned in a text.

Pronouns are useful when writers do not want to repeat a noun or noun phrase in a sentence or paragraph.

> The female polar bear used **her** keen sense of smell to locate a seal nest hidden beneath the snow. Quickly **she** pushed on the snow, pouncing with all **her** weight, and digging frantically with **her** claws.

The pronouns in this example are *her* (replacing the noun *bear's*), *she* (replacing the noun *bear*), and *her* (replacing the noun *bear*). If the author had not used pronouns, she would have repeated the words *female polar bear*. This would have made the writing sound clumsy and boring.

> The female polar bear used **the female polar bear's** keen sense of smell to locate a seal's nest hidden beneath the snow. Quickly **the female polar bear** pushed on the snow, pouncing with all **the female polar bear's** weight, and digging frantically with **the female polar bear's** claws.

Pronouns are also important when writers choose whether their writing will be in the first, second or third person.

> When **I** buy canned fish, **I** check to see where it came from. (*first person*)
> When **you** buy canned fish, check to see where it came from. (*second person*)

When **they** buy canned fish, **they** check to see where it came from. (*third person*)

See also **antecedent**; **nouns**; **noun phrases**; **person**.

In grammar, there are special names for different types of pronouns. The following topics give information on different types of pronouns:

Case and number of pronouns
Demonstrative pronouns
Indefinite pronouns
Interrogative pronouns
Personal pronouns
Possessive pronouns
Reflexive pronouns
Relative pronouns

Case and number of pronouns
Pronouns have *subjective, objective* and *possessive* cases. They also have *singular* and *plural* forms.
See also **case**: **Case of pronouns**; **plural**: **Plurals of pronouns**.

Demonstrative pronouns
Demonstrative pronouns are used when the author is pointing out something but does not name it. The demonstrative pronouns are:
that, this, those, these

These are not safe to eat. **Those** are OK.
This is broken. **That** is not my problem.

Indefinite pronouns
Some pronouns, such as *indefinite* pronouns, do not replace nouns in a sentence. They are also singular words, so they need a singular verb for agreement in a sentence. These words include:
anyone, anybody, anything
no one, nobody, nothing
someone, somebody, something
everyone, everybody, everything

Is anybody able to help me?
No one is home.
Everyone needs help sometime.

See also **agreement**: **Agreement in number**; **singular words**.

Interrogative pronouns
Interrogative pronouns ask questions. The interrogative pronouns are:
who, whose, whom, which, what

Whose socks are they?
Which dog is that?
Who broke that window?
Whom do you want to see?
What is your name?

See also **interrogatives**: **Interrogative pronouns**.

Personal pronouns
Personal pronouns replace nouns that name people or things. They are the most common type of pronoun. Some examples of personal pronouns are:
I, me, my, we, us, our, you, your, she, her, he, him, his, it, its, they, them, their

Painting birds is difficult because **they** don't sit still for long.
In this example, the personal pronoun *they* replaces the noun *birds*.

See also **person**.

Possessive pronouns
Possessive pronouns show ownership. They refer to something already mentioned. The possessive pronouns are:
hers, ours, yours, theirs, her, our, your, their, his, mine

The friends took **their** dogs for a walk.
The possessive pronoun *their* refers to the phrase *The friends*. So we know the friends owned the dogs.

Reflexive pronouns
Reflexive pronouns refer to the subject of a sentence. The reflexive pronouns are:
myself, yourself, himself, herself, itself, ourselves, yourselves, themselves

The clown practised by watching **himself** in a mirror.

In this example, the reflexive pronoun *himself* refers to *The clown*, the subject of the sentence.

Relative pronouns

Relative pronouns replace words or phrases, to connect one part of a sentence with another. They are often used to begin a clause. Some examples of relative pronouns are:

> who, whose, that, whom, which

> She wore an old T-shirt. The old T-shirt was streaked with mud.
> She wore an old T-shirt **that** was streaked with mud.

In the second sentence, the relative pronoun *that* replaces the noun phrase *The old T-shirt*. It makes it possible for the author to join the two sentences.

Further examples:

> She had a son, **whom** she named Benjamin.
> This book, **which** is very old, is quite valuable.

Hint

Relative pronouns

Relative pronouns are placed next to the nouns they are related to.

If the clause beginning with a relative pronoun is *not* placed after the noun it relates to, then the meaning of the sentence might be incorrect. Note these examples. Who passed the bundle to the girl?

> The police chased a man, **who passed a bundle to a girl**.

> The police, **who passed a bundle to a girl**, chased a man.

See also **clauses**: **Subordinate clauses**; **who / whom**.

---

proofreading

Proofreading is the last stage of the editing process before a piece of writing is published. Proofreaders check the text to see if there are errors in details such as spelling, punctuation and capitals.

See also **writing process**: **Editing**.

proper nouns

Proper nouns are the names of particular people, places and things. They always begin with a capital letter.

> Angela, New York, Saturday, September, England

See also **capitals**: **Proper nouns**; **nouns**: **Proper nouns**.

prose

Prose is any form or style of writing or speech that does not have a regular rhythm or sentence length.

> As the intruder leaped over the fence, he was confronted by a guard dog. The large, black beast bared its teeth and uttered a low growl. The intruder knew he was in trouble.

In this example, the writer describes an event without using a regular rhythm in the sentences. The sentences also vary in length.

> The night was dark and held suspense,
> As the intruder leaped and cleared the fence.
> But before him stood a beast on the prowl;
> A big black dog with a menacing growl.

In this example, the same event is described in verse. The lines have a regular rhythm that suggests stressed and unstressed syllables, and a pause at the end of each line in the verse. This is not prose.

See also **iambic foot**; **style**; **syllable**.

proverbs

A proverb is a short, wise saying that has been popular for a long time. Proverbs are usually so well-known that people use them to express something briefly, knowing that their audience will understand their meaning.

> Make hay while the sun shines.
> Those who live in glass houses should not throw stones.
> Don't cry over spilt milk.

Proverbs are often used as the moral of short stories, such as fables. However, if they are over-used in writing, they can become clichés.

See also **clichés**; **fable**.

publishing

To publish means 'to make public'. There are many ways to publish a piece of writing — display on a wall or notice-board, deposit in a library, place on a web site on the Internet, read over the radio, perform on stage or send to the editor of a newspaper are just a few. A work has been published when it reaches the author's audience.

See also **audience**; **writing process**: **Publishing**.

pun

A *pun* is a humorous play on words. To make a pun you need words that have the same or similar sound, but different meanings or spelling.

> Doctor Bell fell down a **well**
> And broke his collar-bone.
> Doctors should attend the sick
> And leave the **well** alone.

Anonymous

In this example the poet played on the word *well* which has two meanings — 'a water-hole in the ground' or 'healthy'. Because the poem is about a water-hole and a doctor, the poet was able to make a pun in the last line of the poem.

Puns are often used in humorous or clever newspaper headlines.

TREE-DOCTOR OPENS NEW BRANCH
DOG CATCHER HOUNDS STRAY PETS

Some people's names can be used to make interesting puns, for example in humorous book titles.

Get rich quick by Robin Banks.
The firefighter by Iva Hose

See also **ambiguity**; **epitaph**; WORD HISTORIES: **pun**.

punctuation

Punctuation marks are used in writing to make meaning clear for the reader. If a writer does not use punctuation carefully, the reader can get the wrong message.

Punctuation marks are used for different purposes in writing. The different uses of punctuation are described under the following headings:

To make meaning clear
To separate sections of text
To show expression
To show pauses and stops
With shortened words

punctuation

To make meaning clear
The following sentences have the same letters or words but different meanings because of the punctuation.

That dog knows **its** home at last. (The home belongs to the dog.)
That dog knows **it's** home at last. (The dog is home.)

James said, 'Susan is gorgeous.' (James spoke — he thinks Susan is gorgeous.)
'James,' said Susan, 'is gorgeous.' (Susan spoke — she thinks James is gorgeous.)

To separate sections of text
Note how difficult the following sentence is to read and understand.

I did not bring my homework because last night while I was out walking my dog chewed ripped and tore holes in some pages swallowed others and somewhere in our garden dug a hole and buried the rest if you believe that I have an old computer I would like to sell you

Punctuation marks make it easier to read and understand.

I did not bring my homework because, last night, while I was out walking, my dog chewed, ripped and tore holes in some pages, swallowed others and, somewhere in our garden, dug a hole and buried the rest. If you believe that, I have an old computer I would like to sell you.

To show expression
Punctuation marks show readers how to express words when reading them out loud. This is important when someone is reading from a story or play script. The following sentences have the same words, but an actor would read each one differently.

Oh, that would be fun.
Oh! That would be fun.
Oh? That would be fun?

To show pauses and stops
Punctuation is used to show a reader when they should pause in a sentence. Some writers prefer to use a lot of punctuation (*heavy punctuation*). However, too much punctuation can interrupt the flow of the reading.

Some writers prefer to use punctuation only when necessary to make meaning clear (*light punctuation*); they leave it to the reader to decide when to pause. However, too little punctuation can leave the reader confused about the meaning.

A good rule is *keep it simple*. The trend is towards lighter punctuation, although both methods are used around the world. It is a matter of personal taste and style, as long as the meaning is clear to the reader, and the punctuation is used correctly.

With shortened words
Publishers create their own *house style* when they decide to punctuate shortened words, because there is more than one way to do it. A publisher's house style is usually similar to the style commonly used in that publisher's country.

The *Young writers guide* does not use full stops in any shortened forms unless it is essential to make meaning clear. However, some examples throughout this guide come from different books, so a variety of styles is used.

You can decide on your own *house style* for punctuating shortened words. The important thing is to stick to a chosen style throughout any piece of writing.

Three punctuation marks are commonly used in shortened words and phrases — the *apostrophe*, the *full stop* and the *slash*. People around the world mostly agree on how to use the apostrophe and the slash in English shortened forms. The full stop, however, causes great debate! Some say full stops should be used for all shortened forms; some say they should not be used at all, and for others either method is acceptable.

Apostrophe
See **apostrophe: Apostrophe for contractions**.

Full stop
There is a trend towards using full stops less in most shortened forms, especially in addresses on envelopes. Some people believe it would be better to leave out full stops altogether.
Three common styles for using full stops in shortened forms are:
- *no full stops in shortened forms of any type*. This is a worldwide trend, and the Internet is speeding up this trend, because people want to save time in communication.
  abbreviations — *Capt, Prof, am*
  contractions — *Mr, Mrs, Dr*
  acronyms — *UK, NASA, USA*

- *full stops for abbreviations, but not contractions, or acronyms with more than one capital letter*. This is the most common style in the United Kingdom, South Africa and Australia.
  abbreviations — *Capt., Prof., a.m.*,
  contractions — *Mr, Mrs, Dr*
  acronyms — *UK, NASA, USA*

- *full stops for all shortened forms except acronyms written in capitals when they are the names of organisations or countries.* This is the most common style in the United States.

  abbreviations — *Capt., Prof., a.m.*
  contractions — *Mr., Mrs., Dr.*
  acronyms — *UK, NASA, USA*

Slash

Some abbreviations are formed with a slash. These abbreviations are common in classified advertisements in newspapers, because they save space.

  c/o or c/- — *care of*
  w/o — *without*
  w/w — *wall to wall*
  a/c — *air conditioning*

The slash means 'per' in abbreviated units of measure.

  km/h (kilometres per hour)
  The wind speed changed rapidly from 0–200 **km/h**.

See also **measures**; **slash mark (/)**.

Hint

When punctuation gets too hard!

If a sentence is hard to punctuate, think about rewriting it. Perhaps it is too long or complex anyway?

For more information about particular punctuation marks, see:
apostrophe (')
asterisk (*)
brackets ( )
bullet points (•)
colon (:)
comma (,)
dash (—)
ellipsis (…)
exclamation mark (!)
full stop (.)
hyphen (-)
question mark (?)
quotation marks (' ' and " ")
semicolon (;)
slash mark (/)

quatrain

A quatrain is four lines of rhyming verse. It can be a whole poem or just one verse in a longer poem. It usually has an A B A B rhyming pattern, but A A B B and A B C B patterns are also used.

question-and-answer text

Question-and-answer text is writing that is based on a series of questions followed by statements or answers to those questions.

Question-and-answer text is used in interviews and quiz books. There are many ways writers can write questions.

See also **question mark (?)**; **report**: **Question and answer — interviews**.

question mark (?)

A *question mark* is a punctuation mark (?) used at the end of a sentence where a question is being asked. It tells the reader that the sentence should be read or spoken as a question.

> 'What did she want**?**'
> 'Nothing.'
> 'Nothing**?**'
> 'Well, nothing important anyway.'

In this example, the question mark and the full stop tell the reader how to read the word *nothing* in two different ways.

See also WORD HISTORIES: **question**.

Further information is under the following topics:
When to use
Direct speech
Questions within a sentence
Rhetorical questions
Tag questions
To emphasise a question
To show doubt
When *not* to use
Dramatic statements
Favours or demands
Indirect questions
With other punctuation
Brackets
Ellipsis
Quotation marks

question mark (?)

When to use

Direct speech
Question marks are used for questions in direct speech. The question mark is written inside the quotation marks.

> '**Are you sure?**' I asked.

See also **direct speech**.

Questions within a sentence
A question mark can be placed at the end of a question even if it is not the end of the sentence.

> **Is this what they think is exciting?** thought Nicholas.
> **What clues did I expect to find? footprints? tracks?**

Rhetorical questions
Rhetorical questions are questions to which the speaker or writer does not expect an answer from the audience. They have a question mark anyway. Sometimes rhetorical questions are asked *and* answered by the speaker.

> "**Andrew bring me flowers?**" She laughed. "You must be joking!"
> **But, Olivia help us?** Oh, no! She just lay coiled up, reading all day.

See also **rhetorical questions**.

Tag questions
Tag questions are questions that the speaker or writer 'tags onto' the end of a statement to turn it into a question.

> We can be friends, **can't we?**
> Oh, it's you **is it?**

To emphasise a question
A question mark can be doubled (??) to emphasise a question. Some authors use a question mark together with an exclamation mark (?!). This technique is used mostly in personal writing such as correspondence and journals, but not in formal writing.

> Do I *just* have pneumonia**??** What a question!
> What about me? Don't I mean anything to you**?!**

question mark (?)

To show doubt
A question mark sometimes shows that an author is unsure of a fact.

> Aesop (**600?** BC)

In this example, the author is not sure about the year 600. There is no doubt about the period BC.

A question mark can also show that the meaning of a word may not be accurate. This often suggests that a word was used in fun. A question mark used this way is placed in brackets.

> My baby brother was ready to **help (?)** me tidy my room.

When *not* to use

Dramatic statements
Dramatic statements do not have a question mark, even if the word order in the sentence is written as a question.

> Oh Henry, isn't this book fantastic!

Favours or demands
Sentences in which a favour is being asked, or a demand made, do not have a question mark.

> "**Please keep your voice down**," replied my father.
> "**Please get in the car**," said Mum. "We're late already."

Indirect questions
Indirect questions do not have a question mark because no one is actually asking a question. Someone is reporting about a question that has been asked.

> **Mr Denton asked me if I'd heard any news** but I hadn't.
> **I asked him why he was late.**

With other punctuation

The question mark is sometimes used with other punctuation marks such as brackets, the ellipsis and quotation marks.

Brackets

If a question is in brackets, then the question mark is also placed inside the brackets.

> (So that's where the chocolates were hidden, eh**?**)
> I told you (didn't I**?**) that I would be late.

Ellipsis

The question mark is placed *before* an ellipsis.

> "Why**?**..." Jessie began.
> "What**?**..." said Mai Ling.
> "No questions," said their teacher.

Quotation marks

If a question is asked in direct speech, the question mark is placed *inside* the quotation marks.

> "Do the patterns mean anything**?"** asked the visitor.
> "What's that writing on the wall**?"** asked Michel. "Secret code**?"**

See also **brackets ( )**; **direct speech**; **ellipsis (...)**;
quotation marks (' ' and " ").

questions

Questions are sentences in which the reader is asked for information or action. Careful writers usually try to keep questions short so they do not confuse the reader. Questions can be written in many ways. Details on different styles of questions are under the following headings.

> **Multiple answer questions**
> **Multiple choice questions**
> **One-word questions**
> **Open and closed questions**
> **True or false questions**

Multiple answer questions

Some questions can have more than one correct answer.

> What are the names of three whales that have teeth?

In this example, the question asks for only three names, but there are about thirty different toothed whales in the world. Two readers could each choose different answers and both readers could be correct.

Multiple choice questions

In multiple choice questions the writer makes the reader choose from three or more possible answers. Only one of the choices will be correct.

> The blue whale is found mainly in:
> A. the Atlantic Ocean
> B. the Pacific Ocean
> C. the Indian Ocean
> D. any ocean

In this example, the writer makes a statement and gives four possible answers for the reader to complete the statement. Points to note about this example:

*   This type of question does not necessarily use question marks. The question in this example is really a statement.
*   The possible answers form a list. Each possible answer is a phrase that completes the introduction, *The blue whale is found mainly in*.

See also **lists**; **sentences**: **Statements**.

One-word questions

Questions can be as short as one word.

> Who? What? When? Where? Why?

One-word questions are usually used in speech or dialogue.

Open and closed questions

Open questions are questions that cannot be answered with a simple *yes* or *no*. Closed questions *can* be answered in this way. Open questions are useful in interviews and conversations because they encourage people to give more detail and express themselves.

> Are you going out tonight? (closed question)
> Where are you going tonight? (open question)
> Why are you going out tonight? (open question)

Open questions often begin with the interrogative pronouns *where*, *why*, *what*, *which*, *when* and *who*.

A useful way of practising open questions is to play the 'yes/no' game, in which players ask each other questions which do not allow the other player to answer *yes* or *no*.

See also **argument**: **Interviews**; **interrogatives**: **Interrogative pronouns**.

True or false questions

True or false questions are in fact statements or commands, but they still ask the reader for information or action.

> The blue whale is the largest animal to have ever lived.
> **True or false?**

In this example, the writer makes a statement then follows it with the question *True or false?* Clever writers choose statements that make the reader really think about the answer. Words like *largest* and *ever* are used to trick the reader. For example, we know that the blue whale is the world's largest animal, but is it the largest *ever*? Maybe some dinosaurs were larger?

For information on the grammar of different questions see **mood**: **Interrogative**; **question mark (?)**; **sentences**: **Questions**.

quiet / quite

Quiet is an adjective. It means 'silent'. It is pronounced /**kwi**-et/.

> The police asked people to remain **quiet**.
> Liu spoke **quietly** to her friend.

Quite is an intensifier. It means 'completely; absolutely'. It is pronounced /kwite/ to rhyme with *kite*.

> After a while, it seemed **quite** easy.
> The artist said the painting was not **quite** finished.

See also **intensifiers**; **modifiers**.

quotation marks (' ' and " ")

Quotation marks (also called *speech marks*) are used for words that are spoken or quoted. They are sometimes called *inverted commas*, because the beginning mark is an upside-down comma.

There are *single* quotation marks.

> 'The baby snake will grow fast if there is plenty of food,' he said.

There are *double* quotation marks.

> "Time to clean your room," my mother declared.

Some people prefer double marks while others prefer single marks; there is no reason why one is better than the other. It depends on the writer — as long as they are consistent within the writing.

The use of quotation marks is explained under the following topics:

> **Direct speech**
> **Names**
> **Quotations**
> **Quotations within quotations**
> **Special words**

quotation marks (' ' and " ")

Invented or unusual words
Slang words
Words being explained
Words used humorously
When not to use
Indirect speech
Play scripts
Transcripts

Direct speech
Quotation marks are used for the actual words spoken in direct speech. Words not actually spoken are placed outside the quotation marks.

"**What a fuss about nothing!**" observed my mother.

Further examples:

"**Don't stop here,**" said Dad. "**It looks dangerous.**"
The other students shouted, "**Well done! Great game!**"
"**We'll be home soon,**" she said. "**Only four months to go.**"

See also **direct speech**.

Names
Quotation marks are sometimes used for the names of people and things when they are first used in writing. These include:

*   *Names of pets*
    When '**Daniel**', a homeless kitten was found eight years ago, the vet said it would never survive.
    '**Jessie**', my gorgeous dog, waits for me by the gate.
*   *Names of ships* (These can also be written in italics.)
    A Russian tourist ship, '**Kapitan Khlebnikov**', arrived in port.
*   *Nicknames for people, places and things*
    The Apollo 11 crew were Neil Armstrong, aged 38, Michael Collins, aged 34 and '**Buzz**' Aldrin, aged 35.
*   *Titles of books, plays, songs, films, poems and other creative titles.*
    These titles are usually written in *italics*, but quotation marks are often used in informal writing.
    A film crew is making a film called '**The Last Flight Home**'.

Quotations
Quotation marks are used to point out words that are quoted from a book or another person.

"We need safe products which don't produce poisons." (Lynette Thorstensen, Greenpeace)

See also writing samples under **report: Question and answer — interviews**.

Quotations within quotations

When a book or person is quoted within another quotation, the quotation inside the main quotation is placed in marks of its own. If single quotation marks are used for the main quotation, double marks are used for the second quotation, or vice versa. This helps to separate the two quotations.

'You don't always get paid. Sometimes they do a runner.'
'What d'you mean, **"do a runner"**?'

In this example, the second speaker is quoting the words *do a runner* of the first speaker. Single marks are used for the main quotation, so double marks are used for the second quotation.

Further examples:

'What does she mean, I must **"claim"** it?' she said.
'The others didn't agree with the umpire. **"Cheat"** they said he was.'

In the United States, double quotation marks are used for the main quotation and single marks for the second quotation.

In the United Kingdom, single quotation marks are more often used for the main quotation and double marks for the second quotation.

In countries like Australia, New Zealand and Canada, both methods are used.

Special words

When pointing out a word to readers, a writer may use quotation marks. This technique is used for:

Invented or unusual words

Quotation marks are sometimes used to highlight invented or unusual words.

Some factories print **'dolphin-friendly'** on their cans of tuna.

In this example, the cans themselves are not *dolphin-friendly*. These words are a name or title given to the tuna meat.

They spent hundreds of hours in a simulator, which was like a smart video game, where they could **'crash'** their spacecraft without getting hurt.

In this example, the quotation marks show that the astronauts did not really *crash* their spacecraft.

Staghorn ferns live on rotting plant matter and water that falls into the **'bowl'** formed by the leaves.

In this example, the word *bowl* is a metaphor for the shape of the plant. The leaves do not form a real bowl.

See also **metaphor**.

quotation marks (' ' and " ")

Slang words

Quotation marks are often used for slang words and other informal sayings.

> Waste is created by our **'throw-away society'**.
> They were invited to a **'barbie'** for lunch.

Words being explained

Quotation marks are used for words that are being explained, or for words that are used to explain another word.

> The word *taipan* meaning **'boss'** comes from the Cantonese language. However, *taipan* meaning **'poisonous snake'** comes from the Aboriginal word *dhayban*.

Words used humorously

Quotation marks are often used for words that are used in a humorous or sarcastic way.

> A group of young **'minstrels'** sang for the class.

In this example, the use of quotation marks suggests that the singers were not really minstrels, but young people pretending to be minstrels.

> Jemma planned a nasty surprise for her **'friend'** Meg.

In this example, the character is using the word *friend* in a sarcastic way.

When not to use

Quotation marks are not used for:

Indirect speech

Indirect speech does not have quotation marks because it is reported — nothing is actually being said. The words *that* and *if* are usually used in indirect speech.

> The wolf replied **that** he was in charge of the woods.
> The wolf asked **if** she lived nearby. The little girl said **that** she did.

Play scripts

The direct speech in play scripts does not have quotation marks.

> SU LING: So what do you say? Should I do it?
> TAN GEK: Why not? You have nothing to lose.

Transcripts

Transcripts are written the same way as play scripts and do not have quotation marks.

> Ground control: We copy you down Eagle.
> Eagle: Houston, Tranquillity Base here. The Eagle has landed.

See also **indirect speech**; **narrative**: **Play script**; **transcript**.

quotations

A quotation is a word or a group of words that were first used by one person or character, then repeated or used by another person or character.

> The last time I saw Mr Dawson before he left on his journey, he said, and I quote, "Do not search for me unless you hear nothing for more than a month."

See also **quotation marks: Quotations**.

raw / roar

Raw is an adjective. It means 'not cooked'.

> The steak was **raw**. All the other meat was well-done.

Roar can be a verb. It means 'to make a loud sound, like a lion's roar'.
> The tiger **roared**.
> In Antarctica, blizzards **roar** with cutting winds and driving snow.

real / really

These words are confused by many people. The word *real* is often used when *really* should be, especially when the speaker or writer means 'very'. Sport commentators commonly misuse these words.

> The footballer played **real** well. (X)
> The footballer played **really** well. (✓)

Real is an adjective. It means 'true, not imaginary'.
> It was a **real**-life problem, not like actors on TV.
> It wasn't a **real** spider — just a toy to frighten people.

Really is an adverb. It means 'truly, actually'.
> The movie was **really** scary.
> I had **really** grown to like my neighbour.

Really can be used as an adjective meaning 'very'.
> The giraffe was **really** tall.

See also **adjectives**; **adverbs**; **intensifiers**.

real / really

If you mean 'very', then use *really*. They both end with the letter *y*.

recount

When a writer tells someone about something that has already happened, then the writer is recounting events. A *recount text* is a record of past experiences or events. They could be true events (*non-fiction*) or imaginary events (*fiction*). The events are usually written in the order of the time they happened (*chronological order*). The writer usually records when and where events took place and who was involved.

Recounts can be written as journals, diaries, biographies, personal letters or newspaper stories.

See also **audience**; **journalism**.

The following topics describe different recounts:
Fiction
    Correspondence — fax
    Correspondence — letter
    Correspondence — personal email
    Journal
Non-fiction
    Autobiography
    Biography
    Historical event
    Journal
    Media articles (journalism)
    Oral history
    Transcript

Fiction
Authors sometimes write fiction in the form of characters writing letters. In these letters, the characters write about things that have happened. They *recount* events.

Correspondence — fax
In the following example, a father sends a fax to his children to tell them about things that have happened in Antarctica, where he is working.

recount

DATE: 23 October 1990
FAX TO: Sue and Peta, 61 8 8234 1234
FROM: Dad, Mawson Base, Antarctica
No. OF PAGES:1
SUBJECT: Another fax to my darling daughters

Dear Sue and Peta,
Your turn for a fax. Thank you very much for your lovely letters
and drawings. I have pinned them all up by my bed - a gallery!
Filming was exciting today. The females returned after months
away fishing. Each heard her mate call and waddled straight up
to him. How they can hear each other when all the others are
racketing on, I don't know!
Some of the eggs have hatched. Others will hatch in the next
few days. Now it is the males' turn to go fishing.
I can't wait to see you! How much have you grown? How heavy
is Harry? I'm looking forward to seeing all the photos.

Much love to you all, DAD

Voices, p. 28

- The 'header' of the fax has information on date, receiver (and fax number), sender, length (pages) and subject. The author uses abbreviations in this section to save space.
- Dad wrote in the past tense when he described events. (*Filming was exciting …*)
- He used the present tense when he described his feelings. (*I'm looking forward …*)
- The language is informal because the character is writing to family members. He uses sentence fragments (*Your turn for a fax.*) and signs it *Much love.* He also uses a lot of exclamation marks and questions which make it more informal.
- He wrote information about penguins in the order that things happened.

See also **correspondence**: **Correspondence**; **formal / informal writing**; **verbs**: **Tenses (time)**.

Correspondence — letter
Authors sometimes use correspondence between characters as a way of telling a story. In this example, a character named Tess writes to a friend, Leah, and tells her about things that have happened at school.

~ *Friday 18th* ~

Dear Leah,

Our class photos came back today. I didn't look at mine. I just left the package on the dining-room table. I don't want to look at a class photo without you in it because without you it's not the whole class.

The disco's on tonight — the one that you suggested to raise funds for Saving the Whales. I feel a real traitor for not going. I paid for my ticket out of my own money so I've contributed to the fund but I didn't show the notice to my parents because they'd have hassled me into going.

I looked in the letterbox as I came in after school. Just junk mail and bills as usual. A letter from you would have helped improve my rotten day.

Your loving friend,

Tess

Letters to Leah, pp. 42, 43

- The letter is in the past tense.
- The writing is very informal and personal. The writer uses contractions (*I've, didn't, they'd*), and signs the letter *Your loving friend.* So the character obviously knows the other person well.

See also **contractions**; **chronological**; **formal / informal writing**; **verbs: Tenses (time)**.

recount

Correspondence — personal email

The writer of personal correspondence in email is often recounting events that have happened. In the following example, a father writes to family members about what his children have been doing.

To: Grandparents@XXOO.com
Cc:
Subject: The latest adventures of James and Olivia

Hi Mum and Dad
James played his first soccer match today. Of course the whole family was there to watch him. His team scored three goals (James kicked one). Next time they hope to win the game!

Olivia performed on stage last night with her gymnastics group. We were impressed by the exercises they did. Of course Olivia was dressed in a wonderful sparkling gym outfit. She looked like a little fairy (until she began an argument with one of the judges!) Our little girl was not impressed with the scores they gave her. I felt sorry for the judges!

That's all the news for now. Keep in touch.
Love, David

- The topic of the email is written in the 'Subject' line.
- Personal recounts are usually informal. The writer began with an informal greeting (*Hi*) and signed off with a personal word (*Love*).
- The writing is in the past tense (James *played*; Olivia *performed*), except for the closing comments (That*'s* all … *Keep* in touch.).
- The recounts are structured with an *introduction* announcing who and what it is about (*James played his first soccer match today.*), *details of events* (His team scored three goals) and a *concluding comment* (*Next time …*).
- Emails tend to be short messages, but this depends on the writer and the audience.

See also **chronological**; **correspondence**: **Appointments**; **formal / informal writing**; **verbs**: **Tenses (time)**.

Journal

Authors sometimes write fiction in the form of a character's diary or journal. In diary entries, the characters write about things that have happened. They recount events. In the following example, the character 'Louisa' recalls things that have happened while she is trapped underground.

recount

> Dear E,
>
> Heard a noise, a scratching sound, like a mouse or cricket. Hoped it was someone. Yelled and yelled.
>
> Saw it! A tiny brown mouse! Nibbling at the apple. Couldn't believe my eyes. Now I know everything will be OK. Something else is alive down here.

'Tomorrow' is a great word, p. 21

- The writer begins each entry with *Dear E* (the name of her diary).
- The writing is about herself, so she writes in the first person. (*I*, *my*)
- She uses contractions (*couldn't*). She also uses incomplete sentences — her language is in the form of short notes to herself. This makes her writing informal.

See also **contractions**; **emphasis**; **formal / informal writing**; **person**.

Non-fiction
Many recounts are non-fiction. Non-fiction events can be recorded in many ways.

Autobiography
In an autobiography, authors recount what has happened in their own lives. They write about themselves.

The following example is the introduction to *Memories: An autobiography* by Mem Fox, an author of children's books. Mem writes about her family.

My family

Hello! My name is Mem Fox. Let me tell you something about my life and about how I became a writer of children's books.

I was born in Melbourne, Australia on 5 March 1946. My parents are Wilfrid Gordon McDonald Partridge and Nancy Walkden Partridge. I have two younger sisters, Jan and Alison.

Nan & Wilfrid Partridge with Mem, 1946

Memories: An autobiography, p. 3

- The author uses first person pronouns (*I, me, my*).
- When the author recounts events, she writes in the past tense (I *was born* in Melbourne).
- The text begins with the author's birth, then moves on to later events. It is in chronological order.

See also **chronological**; **pronouns**; **person**; **verbs**: **Past**.

Biography

In a biography, authors recount the main events or achievements in another person's life. They write about someone else. The following example is from the introduction to the book *Cousteau: An unauthorized biography* by Kevin Comber.

During his school life and as a young man, Cousteau developed a keen interest in diving. In 1930 he joined the French Navy. On one trip he saw a Chinese fisherman dive underwater and catch a fish with his bare hands. Cousteau thought this was amazing. When he returned home, a friend gave him some goggles for underwater diving. Cousteau was fascinated by how many beautiful things he could see.

Some of Cousteau's important achievements are:

- inventing Self-Contained Underwater Breathing Apparatus (SCUBA) [see page 5];
- filming underwater;
- exploring the oceans;
- teaching people about conservation;
- being a peacemaker.

Cousteau: An unauthorized biography, p. 4

- The verbs are in the past tense. If Cousteau were still alive, then some verbs might have been in the present tense.
- Most events are in chronological order.
- The author uses third person pronouns (*he*, *him*, *his*).

See also **chronological**; **person**; **pronouns**; **verbs**: Tenses (time).

Historical event
In a text about a historical event, authors recount important things from the past. The author usually has to research the information to write a historical recount.

In the book *The first lunar landing*, the author recounted the events that led to the first humans landing on the moon. In this example, the *Contents* page shows how the author organised the information into chapters.

Contents	Page
Introduction	3
Apollo Spacecraft/Saturn V Rocket	4
The Astronauts	5
Training for the Journey	6
Journey to the Moon	8
At Work on the Moon	12
Returning to Earth	14
Lesson from Apollo 11	16
Apollo Lunar Landings	18
Index	19
Glossary	20

In the following page, the author recounts details of one part of the event.

recount

Returning to Earth

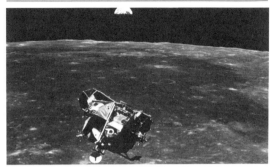

Eagle returning from the moon

Nearly twenty-two hours after landing, the Eagle blasted off the moon and back to the Columbia. Collins was excited to see Armstrong and Aldrin again. He had used a telescope to look for Armstrong and Aldrin on the moon, but he couldn't find them.

The engine was fired and they headed towards the Earth. Everyone was very anxious then, because if the engine failed, they would be left orbiting the moon, unable to get home.

The first lunar landing, pp. 2, 14

- The contents page shows the structure of the book. The topics are listed in chronological order.
- The text is in the past tense (*blasted*, *was excited*, *had used*, *headed*).
- The author writes in the third person (*he*, *them*, *they*).
- The text has compound sentences (clauses joined by *and* and *but*) to join or compare ideas.
- The author uses conditional clauses (*if* …) to explain relationships between facts.

See also **chronological**; **clauses**; **conditional clauses**; **person**; **verbs**: **Past**.

Journal

In a nonfiction journal, writers record their experiences or observations. Scientists and travellers often keep journals. The journal entries are usually dated and may have other background information such as the daily weather. The journal entries are often short.

The following example shows two entries from the journal of an expedition leader in Antarctica. He records weather conditions each day, the end of a journey and a description of the environment.

Date: Thursday, 6th February, 1992
Temperature: -3°C
Weather: Another cloudy day with some wind
    Returned safely to Mawson with tractor train.

Winter freeze sets in

Date: Friday, 13th March, 1992
Temperature: -12°C
Weather: A little cloudy and
           almost no wind
    The sea has begun to freeze.
Some 'pancake' ice has formed
in the harbour.

Antarctic journal, p. 5

- The entries begin with subheadings (Date, Temperature, Weather, Location). Each subheading is followed by a colon.
- The author records measures — details that might be useful for observation later. Such details are important in scientific journals. He uses abbreviations to save space and time.
- The information is recorded in chronological order.
- The text is brief. The author is making short notes about the main events and conditions of each day. Some words are left out of sentences. *'[We] Returned safely to Mawson ...'*

See also **chronological**; **colon (:)**; **measures**; **sentence fragments**.

Media articles (journalism)
Writers for newspapers and other media are called *journalists*. They often recount events that have already happened. They get their information by observing, interviewing and researching. In the following example, the writer recounts the story of the rescue of a cockatoo.

Hello Cocky!

Rosedale, South Australia, 1992: When 'Cocky' a featherless, sulphur-crested cockatoo was found eight years ago, the vet said it would never survive.

Cocky

Cocky had an incurable disease, which stops new feathers from growing. The bird's rescuer decided to knit it woollen coats to keep it warm. Winter coats are made of thicker wool and have higher necks than summer coats. All the coats have little leggings, a hole at the back and are shaped around Cocky's wings. One coat had a Superman emblem, but Cocky didn't like it and picked it off. The coats have to be stitched round the cockatoo while it lies on its stomach.

When first rescued, Cocky was spoon-fed baby cereal. It now eats almost anything, including nibbles from the dog's plate. Its biggest treats are walnuts from the garden.

Cocky cannot fly, but plays with the family dog and cats. At night, it sleeps in an aviary, safe from foxes and other predators.

Rescues, p. 15

- The story has a headline — a short phrase that tells what the story is about. The author has used an exclamation mark to give the impression that the story might be exciting.
- The text begins in the past tense but finishes in the present — the author summarises the recount by giving a short report of ongoing events.
- The first sentence gives the place and time, and a summary of what the story is about. It is in larger type than the main text. This is sometimes called *banner text*.
- The sentences after the banner text give details about the event. The last sentences in the article are less important than the rest. They could be left out without changing the sense of the article.

See also **exclamation mark (!)**; **journalism**; **verbs**: **Tenses (time)**.

recount

recount

Oral history
An oral history is a record of a person's life memories. A writer usually records an interview with the person whose life the writing is about. So the writing is based more on the *person's* words than the *writer's* words.

In the following example, a woman, named Pilawuk, recounts her childhood and school life.

> I went to a lot of schools. I loved school. I don't remember much of the schoolwork. I think I looked forward mostly to being with the other kids. But I did love sewing, singing, art and sport. After second year high school, I left the second family and boarded at Cabra College.

Pilawuk: When I was young, p. 12

- Pilawuk is recording her own experiences, so the writing is in the first person — she uses the pronoun *I*.
- The author uses informal words. The word *kids* is used rather than *children*, because this was the language of the interviewee.
- Contractions are used (*don't*). This makes the text sound more informal and true to the interviewee's language.
- The story is told in chronological order.
- The verbs are in the past tense.

See also **chronological**; **contractions**; **formal / informal writing**; **person**; **verbs: Past**.

Transcript
A transcript is an accurate written recount of a conversation. It is a form of oral history. The following conversation between the 'Eagle' spacecraft and ground control station on earth was recorded during their pioneering journey in 1969. The actual words they said are presented as a transcript.

> were landing on the Moon at a place called the *Sea of Tranquility*. This is what they said:
>
> | | |
> |---|---|
> | Eagle: | Coming down nicely...200 feet, 4½ down...5½ down...5 percent...75 feet...6 forward lights on...down 2½...40 feet, down 2½, kicking up some dust...30 feet, 2½ down, faint shadow...4 forward...4 forward...drifting to right a little...OK. |
> | Ground control: | Thirty seconds. |
> | Eagle: | Contact light. OK engine stop...descent engine command override off. |
> | Ground control: | We copy you down Eagle. |
> | Eagle: | Houston, Tranquility Base here. The Eagle has landed. |
> | Ground control: | Roger, Tranquility. We copy you on the ground. You got a bunch of guys about to turn blue. We're breathing again. Thanks a lot. |

The first lunar landing, p. 11

- A transcript is set out like a play script. The names of the speakers are in the left-hand column and are followed by a colon.
- The text has incomplete sentences (*sentence fragments*) because that is how people speak. In this transcript the speakers are using technical language.
- Some of the verbs are in the present tense because the people speaking are describing things as they happen.
- The grammar is not always standard English or formal writing. (*You got a bunch of guys about to turn blue.*)

See also **colloquial language**; **colon (:)**; **formal / informal writing**; **sentence fragments**; **technical language**; **transcript**; **verbs**: **Present**.

redundancy

A redundancy is the use of more words than necessary in writing or speech.

> They are busy **at this point in time**. (X)
> They are busy **now**. (✓)

The phrase *at this point in time* uses more words than necessary. The word *now* expresses this meaning more simply.

> The reason for the heatwave is **because of** global warming. (X)
> The reason for the heatwave is global warming. (✓)

In this example, the words *because of* are unnecessary.

> The tree **fell and crashed** to the ground. (X)
> The tree **crashed** to the ground. (✓)
> The tree **fell** to the ground. (✓)

In this example, the words *fell* and *crashed* are so similar in meaning, that only one is needed.

See also **oxymoron**; **tautology**.

reference text

Reference texts are a form of report text. They present facts about a topic in an organised way. Reference texts usually have a lot of small pieces of information on many headings within a topic. Dictionaries, thesauruses and encyclopedias are all reference texts. The *Young writers guide* is a reference text.

Readers do not usually read reference texts from front to back like a story. They usually look for certain information, then put the text away until they need it again. The way the reader uses the text makes a difference to the way the writer organises the information. To make information easy to find, reference texts are usually organised in small parcels of text called *entries*. Each entry has a *headword*. The headwords are organised in alphabetical order, or in topic categories (*chapters*).

See also **headwords**; **report**: **Reference texts**.

reflexive pronouns
See **pronouns**: **Reflexive pronouns**.

relative clauses
Relative clause is a term used in grammar. It means a clause that begins with one of the relative pronouns — *who*, *whom, which* or *that*. Relative clauses are used to describe a noun or pronoun. Because they describe people or things, they are also called *adjectival clauses*.

> She painted a picture **that made the room glow.**

In the example above, the relative clause *that made the room glow* describes the noun *picture*.

Further examples:
> They drove to an address **that was not there**.
> The fish was caught by methods **that do not harm dolphins**.
> Tzu Cheng, **who plays the bassoon**, is in the orchestra.
> They met an old friend, **whom they had not seen for years**.

See also **adjectival clauses**; **pronouns**: **Relative pronouns**.

relative pronouns
See **pronouns**: **Relative pronouns**.

report
A report gives information on a topic. The topic may be on one thing (eg *the blue whale*) or a group of things (eg *whales*). A report does not explain how or why something happens — it just gives facts. The facts are organised in different ways to give the report structure. This makes it easier for the reader to find information and to understand it.

Reports usually have two main parts:

- *Introduction or general statement*

The introduction or general statement introduces the reader to the topic. The writer may define the subject and describe the focus of the writing. The introduction should get the reader interested in the subject.

- *Detailed facts*

The body of a report gives detailed facts, which can be structured in different ways. The facts in reports are usually grouped under headings, subheadings and paragraphs. Information can be presented as illustrations, diagrams, sketches, charts, maps or photos with headings, labels and captions.

See also **case study**; **cause and effect**; **compare and contrast**; **question-and-answer text**.

Details about the text features and structure of reports are given under the following headings:

Language features
Structure
> *Case studies*
> *Cause and effect*
> *Classification*
> *Compare and contrast*
> *Question and answer — interviews*
> *Question and answer — quiz*
> *Reference texts*

Language features

Points about the language features of reports:

- The nouns, especially in the introduction, are plural (*whales, mammals, snakes*) or general (*a whale, a mammal, a snake*).
- The verbs are usually in the simple present tense. (Whales *are* mammals.)
- The writing tends to be formal. Third person pronouns (*he, she, it, they, them*) are used rather than first person pronouns (*I, me, we, us*).
- Adverbs that tell 'how much or how many' (*all, most, some, few, only, mainly, often, sometimes*) are used. These adverbs are called *modifiers* and *intensifiers.* They allow the author to begin with general information (*all, every*), then become more focused (*some, few, mainly, many*) and finally go to details (*each, only*).

> **All** whales are mammals. **Some** whales have teeth. **Only** the narwhal has a tusk.

See also **intensifiers**; **modifiers**; **nouns**; **person**; **plural**; **verbs**: **Present**.

report

Structure
There are different ways to organise and plan the body of a report:

Case studies
Writers use case studies when they cannot fit everything known about a topic into one book. Case studies give readers facts through examples.

In the following example, the contents page from a report called *Investigating fungi* shows how the author organised the information. It has been organised under chapter headings *(What are fungi?)* and sub-headings *(Gill fungi, Caterpillar fungi)*. Each sub-heading is a case study — information on just one kind of fungus.

* The book begins with an introduction and general information about fungi — *What are fungi?*
* The facts are organised into case studies that give particular examples — *Puffballs, Stinkhorns, Luminous fungi* ...
* The photos have captions.
* The author writes in the present tense.
* Conditional clauses *(If ...)* are used to explain relationships between facts.
* Measures are used to explain size.

Contents

Puffballs

Puffballs are like pouches of spores. If you step on a ripe puffball, it sends up a cloud of spores. Some puffballs are very large, up to about 1.8 metres (5.9 ft) in circumference!

◄ Common puffballs, *Lycoperdon sp.* Usually found in grasslands and forests.

Earthstar, *Geastrum indicum* ⱽ

Puffballs called *Earthstars* can be used as weather forecasters. If wet weather is coming, the points open so that spores can spread, but if the weather is very dry, they close.

Investigating fungi, pp. 2, 10

The next example of a case study, from a book called *A checkup with the doctor*, gives facts about one instrument a doctor uses. Not all doctors' instruments were included in the book — only case studies that were suited to the topic of the book.

Ophthalmoscope (off-**thal**-ma-skope)

Inside the eye

The doctor uses an ophthalmoscope to look inside your eyes (see diagram opposite). She can see the back of your eye with the magnifying lens. The doctor also checks the movement of your pupils by shining a light onto them and watching to see if they become smaller.

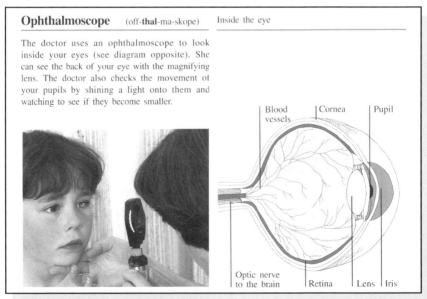

Blood vessels | Cornea | Pupil

Optic nerve to the brain | Retina | Lens | Iris

A checkup with the doctor, pp. 8–9

- A pronunciation guide is used for a technical word.
- The author explains what the instrument is used for.
- A labelled cross-section diagram shows the individual parts of the instrument.
- A photograph shows what the instrument looks like and how it is used.

Cause and effect
The following example comes from a book that reports on natural disasters. The author gives facts about cyclones — why and where they happen (*the cause*) and what is the result (*the effect*).

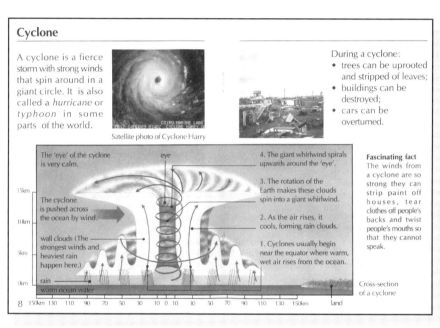

Cyclone

A cyclone is a fierce storm with strong winds that spin around in a giant circle. It is also called a *hurricane* or *typhoon* in some parts of the world.

Satellite photo of Cyclone Harry

During a cyclone:
- trees can be uprooted and stripped of leaves;
- buildings can be destroyed;
- cars can be overturned.

The 'eye' of the cyclone is very calm.

eye

The cyclone is pushed across the ocean by wind.

wall clouds (The strongest winds and heaviest rain happen here.)

rain

warm ocean water

4. The giant whirlwind spirals upwards around the 'eye'.

3. The rotation of the Earth makes these clouds spin into a giant whirlwind.

2. As the air rises, it cools, forming rain clouds.

1. Cyclones usually begin near the equator where warm, wet air rises from the ocean.

Fascinating fact
The winds from a cyclone are so strong they can strip paint off houses, tear clothes off people's backs and twist people's mouths so that they cannot speak.

Cross-section of a cyclone

15km 10km 5km 0km

8 150km 130 110 90 70 50 30 10 0 10 30 50 70 90 110 130 150km land

Natural disasters, pp. 8-9

- The verbs are in the simple present tense — *is, spin, is called, can be*.
- The text is written in impersonal language. The author uses the pronoun *it* when explaining what a cyclone is and what causes it. Impersonal language makes the writing sound more official or scientific.
- A cross-section labelled diagram is used to explain the process of the weather system that causes cyclones. It is often easier and better to present facts in diagrams.
- Facts on the effects of cyclones are presented in a bullet point list. Lists are useful for giving a lot of information in a small space.
- The author uses arrows, scales and numbered captions to help the reader understand the diagram.

- The author gives extra information (*Fascinating fact*) to make the report more interesting.

See also **captions and legends; impersonal writing; lists; verbs: Tenses (time)**.

Classification

The following example shows how an author reports information on a whole class of things by grouping the information into categories. In this case the categories are three main levels of the flora and fauna found in a rainforest. The author presents the information as a guidebook or a field guide for tourists.

Contents	Introduction

Contents

Introduction

A rainforest is a special kind of forest:
- It is wetter than other sorts of forests.
- Tree tops form a canopy which blocks out most of the sunlight.
- Trees are usually evergreens with broad leaves.
- Plants grow on other plants from the forest floor to the canopy.
- More kinds of plants and animals are found in a rainforest than other forests.

This book is a guide to a walk in a sub-tropical rainforest called Lamington National Park. The 'tree top' walk takes you from the forest floor to the top of the trees.

Forest canopy

Forest understory

Forest floor

Life in a rainforest, pp. 2–3

- The *contents* page shows how the author classifies the information in the book into different categories — the three main layers of a rainforest.
- The *introduction* defines the tropical rainforest by listing information in bullet points. The clause introducing the list ends with a colon. The list is made up of a series of sentences that each complete the opening clause *A rainforest is a special kind of forest*.
- Each point begins with a lower case letter because it continues from the opening clause.
- Each point (except the last) ends with a semicolon, because it is not the end of the whole sentence.
- The opening clause together with the bullet points form one sentence.
- The verbs in the list are all in the simple present tense — *are*, *grow*, *is*.

- Most nouns in the list are plural — *plants*, *trees*, *leaves*. This makes the information general.
- In the closing paragraph of the introduction, the author uses the second person pronoun (*you*) because the text is addressing the audience (*tourists*) directly. It makes the writing more informal and friendly.

See also **bullet points (•)**; **colon (:)**; **full stop (.)**; **person**; **plural**; **sentence beginnings**: **Lists**; **verbs**: **Present**.

Compare and contrast
In the following example, an author compares one group of whales to another.

All whales are mammals and so have warm blood. They mate and produce live young which drink milk from the mothers.

In place of arms, whales have flippers. All whales have a tail with two horizontal sections called *flukes*. Some whales have a back *(dorsal)* fin.

There are two main groups of whales - *baleen* whales and *toothed* whales. Today there are 11 known species of *baleen* whale and about 30 species of *toothed* whale. Toothed and baleen whales differ in several ways.

Baleen whales:
- have plates of baleen (whalebone) which hang down from the upper jaw - the baleen have small fibres which help to sieve food from the water;
- may use sonar; but if so, to a lesser degree than toothed whales;
- move from food-rich waters, which may mean going without food for many months;
- have no recorded live mass stranding;
- are usually born head first (not fully known);
- eat mainly krill;
- make sounds including moans, rumbles and chirps.

Toothed whales:
- have teeth which are usually all the same size and shape - they keep the one set throughout their life;
- use sonar to explore their surroundings - the sounds used are called clicks;
- tend to stay in food-rich waters throughout the year;
- (some species) are sometimes seen in live mass strandings;
- mostly seen to be born tail first;
- eat mainly squid, octopus, cuttlefish and fish;
- make sounds including whistles, clicks and groans.

Baleen, p. 39

- The introduction begins with general statements about whales. It uses the words *all* and *some*, then describes *two main groups*.
- The information is organised into lists that compare facts.
- Each list has a heading (a noun phrase), followed by a colon.
- Each dot point completes a sentence from the heading of each list.
- The main points in each list end with a semicolon, except the last point, which ends with a full stop.

- The author uses the impersonal tone in the report, writing about whales generally and not giving them character names.

See also **colon (:)**; **impersonal writing**; **noun phrases**; **semicolon (;)**.

In the next example of compare and contrast, an author uses illustrations to compare the size of a landform with other objects. This gives the reader a clear understanding of size. The author also compares two different cultural explanations for the same facts, to tell the reader about different cultures.

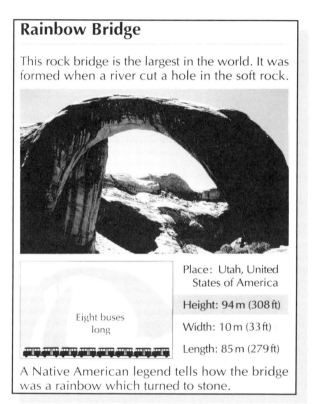

Rainbow Bridge

This rock bridge is the largest in the world. It was formed when a river cut a hole in the soft rock.

Eight buses long

Place: Utah, United States of America

Height: 94 m (308 ft)

Width: 10 m (33 ft)

Length: 85 m (279 ft)

A Native American legend tells how the bridge was a rainbow which turned to stone.

Amazing landforms, p.16

- An illustration is used to compare the rock to the length of eight buses.
- Data (*measures*) are given under subheadings (*place, height, width, length*). A colon is used after each subheading.
- Abbreviations are used for units of measure in a data list.
- The text explains from two different points of view, how the rock was formed, so the reader can compare different cultures. This statement is brief, because the main focus of the text is to give facts, not explain how things happened.
- Capital letters are used for the name of an ethnic group (*Native American*).

report

See also **capitals**: **Proper nouns**; **colon (:)**; **measures**: **Abbreviations**; **quotation marks**: **Words being explained**.

Question and answer — interviews
Writers often get information for a report by interviewing the person or people they want to write about. When writers want to get information from interviews, they prepare questions that will focus on the information they need to write about the topic. Their writing is then based on the answers from the interviewee.

In the following example, the author interviewed a clown.

- In the introduction, the author describes the topic (*entertainers*) and how he got the information (*interviews*). He lists the facts he searched for in the interviews — How did the clown become an entertainer? What does he enjoy about his job? What special skills does he need?
- The author uses third person pronouns (*his, he, him*) when talking about the clown.
- The clown's words from the interview are put in quotation marks.
- The clown uses first person pronouns (*my, I*) because he is talking about himself. But when the author writes about the clown, he uses the third person (*he, his, him*).
- When the author first refers to the clown's stage name, he uses single quotation marks (*'Fritz Sandwich'*). Further use of his stage name is not surrounded by quotation marks.
- When the author writes about a word and wants to draw attention to it, he uses single quotation marks. (*'Peter' is his real name.*)
- The author does not write the actual interview questions he asked. The topics the clown comments on, are introduced as statements.

See also **person**; **pronouns**; **quotation marks**: **Quotations**; **sentences**: **Questions**, **Statements**.

Entertainers are people who amuse us. They might be paid entertainers or friends who are clever and can make us laugh.

Magician
Ray Crowe

Storyteller
Dorinda Hafner

Clown
'Fritz Sandwich'

This book is based on interviews with three people who are paid entertainers. It describes how each person became an entertainer, and what they enjoy about their jobs. Each entertainer also gives hints or trade secrets about his or her work.

'Fritz Sandwich' is a clown. His main job is to make people smile, laugh and feel happy.

Fritz ('Peter' is his real name) became a clown while delivering singing telegrams. His boss dared him to do a clown's job for a children's party! Peter had no idea that he would become a clown.

"It is my whole working life. It is what I do."

Question and answer — quiz

In the following example, an author uses a question-and-answer report to create a quiz text.

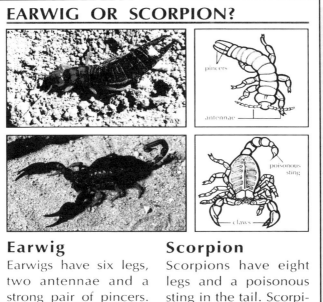

EARWIG OR SCORPION?

Earwig
Earwigs have six legs, two antennae and a strong pair of pincers. They do not have a sting or claws.

Scorpion
Scorpions have eight legs and a poisonous sting in the tail. Scorpions do not have antennae. They use two large pairs of claws for holding prey.

Which is which?, p. 8

- The report compares pairs of animals that look similar.
- The heading for each section is a question.
- Photographs and drawings give the reader clues.
- Details about each animal are grouped under subheadings.
- The text is impersonal — the author does not give the animals pet names or treat them as characters.
- The text about each animal is in the plural because the author refers to the animals in general.
- The verbs are in the simple present tense (*have, do, use*).
- The pronouns in the body of the report are all in the third person plural (*they*).

See also **impersonal writing**; **plural**; **pronouns**; **question mark (?)**; **sentences**: Questions; **verbs**: Present.

Reference texts

Facts in reference texts are usually organised under subheadings called *headwords*. Encyclopedias, dictionaries and this *guide* are reference books.

The following example from an encyclopedia, gives medical facts. Each headword is about a different topic, but all the topics are medical. Publishers use different rules and styles for different reference books, so the following points may not be true for all reference books.

---

ge-im

German measles: (See RUBELLA)

goose bumps Many tiny bumps on the skin. Caused by muscles in the skin tightening and making hairs stand on end. Happens when people are cold or frightened.

hay fever Allergic reaction to smoke, dust, pollen from hay grasses etc. getting in the nose. Causes sneezing, 'runny' nose and watery eyes.

hiccup; hiccough Sound which happens when air pushes suddenly on the voice-box and closes it. This makes a 'hic' sound. May be caused by many things, e.g. full stomach, tiredness etc.

immunization Use of medicine to help the body resist diseases like measles, mumps, polio and hepatitis. Medicine can be injected or taken as a syrup.

A children's medical encyclopedia, p. 15

- The headwords are listed in alphabetical order.
- The headwords are in bold type so they are easy to find.
- The headwords do not begin with a capital letter unless they are proper nouns.
- Sentence fragments are used to fit more information into the encyclopedia, and make it quicker to read.
- Cross-references are in brackets.
- Headwords in cross-references are in small capitals.
- Abbreviations such as *eg* and *etc* are used to save space.

See also **cross-references**; **emphasis**; **headwords**; **Latin abbreviations**; **nouns**: **Proper nouns**; **sentence fragments**; **small capitals**.

reported speech

See **indirect speech**.

research

Research is a part of the writing process. It is the stage when authors find the information they need so they can write with confidence. Research includes interviews, reading, note taking and experimentation with ideas and methods (eg testing recipes).

See also **procedure**: **Recipe**; **writing process**: **Researching**.

response text

See **review**.

review

A *review* is a text in which the author gives a professional or expert opinion about an event or product. Reviews can be about books, music, performances, paintings, movies, web sites, government policies or consumer products (eg washing machines, cars, foods etc). Reviews are sometimes called *critical reviews* or *response texts*.

A review usually has three main parts:

Introduction
The author defines the topic of the review. The introduction can include facts that give background information on the topic.

Critical opinion or questioning
The author gives expert opinions about the strengths and weaknesses of the topic.

Summary
The author summarises the strengths and weaknesses and makes a judgment about the topic. It can include recommendations to the reader.

Future World
'Future World', the latest movie by Global Studios, stars Rick Wycket and Amelia Lightheart. This high-budget, futuristic fantasy broke box office records in its first week. The story is based on the idea of the world being plunged into an ice age by a nuclear war. The few remaining humans face life in a harsh environment without technology.

The producers obviously spent much of their budget on stunning visual effects. The techno-wizards used the latest digital techniques to create an impressive setting that is completely believable.

Less believable is the wicked performance of Wycket, who was reputedly paid (or *over-paid*) three million for his role. For a fantasy, his acting is not fantastic, in contrast to Lightheart, a fresh talent who will undoubtedly become a star.

The screenwriters fail to provide a credible story-line. The plot has more holes than a Swiss cheese and leaves too many questions unanswered. This is the real downfall of this expensive project.

Overall, this is a very average movie. The only benefit of seeing it on the big screen is the visual effects. Save your money and see it at home for half the price when it reaches the small screen. Rating ☆☆

- In the first paragraph, the writer gives background facts about the topic — the title, the people involved, statistics (numbers, money or records) and a summary of the theme.
- In the next three paragraphs, the writer gives opinions about strengths and weaknesses. Use is made of puns and other clever or witty use of words. This makes the writing entertaining or more interesting to the reader. Often this witty language becomes sarcastic:
  the *wicked* performance of *Wycket*
  paid (or *over-paid*)
  For a *fantasy*, his acting was not *fantastic*.
  The plot has *more holes than a Swiss cheese*.
- The last paragraph is the summary. It includes the reviewer's or critic's recommendation. The writer uses commands (*Save your money* and *see it at home* …) when recommending what action the reader should take.
- The writer uses the present tense when describing the movie (*stars*, *is based*, *fail*, *has*, *leaves*, *is*) and the past tense when recalling facts (*broke*, *spent*, *used*).

See also **pun**; **sentences**: **Commands**; **verbs**: **Tenses (time)**.

revising

Revising is part of the writing process. After writing a rough draft, an author needs to revise the work to improve the style and to make it ready for other people, such as editors, to read. When revising, the author is mainly concerned with the main ideas and organisation of the writing. Spelling, punctuation and grammar are not so important at this stage.

See also **writing process**: **Revising**.

rhetorical questions

Questions to which the speaker or writer does not expect an answer are called *rhetorical questions*. They are sometimes asked and answered by the speaker.

> My dog had ten pups. **Did you hear me?** Ten pups!
> **Remember what the guide said?** Don't wander off the track.

A rhetorical question can be a single word.

> They said I was disqualified. **Why**?

rhyme

Rhyme is the linking of words with similar end sounds. The following word pairs rhyme.

> game/claim, hero/zero, see/agree, fiesta/siesta,
> alligator/commentator

Words that rhyme do not always end with the same letters (*game/claim*). They do not always have the same number of syllables (*see/agree*).

Rhyme is most commonly used in verse. The poet places the rhyming words at the ends of lines in a verse.

> A young girl was walking in **Kent**,
> When she stepped on some fresh-laid **cement**.
> To her shock and **dismay**,
> It set **straightaway**,
> And now she's a street **ornament**.

There was a big fish, p. 11

Verse can be written with different rhyming patterns. This example is a limerick. Limericks have a rhyming pattern of AABBA. This means that lines one, two and five rhyme, and lines three and four rhyme.

> They sawed the giant **trunk**,
> And toppled it to the **floor**.
> Into the bark were **sunk**,
> Steel teeth — a monster's **jaw**.

This example has an ABAB rhyming pattern. This means that every second line of a verse rhymes.

> They sawed the giant trunk,
> And felled that great old **tree**.
> And on its giant stump,
> A ringed history I could **see**.

This example has an ABCB rhyming pattern. This means that only the second and fourth lines of a verse rhyme.

Rhyme is also used in narrative texts where the rhyme is within a sentence. This is called *internal rhyme*.

Like a tower of **green** so rarely **seen**, the great old tree toppled.

See also **poetry**.

rhyming couplet
See **couplet**.

RIP

RIP means 'may he/she rest in peace'. It is used on tombstones and at the head of an obituary.

See also **acronyms**; **obituary**; WORD HISTORIES: **RIP**.

road / rode
Rode is the past tense of the verb *to ride*.

The young whale **rode** on its mother's back!

A *road* is a way that has been cleared for vehicles to travel on.

That **road** leads to a lake on the other side of the forest.

roar
See **raw / roar**.

sauce / source

These words sound the same, but their spellings and meanings are quite different.

Sauce is a noun. It means 'anything liquid or soft that is poured on or mixed with food to add flavour'.

The cook added the meat **sauce** to the pasta.

Source can be a noun. It means 'the place anything comes from'.
> The explorers tried to find the **source** of the River Nile.
> The **source** of the information was a secret.

See also **nouns**.

saw / soar / sore

Saw can be:

* a noun meaning 'a tool used for cutting'
  > The carpenter had to sharpen his **saw**.

* the past tense of the verb 'to see'
  > We **saw** a giant dog on the track at night.

Soar is a verb meaning 'to fly'.
> Along the cliff face, the winds allowed the eagle to **soar**.

Sore can be:
* a noun meaning 'a wound'
  > The **sore** took weeks to heal.
* an adjective meaning 'painful'
  > She had a **sore** throat from yelling all day at the football.

See also **adjectives**; **nouns**; **verbs: Tenses (time)**.

scared / scarred

Scared and *scarred* look similar — but they sound different and they have different meanings.

Scared can be an adjective. It means 'afraid'.
> The pet rabbit shivered whenever it was **scared**.
> "I feel **scared** when it is dark," said the child.

Scared can be a verb. It is the past tense of 'scare'. It is pronounced /skaird/ to rhyme with *shared*. It means 'to frighten'.
> The noise of the gun-shot **scared** the birds away from the fruit trees.

Scarred is a form of the word *scar*. It is pronounced /skard/ to rhyme with *card*. *Scarred* can be an adjective. It means 'marked with a scar'.
> The girl's **scarred** hand was protected by a glove.

Scarred can be a verb. It means 'to cause an injury that leaves a scar'.
> Hannah **scarred** her hand when she burnt it on the oven.

scene / seen

Scene is a noun. It means 'a place where something happens; a view'

> Firefighters, ambulance teams and police rushed to the **scene**.
> The artist painted a **scene** of the hills and a lake.

Seen is a form of the verb to see.

> Germs are too small to be **seen** without a microscope.

seam / seem

Seam is a noun. It means 'a line where two edges are joined'.

> The **seam** in her cloak had pulled apart and looked ragged.

Seem is a verb. It means 'to appear to be'.

> Now that you have explained it, things **seem** very clear to me.
> Magicians **seem** to make things appear and disappear.
> They **seem** to be very honest people.

seas / sees / seize

These three words all sound alike, but their spellings and meanings are different.

Seas is the plural of the noun sea. It means 'oceans, great areas of salt water'.

> Transport ships sail the **seas**.

Sees is the present tense of the verb to see.

> Put it back before someone **sees** it is missing.

Seize is a verb. It means 'to grab, hold, take'.

> **Seize** them and search the ship!

semicolon (;)

The semicolon marks a break in a sentence — it is a stronger pause than a comma. It gives a more dramatic introduction to the words after it.

A semicolon *links* ideas. A comma *separates* ideas. Ideas linked by a semicolon could also be written as separate sentences.

> The first attack was a surprise; next time it would be different.

This example could be written as two separate sentences. However, the semicolon links the two ideas more strongly and makes the second part of the sentence sound more exciting.

Further examples where the semicolon makes the second idea more dramatic:

> Hundreds of voices were calling; hundreds of people were parting.
>
> He wished he could help; he'd feel much more useful.

Semicolons are also used:

In dictionary and glossary definitions
In lists
In series

In dictionary and glossary definitions

The semicolon is often used to separate the main ideas in dictionary and glossary definitions.

> **CFC** Chlorofluorocarbon; chemical that harms the ozone layer.
>
> **granite** Very hard rock; formed from magma.

In lists

Semicolons are used to separate the ideas in a list (unless the items are single words, or short phrases). When semicolons are used in lists, the last item ends with a full stop.

> For example, people can:
> * buy non-toxic products and refuse to buy goods in unnecessary packaging;
> * persuade politicians to protect the environment;
> * recycle waste.

See also **report**: **Compare and contrast**.

In series

Semicolons are often used to separate the ideas in long sentences with a series of thoughts.

> She thought about home, and how she hoped she could return some day; about Dad, her life-long helper; about Mum, who had been so patient; and about her brother, whom she'd often teased.

sentence fragments

Sentence fragments are groups of words that are incomplete sentences. They are missing either a subject or a complete verb — or both.

Sentence fragments are common in speech and informal writing (diaries, notes etc). They are punctuated the same way as complete sentences.

> "Saw a satellite! A speck in the night sky! Gliding across the stars."

In this example, none of the groups of words is a complete sentence; they are all sentence fragments. The author has used sentence fragments to make the language more realistic for a character's speech — a series of thoughts in which parts are taken for granted and not put into words.

Sentence fragments are often used in reference books such as dictionaries and encyclopedias, where writers need to fit a lot of information in a small space. Unnecessary words are left out.

> **rabbit** Small, furry four-legged mammal. Eats grass.

In this example, *Small, furry four-legged mammal* has no verb. *Eats grass has no subject* (it is assumed from the headword that the reader knows the subject is *rabbit*). So they are both sentence fragments.

Captions to pictures, charts and diagrams are often sentence fragments.

> Giraffe in shade of a tall tree
> Zookeeper feeding a python

See also **captions and legends**; **report: Reference texts**; **sentences**; **recount: Transcript**.

sentences

A sentence is usually a group of words that has a main clause — a subject and a finite verb. The finite verb and any words adding to it are called the *predicate* of the sentence.

> The bird [*subject*] sang. [*predicate*]
> The tiny bird [*subject*] sang its tune from the tree. [*predicate*]

Sentences begin with a capital letter and end with some form of punctuation. The punctuation mark could be:
- a full stop (.)
  > Jonno was the fittest member of the team.
- a question mark (?)
  > Who took my toothbrush?
- an exclamation mark (!)
  > "Help! I can't swim!"
- or an ellipsis (…)
  > "We were happy, until …"
  > "Until what?" asked Jin Yoon.

The following topics show you details on the main sentence types and some hints on ways to structure them and use them in your writing.

Commands
Exclamations
Interjections
Questions
Statements
Sentence structures
> *Sentence fragments*
> *Simple sentences*

sentences

Compound sentences
Complex sentences
Order of words, phrases and clauses
Sentence length

Commands

Sentences can be used to give commands, orders or directions. These are sometimes called *imperative sentences*. The subject of a command is often not written — it is understood that the subject is *you*.

> Apply here for a job.

In this example, the sentence begins with the verb *apply*. The subject is understood to be *you*.

Commands usually end with a full stop, unless a writer wants to say something forcefully — then an exclamation mark would be used.

> Get out!

Further examples of commands:

> Tie a knot in one end of the rope.
> Don't buy products with unnecessary packaging.
> Always wash your hands before cooking.

See also **argument**: **Advertisements**; **procedures**: **First aid procedure**.

Writing tip

Commands

Commands are useful in particular kinds of writing, such as:

- procedures — recipes, rules to games, manuals for using equipment, instructions for making or doing something etc.

  Add the sugar and butter, and mix the ingredients.

- persuasive texts

  Hurry, before it's too late! Get your free sample today.

- morals in *fables* — stories with a lesson

  Make hay while the sun shines.

See also **argument**; **narrative**: **Fable**; **procedure**.

Exclamations

Exclamations are sentences that express strong feelings such as surprise, excitement, fear, pain or happiness. They usually end with an exclamation mark (!).

> I've been robbed!
> We won the race!
> My leg is broken!

See also **argument**: **Advertisements**; **exclamation mark (!)**.

Writing tip

Using exclamations

Here are some ways you can use exclamations.

• Emphasise a point in an argument

> Don't buy fish from countries that use driftnets. It costs too much!

• Attract attention in an advertisement

> Our discount specials will amaze you!

• Make a newspaper headline seem dramatic or sensational

> IT'S WAR ON DRUGS!

Interjections

This is a special group of words that are often one-word sentences. They are sounds that express feelings, but they are not necessarily listed in dictionaries. People can invent them to suit their needs.

> Yee-ha! Yahoo! Wow! Ssh! Zowie! Zipitty-do!

See also **interjections**.

Questions

Sentences can be used to ask questions. These are sometimes called *interrogative sentences*. Questions (except for indirect questions) end with a question mark.

> What is the price of that book?
> You could help me, couldn't you?
> Who discovered penicillin?

Some questions cannot be answered with yes or no. They are called open questions.

> What do you think of the new school principal?
> Why won't you help me?
> Where is the nearest shop?

Open questions are useful for getting people to talk more or for finding out information.

See also **argument**: **Debate**; **interrogatives**; **question mark (?)**; **questions**: **Open and closed questions**.

Statements

Sentences can be used to make statements. These are sometimes called *declarative sentences* because they declare or state something. Most statements end with a full stop.

> Once upon a time there was a river in this valley.
> Some people actually enjoy shopping.
> Antibiotics kill germs, especially bacteria, or stop them from growing.

See also **argument**: **Letter to the editor**; **explanation**.

Sentence structures

Sentence fragments

An incomplete sentence is called a sentence fragment. A subject without a predicate, or a predicate without a subject, is not a complete sentence.

> the bird (This is a subject without a predicate. What happened about the bird?)
> sang in the tree (This is a predicate without a subject. Who or what sang?)

There are three main types of complete sentence. You know the structure of a sentence by the number and kind of clauses it has.

Simple sentences

Simple sentences are made with just one main clause.

> The bird sang.

In this example, the subject is *The bird*; the verb is *sang*. Together, this group of words forms a main clause and makes a simple sentence.

Compound sentences

Compound sentences are made from two or more main clauses, joined with a conjunction (*and, but, or, so, yet*). Each clause in the sentence is equally important.

> The bird sang in the tree, **but** no one was listening.

The conjunction *but* joins the two main clauses *The bird sang in the tree*, and *no one was listening*, to make a compound sentence.

> The woman had matted hair and a tired face, **and** some of her teeth were missing.

In this example, the two main clauses *The woman had matted hair and a tired face* and *some of her teeth were missing* are joined by the conjunction *and* to make one compound sentence.

Complex sentences

A complex sentence is made from a *subordinate clause* and a *main clause*. In a complex sentence, the main clause is the most important part of the sentence. The subordinate clause adds meaning to the main clause — but it cannot be a sentence by itself.

> As usual he gave a big grin [*main clause*] that made everyone happy [*subordinate clause*].

> But when her father was not at home, [*subordinate clause*] she began to worry. [*main clause*]

> When the game was over, [*subordinate clause*] she would celebrate. [*main clause*]

See also **clauses**: **Main clauses**, **Subordinate clauses**; **conjunctions**.

Order of words, phrases and clauses

The order of words, phrases and clauses in sentences can be varied to make your writing more interesting. Even the position of the subject and the verb can sometimes be changed without changing the meaning of the sentence.

- It is common in an English sentence, to place the subject before its verb.
  > The terrified rider tumbled down the hill.

In this example, the subject *The terrified rider* comes before its verb *tumbled*.

- It is possible to place the subject *after* the verb.
  > Down the hill tumbled [*verb*] **the terrified rider**. [*subject*]

In this example, the subject of the sentence *the terrified rider* has been placed after the verb *tumbled*. The sentence begins with the adverb phrase *Down the hill*. This makes the sentence sound more dramatic.

- A sentence can begin with an adverbial phrase.
  > **Beyond the hills**, a barren desert awaited the explorers.

The phrase *Beyond the hills* tells *where* a barren desert awaited.

- A sentence can begin with an adverbial clause.
  > **Before she knew it**, she'd lost her way.

The clause *Before she knew it* tells *when* she'd lost her way.

* A sentence can begin with adjectives.
    Dark and sinister, the storm clouds gathered.

The adjectives *dark and sinister* describe the subject *the storm clouds*.

* A sentence can begin with a series of noun phrases.
    The bold rider, **the brave horse** and **the eager dog** plodded on into the desert.

This sentence has a compound subject (more than one noun phrase): *The bold rider, the brave horse*, and *the eager dog*. In this example, the author has also made the sentence interesting by using a different adjective (*bold*, *brave* and *eager*) for each noun in the subject.

* A sentence can begin with a noun clause.
    How we will solve this problem, I don't know!

In this example, *I don't know* is the main clause. *How we will solve this problem* is a noun clause saying what I don't know. The author decided to place the noun clause *in front of* the main clause. This makes the sentence sound more interesting than if it begins with the main clause.

    I don't know how we will solve this problem.

See also **adjectives**; **adverbial clauses**; **adverbial phrases**; **noun clauses**; **subject**.

Hint

Word order in sentences

One of the interesting things about the English language is that you can often change the word order in a sentence without changing the meaning.

The important thing to remember about the position of words in a sentence is that the link between a subject and its verb must not change. If you change this link, then you change the meaning of the sentence.

To make sentences interesting, experiment with the position of words, phrases and clauses. Move them around to see how many different ways you can say the same thing.

See also **clauses**; **grammar**: **Word order and links**; **phrases**.

Sentence length
Sentences can be short or long, depending on a writer's style and purpose.

You can use short sentences to create a sense of urgency and excitement in a story.

> The shark swam towards him. He watched its fin. It circled. Could he make it to the boat in time?

In this paragraph, the short sentences make the story sound more dramatic. They suggest that something important is about to happen.

> Beautiful and sad, the notes spilled into the water, telling the tale of the whale who had helped him and, from somewhere far off, the sounds came back as though others were singing too.
>
> *Baleen, p. 36*

In this example, a long sentence makes it possible for the author to link ideas. This is important when describing a scene, a character or summarising ideas in a text.

Hint

Short sentences

Too many short sentences together can make a text jerky and difficult to read. It is a good idea to use both short and long sentences.

You can use long sentences to create rhythm in your writing.

> Crouching in the corner of the room, the mouse waited, watching the crowd of humans prepare to leave the room and, hopefully, some tasty morsels behind them.

Hint

Long sentences

Too many long sentences together, or sentences that become too long, can make your writing hard to understand. Readers may lose track of the ideas you are presenting.

See also **ellipsis (…)**; **full stop (.)**; **predicate**; **sentence fragments**; **subject**; **verbs: Finite and non-finite verbs**; WORD HISTORIES: **sentence**.

serial

See **cereal / serial**; WORD HISTORIES: **cereal**; **serial**.

sexist language

Sexist language is the use of words in ways that make either males or females feel that they have been excluded or ignored.

In writing, this means what authors say about males and females and how they say it. If writers suggest that only males (or females) can do certain things, then the writer is regarded as being 'sexist'.

> Soccer is a boys' game.

This statement is sexist because the author suggests that only boys should play soccer. It is better to avoid sexist language.

> The **firemen** put out the blaze.

This statement suggests that all people who fight fires are men. *Firemen* is a sexist word. Words like this have alternatives that are preferred in modern writing.

> The **firefighters** put out the blaze.

Firefighters could be men or women, so this word is not sexist.

Other words that many people think are sexist, include:

> chairman, policeman, spokesman, mankind, actress, waitress

Words that can replace these words are:

> chair or chairperson, police officer, spokesperson, humans, actor, waiter

See also **agreement: Agreement and gender**; **gender**; **he / she**; **pronouns**.

shall / will

Shall and *will* are both auxiliary verbs used to make future tense verbs.

> I **shall finish** the job tonight.
> We **shall meet** again next week.
> You **will get** lost if you go that way.
> They **will help** to clean up after the party.

It used to be a rule of English grammar that for a simple future tense, *shall* was used with the first person pronouns (I, we) and *will* was used with second and third person (you, he, she, it, they). However, since its beginnings, the English language has gone through changes that make it simpler to use. Unnecessary words are left out. During the last half of the 1900s, English speakers and writers gradually seem to have decided that the word *shall* is not so necessary or useful. Careful writers still use it in formal language.

Shall is mainly used for emphasis.

> I **shall** finish the essay, even if I have to work all night.

In this example, *shall* is used to suggest that the essay will certainly be finished.

Shall is often used in tag questions.

> Let's eat dinner early, **shall** we?

See also **auxiliary verbs**; **question mark (?): Tag questions**; **verbs: Future**.

shortened words

Speakers and writers often shorten words by leaving out letters from the middle or end of a word. For example, *Mister* becomes *Mr*, and *do not* becomes *don't*.

Shortened words include abbreviations, acronyms, clipped words, contractions, initials and symbols.

Shortened words are useful because they save time and space. They are used more in business writing (*email, faxes, letters, reports, advertising* etc) and technical writing (*science reports, manuals, tables, charts* etc) than in fiction, although fiction writers use shortened forms in dialogue.

For details on particular forms of shortened words, see **abbreviations**; **acronyms**; **clipped words**; **contractions**; **initials**; **symbols**.

See also **abbreviations**: **Correspondence**; **dialogue (US: dialog)**; **punctuation**: **With shortened words**; WORD HISTORIES: **abbreviation**.

should

See **could / should / would**.

should have (of)

See **could have (of)**.

sight / site

Sight can be a noun. It means 'something you can see'.

> The tourists were over-awed by the **sight** of the mountains.
> The tree rising from the lake made an unusual **sight**.

Site is a noun. It means 'a place or ground area'.
> The construction **site** was too dangerous for visitors to enter.
> Waste in landfill **sites** produces gases.

silent letters

Many English words are spelt with letters that are not sounded. These letters are commonly called silent letters.

The best way to deal with silent letters is to remember the words that have them. There are some useful methods you can use to do this.

Remember words as members of groups
List words with the same silent letters. Often you can discover that a word group follows a spelling pattern. If you know the pattern then it is easier to remember how to spell the words in that group. Here are some examples for different letters of the alphabet.

Silent letter b
> bomb, climb, comb, crumb, dumb, lamb, limb, numb, plumber, thumb, tomb, womb
> debt, doubt

Notice how the silent letter *b* has two groups (*-mb* and *-bt*).

Silent letter c
> obscene, scenario, scene, scent, science, scintillating

Notice how in all these silent letter *c* words, the letter *s* comes before the *c*.

Silent letter e
> above, dove, give, have, please, sneeze, some

Notice how the silent letter *e* is at the end of words and follows a single consonant.

Silent letter g
> gnarled, gnash, gnat, gnaw, gnome, gnu
> align, consign, design, feign, foreign, malign, reign, resign, sign
> neigh, neighbour, sleigh
> diaphragm, phlegm, paradigm
> bought, brought, caught, fought, nought, sought, taught, wrought
> fight, light, might, sight, tight

The letter *g* is silent only in words where it is linked to the letters *n (gn)*, *m (gm)* and *h (gh)*.

Silent letter h

> aghast, ghastly, gherkin, ghetto, ghost, ghoul
> rhapsody, rhetoric, rhinestone, rhinoceros, rhubarb, rhyme, rhythm
> whale, wharf, what, wheat, when, where, whether, whey, which, while, whine, whip, whirl, whisker, whisper, whistle, white, whiz, whorl, why

In most words with a silent letter *h*, the *h* follows the letters *g, r* or w.

Some words begin with the silent letter *h*.

> heir, heirloom, honest, honour, hour, hors-d'oeuvre

This is because many of them came from the French language, where the letter *h* was not pronounced.

With some French words like this, most people pronounce the *h*, but some people still prefer to keep the *h* silent when they come after the word *an*. Some examples are:

> hotel, herb, historical

See also **a / an**.

Silent letter k

> knack, knave, knead, knee, kneel, knelt, knew, knife, knight, knit, knob, knock, knoll, know, knowledge, knuckle

The silent letter *k* is always followed by the letter *n*.

Silent letter n

> autumn, column, condemn, damn, hymn, solemn

The silent letter *n* always follows the letter *m* at the end of a word.

Silent letter p

> pneumonia, pneumatic, psalm, pseudo-, psychiatry, psychic, psychology
> receipt, corps, coup

The silent letter *p* is usually at the beginning of the word and is followed by the letters *n* or *s*.

Silent letter s

> aisle, chassis, corps, debris, isle, islet, island

The silent letter *s* is in words that English borrowed from French.

Silent letter w

> wrangle, wrap, wrath, wreath, wreck, wren, wrench, wrestle, wretch, wriggle, wring, wrinkle, wrist, write, wrong, wrote, wry,
> who, whoever, whole, whom, whooping cough, whose
> answer, sword
> two

The silent *w* is most common at the beginning of a word and is usually followed by the letter *r* or the letter h.

Answer and *sword* are the only two words where the silent *w* follows the letter *s*. They come from Old English when the *w* used to be pronounced.

Two is like no other English word. In Old English the *w* was pronounced. It still is in the words *twin* and *between*.

Word histories

Some words with silent letters do not fit a pattern. The silent letters can be explained only by their history. Often these word histories are interesting stories. The word *two* is an example.

See also **spelling**; WORD HISTORIES: **answer**, **between**, **sword**, **two**, **who**.

simile

A simile compares something to something else. Similes are often phrases that begin with *like* or *as*.

> Getting to know people can be **like peeling onions**.
> The shark moved through the water **like a sinister shadow**.
> The pelican lunged at the fish with its **sword-like** beak.
> The leopard seal's eye was **as cold as the ice**.
> The children screamed, their faces **as pale as ghosts**.

Writing tip

Creating word pictures

Similes are a useful way of building images or pictures in the mind of your reader. You use similes to compare things. You can often make something clearer to your audience by comparing it to something else that the reader will know or understand.

---

simple present tense
See **verbs: Present**.

simple sentences
See **sentences**: Sentence structures.

simple verbs
See **verbs**: Simple and compound verbs.

singular

Singular means 'one'. A singular noun is a noun that refers to only one person or thing.

> a computer
> an engineer
> one moment
> the mouse

Nouns, pronouns and verbs all have singular forms. The following sentence is in the singular.

> The **computer** [*noun*] **has** [*verb*] a virus in **its** [*pronoun*] memory.

The following sentence is in the plural form.

> The **computers** [*noun*] **have** [*verb*] a virus in **their** [*pronoun*] memories.

See also **plural**.

singular words

Some words refer to a single person or thing. Some singular words are:

> each, everyone, nobody, nothing, none, no one, anyone

In a sentence, singular words need a singular verb. Otherwise the sentence will not have agreement.

> **Each** one knows its nest and defends it.

In this example, the word *each* agrees in number with the verb *knows* and with the singular pronoun *its*. It would be incorrect to write *each one know their nest.*

Further examples:

> **Everyone was** quiet — no one was moving.

It would be incorrect to write *Everyone were quiet — no one were moving.*

> **Each** female penguin heard **her** partner call and went straight to him.

It would be incorrect to write *Each heard their mate call*. However, there is a trend in English to do this to avoid having to write *his or her*.This is explained under *Agreement and gender* (see cross-reference below).

Mass nouns are singular words, even though they can refer to something that can have millions of parts.

> The **sand was** blowing into their eyes.

It would be incorrect to write *The sand were blowing.*

See also **agreement**: **Agreement and gender**; **anyone**; **nouns**: **Mass nouns**.

slang

Slang is everyday language used in informal speech. It is not accepted as standard English, so it is not used in formal writing (unless it is part of dialogue in a story or a transcript or quotation in nonfiction).

> Please don't send it by **snail mail**. Email the information today.

In this example, *snail mail* is a slang term for the post. It is a metaphor that suggests that the postal system is very slow compared with email.

Slang includes words and phrases that are understood by people in a particular place or group, but not by people outside that place or group.

> Later we c'n learn ya 'ow to find easy **pickins** near the thee-aters when the **toffs** come.

Hannah, p. 30

This example is from a story that is set in the 1790s in London. The dialogue includes slang terms that were used at that time.

*   *Pickins* (short for *pickings*) is a slang word for 'things to steal'.
*   *Toffs* is a slang word for 'rich people'.

Further examples:

> "Johnny will **chuck a wobbly** if you don't invite him," warned Sean.
> "He was caught **nicking** a gnome from someone's garden!"

See also **colloquial language**; **dialect**; **metaphor**; **transcript**.

Writing tip

Give life to your characters

Slang is useful when you want to give life to certain characters in stories by including it in their speech (dialogue). It can make your characters sound authentic or real, because it is how people often speak in real life.

---

slash mark (/)

The slash mark was one of the first punctuation marks used in English. It was used to show a pause in reading. Today this punctuation mark has several other names. (See 'Amazing but true' below.)

See also WORD HISTORIES: **slash mark (/)**.

The slash is now used in several ways in English:

Abbreviations
Alternative words
Dates
Measures
Phonemes or sounds

slash mark (/)

Abbreviations
The slash is used in some business abbreviations.

c/o Seacliff Motel, Seacliff, SA 5101 (meaning 'care of' in addresses)
a/c (meaning 'account')
A/V (meaning 'audiovisual')

See also **punctuation: Slash.**

Alternative words
The main use of the slash is to show 'either/or' words or numbers in a text.

Body temperatures higher than **37.2°C/98.4°F**, mean a fever.
In this example, both temperatures are correct — they are *alternatives*.

Further examples:

Asthma is a tightening of the airway **and/or** blockage in the lungs.
Cyclones/hurricanes/typhoons are circular wind storms.

Dates
The slash is sometimes used to separate the numbers in dates.

5/3/01
5/3/2001
Writers need to be careful when writing the date; this date would mean something different depending on which country you are in.

See also **dates and times: Order.**

Measures
The slash means *'per'* in abbreviated units of measure.

The astronauts travelled at about 40,230 **km/h** (25,000 mph).
In this example, the abbreviated measure *km/h* means 'kilometres per hour'.

Further examples:

25¢/copy (twenty-five cents per copy)
90p/person (ninety pence per person)
5 mg/day (five milligrams per day)
40 ft/s (forty feet per second)

See also **measures.**

Phonemes or sounds
Slashes are placed around letters that represent sounds (*phonemes*) in writing.

Her name is Anna Smyth, pronounced with an /i/ sound as in *wife*.

The punctuation mark with the most names

The / mark has more names than any other punctuation mark in English. Depending on where you are in the world (or to whom you are speaking), it may be called:

a bar, a diagonal, an oblique, a slant, a slash, a solidus, a stroke, a virgule

See also WORD HISTORIES: **solidus**.

slogan

A slogan is a short phrase or sentence often used in advertising to help people remember a business or a product.

People who write advertising slogans have special writing techniques for making them memorable. First, they must keep the slogan short or people cannot remember it. They also use the sounds of English — assonance, alliteration and rhyme.

(assonance, rhyme and rhythm)
Browse on down, to the burgers at Brown's.

(assonance)
Brown's **burgers** go **further**.

(alliteration)
Brown's **b**urgers are **b**igger.

(rhythm and alliteration)
You'll **never get a bigger burger** than Brown's.

See also **alliteration**; **assonance**; **rhyme**; WORD HISTORIES: **slogan**.

slunk

Slunk is the past tense and past participle of the verb to slink.

Then I **slunk** back to my room and pretended to read.
The fox had **slunk** back into the thicket before the hunters arrived.

small capitals

Small capitals are capital letters that are the same height as lower case letters. They have become more common in writing since word processors made them available.

> FULL CAPITALS
> SMALL CAPITALS

They are used for:
> **AD, BC, BCE**
> **Chapter beginnings**
> **Cross-references**
> **Play scripts**

AD, BC, BCE

The abbreviations *AD, BC* and *BCE* are sometimes written in small capitals.
> Aesop lived about 600 **BC**.

See also **dates and time**; WORD HISTORIES: **AD, BC, BCE**.

Chapter beginnings

Designers sometimes use small capitals for the first word or phrase of each chapter in a book.
> **Chapter Six**
> THE VEHICLE crawled along the track wending into the valley.

Cross-references

Small capitals are sometimes used for cross-references in nonfiction texts.
> **virus** (See GERM)

See also **cross-references**; **report**: **Reference texts**.

Play scripts

Small capitals are sometimes used for the character prompts in a play script.
> DETECTIVE: Aha! It's come to me at last!
> (*Enter the butler.*)
> BUTLER: What's the matter, sir? Did you have a bad dream?

See also **narrative**: **Play script**.

soar

See **saw / soar / sore**.

sore
See **saw / soar / sore**.

source
See **sauce / source**.

speech

There are several ways that writers can show speech. The method they choose depends on the audience and purpose of the writing. Putting speech into writing brings characters to life.

Callouts are used for cartoons, comics and advertisements. Most of these texts are dialogue — characters speaking. Callouts are also called *speech bubbles* or *speech balloons*.

Play scripts are used for speech that is to be performed. In a play script, the writer lists the characters' names before each line of words they are supposed to speak.

Quotation marks are used for direct speech within a narrative. They are also called *speech marks* or inverted commas. With quotation marks, writers can add descriptions saying how the characters look, feel and think, as well as what they say in their speech.

Transcripts are like play scripts except they record speech that was actually spoken by someone. This writing is suitable for recording oral history.

See also **callout; dialogue (US: dialog); direct speech; indirect speech; narrative: Play script; quotation marks (' ' and " "); transcript.**

speech balloons
See **callout; dialogue (US: dialog); speech**.

speech marks
See **quotation marks (' ' and " ")**.

spelling

There are about forty-six different sounds made by English speakers — depending on the accent and dialect spoken. But there are only twenty-six letters in the English alphabet. There are not enough letters to make each of these sounds with one letter. Therefore, some sounds are represented by groups of letters. And groups of letters can have more than one sound. For example:

oo (room, book, fool, flood, brooch)
ch (chat, machine, chemist)
sh (shine, dish)
th (that, path)

English spelling has many patterns that can help you to know how to spell a word. However, for any spelling rule, English has words that are exceptions to that rule.

There are four main reasons why the letters of the alphabet have so many different sounds, and why spelling rules have so many exceptions in English.

1. Borrowed words

Most words used in the English language have been borrowed from other languages. Different languages have different spelling patterns. So English is a mixture of spelling from many languages.

Many words come from the languages of conquerors of England. When the Romans left England, the country was invaded by Germanic and Scandinavian peoples called the Angles, Saxons and Jutes. These people brought words like *answer*, *Wednesday*, *window* and even the word for our language, *English*. They also brought words like *knight*, but they pronounced them with German sounds, which were later dropped, but the spelling was kept. This is why English has the silent *k* in this word, and the *-gh* spelling in many other words.

When William the Conqueror won the Battle of Hastings in 1066, the Normans brought French words to the country, including many words for foods. For the animals that the Saxons called *cow*, *calf*, *sheep* and *pig*, the Normans had French names that became *beef*, *veal*, *mutton* and *pork* in English.

Over hundreds of years, scholars added new words to English by borrowing from Latin and Greek. This happened especially for words in science and literature, such as *acronym*, *auxiliary*, *biography*, *chronology*, *drama*, *elegy* and *epitaph*. This is why many words use the letters *ph* for the /f/ sound.

As the English travelled, traded with, and colonised lands all over the world, they borrowed words from many cultures. Such words include *kangaroo*, *kookaburra* and *koala* (from Australian Aboriginal languages); *shampoo*, *dinghy* and *khaki* (from India); *chocolate* (from North America) and *tea* (from China).

spelling

The WORD HISTORIES section of the *Young writers guide* gives you the stories behind these words and many others.

2. The first dictionary writers
Hundreds of years ago, people who could write in English used to spell words in many different ways. There was no regular system for English spelling. In the 1600s and 1700s some people tried to set a system for spelling English words. They wrote dictionaries. The problem is, these writers allowed many exceptions to their own spelling system. Of course, once the words were published in dictionaries, then people believed that these were the correct spellings — even though they were inconsistent!

3. Changing speech patterns
Over many years, the sounds that people give to words, change. Sometimes, for example, certain letters in words are no longer pronounced. So while the spelling might have made sense hundreds of years ago, it seems to make no sense today. This change is still going on and always will.

If a word does not follow any spelling pattern, we can sometimes understand its spelling by finding out about its history. This is one reason for the *WORD HISTORIES* section in this guide.

4. There is more than one 'English' language
Over hundreds of years, as people left England to live in other parts of the world, they took their language with them. However, after a while, these people slowly developed their own versions of English. The most important example of this is the English that is spoken and written in the United States of America, where the spelling of many words has been changed from the spelling used in England.

Further information on spelling is under the following headings.
> **Alternative spellings**
> **Common errors**
> **Compound words**
> **Plurals**
> **Pronunciations**
> **Rules**
> **Same sound / different spelling**
> **Same spelling / different sound**
> **Silent letters**
> **Syllables**
> **Word histories**
> **Word parts**

Alternative spellings

Many English words can be spelt in more than one way. Some examples are:
>colour/color; realise/realize; centre/center;
>haloes/halos; hoofs/hooves; OK/okay;
>traveller/traveler; leaped/leapt; auntie/aunty

For information on words like these, see **alternative spellings**.

Common errors

Some words are often misspelled. For some reason, many people find it difficult to remember the correct spelling of certain words. Here are some of the most commonly misspelled English words.

>accidentally, accommodation, aerial, anoint, benefited, broccoli, cemetery, certainly, chimney, conscious, consensus, coolly, curtain, definitely, desperate, development, dissipate, dumbbell, ecstasy, embarrass, exceed, existence, February, forfeit, fulfil, gauge, harass, independent, inoculate, insistent, irritable, leisure, liaison, librarian, millennium, mischievous, minuscule, mysterious, ninth, occasion, occurrence, parliament, peddler, preferred, privilege, profited, pursue, pursuit, receive, recommend, repetition, sacrilegious, seize, separate, similar, sincerely, suffered, supersede, truly, tyranny, unnecessary, weird

With computer spellcheckers, it is easy to check the spelling of words like these, but this is not so helpful if you are a signwriter, or someone writing a greeting card.

Compound words

Some English words are made of other words joined. Some examples are:
>butterfly, bookkeeper, football, twenty-five

For information on words like these, see **compound words**; **hyphen (-)**: **Compound words**.

Plurals

There are many ways to spell plurals in English. Some examples are:
>bird/birds; branch/branches; hobby/hobbies; half/halves;
>zero/zero(e)s; mouse/mice; fungus/fungi; larva/larvae; axis/axes

For information on words like these, see **plural**.

Pronunciations

Letters can have more than one pronunciation in English. The letter *y* can have at least four different sounds.
>fly, myth, hurry, yes

Further examples:
>u (but, put, busy, bury, puny, rule)
>c (case, recess)
>f (fun, of)
>g (get, gym, damage, garage)
>s (bus, busy, sure)

Often, two or three letters are combined to represent sounds. These letter strings sometimes represent more than one sound in different words.
>ea (beat, dead, break)
>oo (broom, book, blood, brooch, maroon)
>th (bathe, bath)
>sch (school, schnitzel)
>wh (when, who)

Most sounds in English can be represented in more than one way.
>/sh/ (ship, sure, tissue, machine, anxious)
>/k/ (kite, pick, chemist, cancer, cheque, desiccate)
>/f/ (fun, elephant, rough)

See also **consonants**; **-e**; **vowels**; WORD HISTORIES: **who**.

Rules
Some groups of words in English follow a spelling pattern or rule, but there are usually exceptions to the rule. One example is:
>*i* before *e*, except after *c* in words with an /ee/ sound

Words that follow the rule include *receive* and *siege*. Exceptions to the rule include *seize* and *protein*.

Another common spelling rule in English is the -e rule that gives a long sound to vowels placed before a consonant.
>hop / hope

In this example, the o has a short sound in the word *hop*. In *hope*, an e is placed after the consonant p, and the o is given a long sound.

Further examples:
>bit / bite, cop / cope, hat / hate, sit / site

Exceptions to this rule include:
>give, love, dove, shove

See also **-e**; **-ei- / -ie-**.

Same sound / different spelling
Many English words sound the same but have different spellings and different meanings. Some examples are:

   to/too/two, here/hear, hoarse/horse, knew/new, practice/practise

For information on words like these, see **homophones**, or look up the word in this guide or a dictionary.

Same spelling / different sound
Some English words look the same but have more than one pronunciation and meaning. Some examples are:

   bow, row, tear, read, lead, wind

For information on words like this, see **homographs**.

Silent letters
Many English words have letters that are not sounded. This makes the spelling of these words difficult to remember. Some examples are:

   lamb, gnaw, honest, knee, hymn, island, write

For information on words like these, see **silent letters**.

Syllables
Sometimes it is helpful when spelling long words to break them up into syllables.

   acquisition (ac-qui-si-tion)

See also **syllable**.

Word histories
Sometimes English spelling seems to make no sense at all. The spelling of some words is best learned by finding out about their history — why they are spelt the way they are. Knowing the story can help you to understand and remember the spelling. Some examples are:

   answer, cereal, cliché, dialogue, hippopotamus

See also **silent letters**; WORD HISTORIES: **answer**; **cereal**; **cliché**; **dialogue**; **hippopotamus**.

Word parts
Many English words are made by adding different affixes (word endings and beginnings) on to a root word. Some examples are:

   read: reads, reading, reader, readable, readability, unreadable
   picnic: picnicked, picnicker, picnicking
   port: deport, export, import, report, transport, portable, porter

For information on how to add beginnings and endings on to words, see **affixes**; **-ic**; **plural**; **prefixes**; **suffixes**.

split infinitives

For hundreds of years there has been a rule that educated people said must be followed in English grammar — *never split an infinitive!* This means that an infinitive verb like *to run* should never have another word between these words.

Dogs like **to run** freely in a park. (This was considered correct.)

Dogs like **to** freely **run** in a park. (This was considered incorrect.)

This old rule was based on the grammar of Latin, the ancient Roman language. The Latin word for 'to run' was *currere*. In Latin, the infinitive could not be split because it had one word, not two. So the rule doesn't really make much sense in English and nobody seems to bother much about it now. The main rule is to be careful that if you do split an infinitive, you don't change the meaning of your sentence or make the meaning unclear.

See also **verbs**: **Infinitives**.

standard English

Standard English is writing and speech that can be understood by English speakers anywhere in the world. However, English speakers in different parts of the world use different dialects. This means that different regions have their own grammar, sounds, colloquialisms, and slang words and phrases. Dialects are sometimes difficult for people outside that region to understand.

If you are writing for a worldwide audience, it is better to write in standard English and avoid colloquialisms, slang and technical language. Standard usage is becoming more important as email makes it simpler for people to communicate with others all around the world.

See also **colloquial language**; **dialect**; **jargon**; **slang**; **technical language**.

statements

Statements are sentences that state or declare something. They do not ask questions, give instructions or exclaim anything. Statements usually begin with a capital and end with a full stop.

See also **sentences**: **Statements**.

storyboard

A *storyboard* is a plan for the structure of a piece of writing. Storyboarding is a method used by many authors to map out their thinking before they do a first draft. It helps them to organise their thoughts and ideas.

Storyboarding can be used for any form of writing — fiction and non-fiction. Storyboards are often notes or sketches done in a chart or drawn boxes. The *table of contents* of a non-fiction book is a form of storyboarding. It shows how the author decided to organise the information in the book.

strong verbs

See verbs: **Irregular**.

style

Style is the way writers express themselves. Different writers have their own special way of saying things. Many institutions like government offices, churches and businesses have their own sense of style that is used in any writing published by that institution. A writer or institution may use different styles depending on the audience and purpose of each piece of writing.

People often confuse grammar and style. Grammar is about the *meaning* of what is said; style is about *how* it is said. The following sentences have the same or similar meaning — they give the reader the same information about the same subject — but each sentence has a different style.

> The child bit the dog.
> The dog was bitten by the child.
> CHILD BITES DOG!
> "I bit the dog," said the child.
> By the child in a fit,
>   the doggy was bit.
> The youngster bit the pooch.
> The kid sank her teeth into the mutt.

When writers consider style, they think about:

- *Text type* — whether it is correspondence, a newspaper headline, a poem, a story told as a diary, an interview, a play etc
- *Vocabulary* — which words are used and how they are used (*dog, doggy, pooch, mutt* etc)
- *Sentence structure* — word order, sentence length, punctuation etc
- *Point of view* — first, second or third person; active (*bit*) or passive (*was bitten*)
- *Imagery and technique* — simile, metaphor, alliteration, rhyme, compare and contrast, cause and effect etc
- *Tone* — formal (*dog, child*), informal (*pooch, mutt, kid*), persuasive, dramatic, polite (euphemistic), blunt etc
- *Rhythm* — prose or verse

For further information on style techniques used by writers, see **active voice**; **alliteration**; **compare and contrast**; **euphemism**; **formal / informal writing**; **metaphor**; **passive voice**; **person**; **prose**; **sentences: Order of words, phrases and clauses**; **simile**; **tone**.

The grammar and style of different text types is explained in writing samples under these headwords: **argument**; **correspondence**; **explanation**; **narrative**; **procedure**; **recount**; **report**; **review**.

subject

There are two main parts to any sentence — the *subject* and the *predicate*. The subject is the person or thing that the sentence is all about.

> **The intruder** moved through the house like a shadow.

This sentence is all about *the intruder*. So *the intruder* is the subject of the sentence. The rest of the sentence is called the 'predicate' (what is said about the intruder).

The subject can be made up of several words and phrases.

> **The intruder, a silent thief**, moved through the house like a shadow.
>
> **The intruder, looking for loot,** moved through the house like a shadow.
>
> **In black clothing, the intruder** moved through the house like a shadow.

See also **case**; **object**; **predicate**; **sentences**.

subordinate clauses

See **clauses**: **Subordinate clauses**.

suffixes

Suffixes are word parts (*affixes*) that are joined to the end of a word.

Suffixes change the form of words and how they can be used in sentences.

> health — health**y,** wealth — wealth**y**

In these examples, *-y* is a suffix. It changed the nouns *health, wealth* into adjectives *healthy, wealthy*.

Some of the ways in which suffixes change words are shown under the following topics:

Suffixes that change words into adjectives
Suffixes that change words into nouns
Suffixes that describe and name nations
Suffixes that form plurals
Suffixes that form tenses of verbs

Suffixes that change words into adjectives

Suffix	Examples
-able	dependable, enjoyable, likeable, predictable, suitable
-al	central, environmental, musical, mythical, political
-ant	arrogant, dominant, pleasant
-ar	circular, insular, muscular, polar, vehicular
-ary	culinary, hereditary, imaginary, military, solitary
-ate	desperate, irate, passionate
-ed	hooded, webbed
-en	hidden, sullen, wooden, woollen
-ent	apparent, different, impudent, strident
-er	colder, easier, happier, sadder, warmer
-est	coldest, easiest, happiest, saddest, warmest
-ful	graceful, successful, wonderful
-ic	civic, dramatic, electronic, historic, scenic, sonic
-ing	drinking (The drinking water was cold.) swimming (The duck is a swimming bird.)
-ious	delirious, delicious, gracious, infectious
-ish	childish, greenish, sheepish
-ist	alarmist, racist, sexist
-less	harmless, helpless, homeless, sleepless, useless
-some	awesome, handsome, loathsome
-y	easy, healthy, lengthy, shiny, skinny, wealthy

Suffixes that change words into nouns

Suffix	Examples
-age	appendage, baggage, bandage, carriage, marriage
-ance	appearance, distance, remembrance
-ant	applicant, deodorant, servant
-cide	genocide, insecticide, pesticide

suffixes

Suffix	Examples
-dom	boredom, freedom, kingdom, stardom, wisdom
-ence	dependence, difference, experience
-er	carpenter, lawyer, plumber, singer, swimmer, teacher
-ery	colliery, imagery, jewellery
-hood	adulthood, brotherhood, childhood, manhood, sisterhood
-ian	civilian, electrician, magician, musician, politician
-ic	diabetic, fanatic, paraplegic
-ing	driftnetting (Many countries have banned driftnetting.) swimming (Swimming is good for you.)
-ism	chauvinism, feminism, pacifism, racism
-ist	chauvinist, dentist, feminist, pacifist, scientist, soloist
-ity	ability, generosity, mentality, neutrality, stability
-ling	duckling, gosling, hatchling
-ment	equipment, government, judgment, management
-ness	business, itchiness, kindness, sleeplessness
-or	actor, decorator, impersonator, sculptor
-ship	friendship, hardship, kinship
-sion	exclusion, extension
-th	breadth, depth, health, length, stealth, strength, wealth, width
-tion	dictation, inhalation, meditation, preparation
-ure	adventure, exposure, pleasure, scripture, sculpture, tenure

Suffixes that name and describe nations

Suffixes such as *-ian*, *-ity*, *-ism*, *-al*, *-ic*, *-ean* and *-ish* are used in nouns and adjectives that name and describe nations, nationalities, cultural groups and the nature of a culture.

- Aborigine, Aboriginal, Aboriginality
- America, American, Americanism
- Asia, Asian
- Australia, Australian, Australianism
- Austria, Austrian
- Belgium, Belgian
- Britain, British
- Canada, Canadian
- China, Chinese
- Denmark, Danish
- Fiji, Fijian
- Germany, German, Germanic
- Greece, Greek, Grecian
- India, Indian
- Indonesia, Indonesian
- Ireland, Irish
- Italy, Italian
- Japan, Japanese
- Korea, Korean
- Malaysia, Malaysian
- Mexico, Mexican
- Netherlands, Netherlander (but also, Dutch)
- New Zealand, New Zealander
- Norway, Norwegian
- Oceania, Oceanian
- Portugal, Portuguese
- Scotland, Scottish
- Singapore, Singaporean
- South Africa, South African
- Spain, Spanish, Spaniard
- Sweden, Swedish, Swede
- Taiwan, Taiwanese
- Vietnam, Vietnamese

See also **adverbs: Adverb modifiers**; **adjectives: Adjectives of degree**; **nouns: Abstract nouns**; **affixes**.

Suffixes that form plurals
See **plural**.

Suffixes that form tenses of verbs

The suffix -ed is used to form the past tense and past participle of many verbs.
> (help) helped, was helped

The suffix -s is used to form the third person singular in the present tense of many verbs.
> helps, runs, eats
> He helps in the garden.
> She runs in the marathon.
> It eats almost anything.

The suffix -ing is used to form the present participle of verbs.
> helping, running, eating

See also **participles**; **verbs: Tenses (time)**

summary

A summary is a shortened form of a text. It describes the most important ideas, information and meanings in a text, but does not give all the detail.

A summary can be presented in many forms, such as an introduction, a conclusion, an end note or a prologue. A summary should keep the general meaning of the full text, not just the topics or ideas. (Compare with *synopsis*.)

> **Conclusion**
> Given the information in this book, it is still not easy to answer the question Who discovered and developed penicillin? Considering the evidence, many people should have been given recognition for their parts in putting together the jigsaw puzzle. Why did Fleming get the main public credit and recognition? What role did the media play? How did personalities influence who got the credit? How did the war affect what happened?
>
> History is full of puzzles. To understand what has happened in the past, people need to ask questions and seek answers from different sources. In the end, they must decide for themselves.

See also **prologue (US: prolog)**; **synopsis**.

superlative degree

See **adverbs: Adverb modifiers**; **adjectives: Adjectives of degree**.

syllable

A syllable is a single unit of pronunciation. There is always one vowel sound in any syllable. A syllable can have a consonant sound before or after it. A word can have one or more syllables.

> *On* has one syllable.
> *Only* has two syllables (on + ly).
> *Loneliness* has three syllables (lone + li + ness)

A syllable can be made up of one letter or several letters. These words have only one syllable, but they have from one to nine letters.

> a, or, for, poor, sound, itched, knights, screened, squelched

---

Writing tip

Syllables in poetry

To a poet, a syllable is one beat in the rhythm of the writing. Poets often choose a particular word because it has the right number of beats (syllables) to suit the rhythmic pattern of the poem.

Ho, ho! Haw, haw! He, he!

Giggle, giggle, chuckle, chuckle! Dear me!

The verse on these pages,

Is downright outrageous.

Just read some and (ha, ha!) you'll see.

In this poem, the writer used the word *verse* in the third line. He might have used the word *poetry* to create an alliteration with the word *pages*, but *poetry* has three syllables (po + e + try) and this does not fit the rhythm of the line. He wanted only one beat (syllable) at that point, so *verse* worked.

Hint

Syllables and spelling

Sometimes, breaking long words into syllables as you say them, can help you to spell them.

irresponsible (ir + re + spon + si + ble)

symbols

Symbols are used instead of words in some kinds of writing. The symbols *$*, *?, &, %* and *kg* are all used in scientific and business writing. Further information is under the following topics:

Ampersand (&)
Copyright (©)
Degrees (°)
Hash (#)
Measures (' ")
Money ($, £, ¥)
Numbers
  x meaning 'times'
  Per cent (%)

Ampersand (&)

The ampersand is a symbol for the word *and*. It is used in addresses, titles, company names, signs, personal notes, and some business and technical writing. It is not used in formal writing.

  Deadly & dangerous snakes by Ted Mertens
  Fables: A Short Anthology Illustrated by Lisa Herriman & Lesley Scholes.

See also **addresses**: **Abbreviations in addresses**; WORD HISTORIES: **ampersand (&)**.

Copyright (©)

The copyright symbol shows who owns the copyright to a text or picture. This information, and the year the copyright began, is usually printed on the imprint page of a book.

  Text © Josephine Croser, 2002
  Illustrations © Laura Peterson, 2002

Degrees (°)

The ° symbol means *'degrees'*. It is used in measures of temperature, angles in geometry and positions on maps.

  Temperature: -50°C. Wind speed: 20 km/h.
  The spacecraft became very hot (about 28,000°C or 50,700°F), but the heat shield protected the astronauts.

See also **measures**.

Hash (#)

The hash symbol is used mainly in addresses to mean 'unit' or 'floor'.

> Department of Education and Training
> #6, 13 Washbourne Street
> Springfield

The hash symbol is used by editors to mean 'space'. Editors use this mark as an instruction to the typesetter or designer of text being prepared for publication.

Measures (' ")

The single and double quotation marks are symbols for the measures feet (') and inches (").

> Mark Brown: 6'4" tall

This example means that Mark Brown is 6 feet and 4 inches tall.

Money ($, £, ¥)

Symbols are used for currencies all over the world. They are only used with numerals.

> five $ (X)
> $5.00 (✓)

Symbols for money are used in personal notes, newspaper reports and business letters.

Examples of money symbols from around the world:

> ¢ or (cent)
> DM (German Deustchmark)
> $ dollar
> £ (pound)
> d (pence)
> ¥ (Japanese Yen)

In text about a country's currency, the symbol for that country should be written before the dollar or currency symbol and numerals.

> A$500 (500 Australian Dollars)
> CN$500 (500 Canadian Dollars)
> NZ$500 (500 New Zealand Dollars)
> S$500 (500 Singapore Dollars)
> US$500 (500 United States Dollars)

See also WORD HISTORIES: **dollar symbol $**.

Numbers

Symbols are used with numerals in mathematical statements and measures. They are used in nonfiction and technical texts, charts, tables and lists. These symbols include:

x meaning 'times'

The symbol *X or x* means 'times' or *'by'* when used with numerals, for example in measures of sheets of material.

> For this activity, you need thin, stiff cardboard (24cm X 24cm).
> Fungus (magnified 400x actual size)

Per cent (%)

The words *per cent* mean 'per hundred' (from the Latin words *per centum)*. The % symbol is used only with numerals — mostly in tables, and technical or other nonfiction writing.

> **Milk**
> Vitamins and minerals (0.7%)
> Proteins (3.5%)

synonyms

Synonyms are words that are the same or similar in meaning.

> small — little, tiny, narrow, light, short
> big — large, huge, enormous, fat, wide, tall, heavy

Very few words are exactly the same in meaning, but some words have many alternatives that are similar. Writers pay attention to the *shades of meaning* in words that are similar.

Writers and editors use a *thesaurus* to find synonyms. Modern word processors on computers have a thesaurus.

synopsis

A synopsis is a description of the main points in a text. Reviews often begin with a synopsis of the writing or performance that is being reviewed.

> This book discusses the question Who discovered and developed penicillin? The first chapter reports on the people and events that were involved. The second chapter discusses who has been given the credit and recognition.

- In this example, the writer mentions the theme of the book (Who discovered and developed penicillin?)
- The synopsis describes the topics covered in the main sections of the book. (People and events; credit and recognition)
- The synopsis does not give details of the topics. This is given in the book.

See also **review**.

take

See **bring / take**.

tautology

When a writer or speaker says the same thing twice, using different words, it is called a *tautology*. Writers try to avoid tautologies.

An Australian radio announcer, reporting a horse race in 1974, made this comment:

> Here comes the **leader, out in front**!

If a horse is the *leader*, of course it would be out in front!

A lawyer asked a male witness this question in court in the USA:

> Were you **alone** or **by yourself**?

If *alone*, then of course the witness would be by himself!

technical language

People who work, study or have an interest in a special area of knowledge often use specialist words when they communicate with other people who share that knowledge. When people write or speak about their knowledge using specialist words and phrases, they are using *technical language*.

Scientists, lawyers, doctors, musicians, teachers, nurses, florists and other groups all use words that are well-known by others in their group, but not by people outside that area of knowledge. Writers avoid technical language if they are writing for a general audience.

See also **audience**; **jargon**.

tense

The tense of a verb tells when something happened. There are three main tenses — past, present and future.

See also **verbs: Tenses (time)**; WORD HISTORIES: **tense**.

text type

Text type means the different ways an author can write to suit the audience and purpose of the writing. There are several text types for fiction, nonfiction and poetry. They are also called *genres*.

For details on the different text types, see **argument**; **audience: Text type**; **discussion**; **explanation**; **narrative**; **procedure**; **recount**; **report**; **review**.

that / which / who

That, which and *who* are relative pronouns. They are used to begin clauses that describe a noun or a pronoun.

If the noun is a *person*, then *who* is used.

> There was once a poor **farmer who** had many children.

If the noun is a *place, animal* or *thing*, then *which* or *that* is used. Some people argue over whether to use *that* or *which* for different clauses, but it is common now to use *which* or *that* equally.

> They released the **pigeons, which** flew away on their journey home.
> The water reflected the sun in a dazzle **that** blinded the driver.

the

The word *the* is called the *definite article* by people who study grammar. This is because it points to a *particular* thing. *A* and *an* are called the *indefinite articles* because they point to some *general* thing.

> **the** cat
> **the** person
> **the** idea

See also **articles**.

theme

A theme is the idea or thought behind a piece of writing. For example, the moral of a fable is its theme — the lesson that the storyteller wants to communicate to the audience.

See also **audience**: **Theme**; **narrative**.

thyme / time

Thyme is a garden herb used in cooking.

> **Thyme**, rosemary, basil and coriander are popular herbs.

Time is when things have happened, are happening or will happen.

> It was **time** to go to bed.
> She corrected her writing for the last **time**.
> They arrived just in **time** for the meeting.

time

See **dates and time**.

tire / tyre

Tire means 'to grow weary'.

> They began to **tire** of hearing the same old jokes.

A *tyre* is a lining fixed to the outside of a wheel. It is usually made of rubber.
> His bike had a flat **tyre**.

In the USA, the spelling *tire* is used for both meanings; American English does not use the spelling *tyre*.

See also **alternative spellings**.

titles of people

See **abbreviations**: Titles of people; **capitals**: Proper nouns.

toe / tow

A *toe* is one of the digits on your feet.

> It usually hurts when you stub your **toe**.

Tow means to pull or drag by a rope, chain or other type of cable.
> The truck arrived to **tow** away the wrecked car.

to / too / two

To is a preposition. It can mean 'towards'.

> The child ran **to** her parents.

To can be used as part of an infinitive verb.
> He liked **to prove** how smart he was.

Too is an adverb. It has several meanings.
- It can mean 'extremely'.
  > The soup was **too** hot.
- It can mean 'also, besides, as well'.
  > The chicken was tasty, but she ordered the steak **too**.
- It can mean 'more than' or 'beyond'.
  > The mountains were **too** far away to reach that day.

Two means the number 2. It is an adjective that tells how many.
> There were **two** locks on the door.

See also **adjectives**; **adverbs**; **prepositions**; **infinitives**.

tone

Tone describes the manner in which a writer addresses the audience. It is part of a writer's style.

There are many tones writers can use. They can be factual, emotional, personal, impersonal, humble, polite or arrogant. It is important to remember who your audience is and the purpose of your writing. Your tone makes a difference to the way your audience feels about what you have written.

The examples under the following headings show how the same letter can be written in different tones.

Angry or polite
Emotional or factual
Formal or informal

Angry or polite

> Dear Sir,
>
> The book I ordered from you arrived damaged. I'm afraid the damage is so great that I prefer to have the book replaced with a new copy. Please let me know what you wish me to do with the damaged copy.
>
> Yours truly,
>
> S D Abrahams

In this example, the tone is *polite*. The writer has politely asked for action and does not attempt to make the bookseller feel under attack. This tone is communicated with the phrases *I'm afraid that*, *I prefer* and *Please let me know*.

> Dear Sir,
>
> The book I ordered from you arrived damaged. The damage is so great that I demand a replacement. You should improve your delivery service. Let me know what to do with the damaged copy.
>
> Yours truly,
>
> S D Abrahams

In this example, the tone is one of *anger*. The writer is being very assertive towards the bookseller. This tone is communicated with the phrases *I demand*, *You should* and *Let me know* (a command without a modifier such as *please*).

Emotional or factual

> Dear Mr Page,
>
> The book I ordered from you arrived terribly damaged. I feel awful about asking for a replacement, but I like my books to be in perfect condition. I would be happy to return the damaged book. I'm sorry this happened, but I'm eager to receive a new copy so I can enjoy reading it.
>
> Kind regards,
>
> S D Abrahams

tone

In this example, the tone is emotional. The writer expresses different personal feelings about the matter. The writing is also polite. This tone is communicated in the words *terribly*, *feel awful*, *I like*, *I would be happy*, *I'm sorry*, *I'm eager* and *so I can enjoy*. An angry letter would also express emotions (disappointed, annoyed, angry, frustrated).

> Dear Mr Page,
> The book I ordered from you arrived damaged. The damage made it unreadable. If you send a replacement copy, I will return the damaged copy.
> Regards,
> S D Abrahams

In this example, the tone is factual. The writer explains facts and actions, but does not mention personal feelings.

Formal or informal

> Dear Mr Page,
> I wish to inform you that I have received the book I ordered, but it was damaged upon arrival. I respectfully request that a replacement be sent. I shall return the damaged copy for your records. Thank you in anticipation of your action on this matter.
> Yours faithfully,
> S D Abrahams

In this example, the tone is *formal*. The writer is being very businesslike and correct towards the bookseller. This tone is communicated in the phrases *wish to inform*, *I respectfully request*, *Thank you in anticipation of* and *Yours faithfully*.

> Dear Mr Page,
> I've just received the book I ordered from you, but it was damaged when it arrived. I'd like a replacement copy to be sent, please. I'll return the damaged copy, of course. Thanks. I look forward to getting the replacement.
> Cheers,
> S D Abrahams

In this example, the tone is *informal*. The writer is being very casual towards the bookseller. This tone is communicated in the words and phrases *I've just received*, *I'd like*, *I'll return*, *Thanks* and *Cheers*. The writer's use of contractions (*I'll* and *I'd*) adds to the informal tone.

See also **formal / informal writing**; **impersonal writing**; **style**.

transcript

A transcript is a written record of a conversation. The words are usually recorded using a notepad or a tape recorder, and then transcribed (typed or written) into text.

> Ground control: We copy you down Eagle.
> Eagle: Houston, Tranquillity Base here. The Eagle has landed.

In this example, the astronauts in the Eagle spacecraft were telling Ground Control, at Houston on Earth, that they had landed on the moon.

- Transcripts are often written like a play script, so the reader knows who said what.
- Transcripts are supposed to be an accurate record of the actual words spoken.

See also **narrative**: **Play script**; **quotation marks**: **Transcripts**; **recount**: **Transcript**; **speech**.

units of measure

See **measures**.

usage

Usage, in writing and speech, means the accepted ways in which words and the language are used. It is also about making correct choices of words in your writing.

Different forms of English usage occur in different English-speaking countries.

> Please remain seated until the seatbelt sign is switched off. **In a moment** we will **disembark** through the forward door.

> Please remain seated until the seatbelt sign is switched off and we will **de-plane momentarily** through the forward door.

The first example is typical usage by airline workers in England, Australia and New Zealand. The second example is typical usage by airline workers in the USA. The difference is in the use of words and phrases like *disembark* and *de-plane*, and *in a moment* and *momentarily*.

Usage is also about the ways people use grammar.

> I was ill **from Monday to Friday**.
> I was ill **Monday through Friday**.

The first example is typical usage in England, Australia and New Zealand. The second example is typical usage in the USA.

Usage is also about correct choices of words. The various English dictionaries of the world together list over 600,000 words. Many of these words have similar sounds or meanings. This can be confusing — words like *its* and *it's*, *bring* and *take*, *real* and *really*. Using the wrong word can completely change the meaning of a sentence, and possibly cause embarrassment to the writer.

Words like *to, too,* and *two*, that are often confused because they sound alike, are explained under their own headwords throughout this guide. Their meanings can also be found in a dictionary.

If a writer needs to know the meanings of words that sound the same (eg *weather, whether* and *wether*), then the dictionary is the best reference. If a writer needs to know how to use a word in a particular piece of writing (eg *real, really* or *bring, take*), or compare the use of different words (eg *discrete, discreet* or *its, it's*), then a writer's guide is usually the best reference.

verbal adjectives

See **adjectives**: **Verbal adjectives**.

verbal nouns

Words ending in *-ing* are called *present participles* — a form of a verb. Present participles can be used as nouns.

> They like **swimming**. **Swimming** is their favourite sport.

In this example, the verb form *swimming* has been used as a noun — a thing they like. When *-ing* words are used as nouns, they are called *verbal nouns* (because they are a verb acting like a noun).

See **nouns**: **Verbal nouns**.

verbs

A verb is a word that tells what the subject of a sentence is *doing, being,* or *feeling.*

> The lions **moved** through the herd like a trained team as they **searched** for a victim. One lioness **grasped** a slower beast and **dragged** it to the ground.

The verbs *moved, searched, grasped* and *dragged* in these sentences tell what the subjects (*The lions* and *one lioness*) did.

> Rusty **had been** a family pet since the children were babies.

The verb *had been* tells about Rusty being or existing.

verbs

'I **wonder** how they **feel** about losing the game?' **mused** Greg.
The verbs *wonder*, *feel* and *mused* tell about thinking and feeling.

Verbs are probably the most important words in a sentence, because a verb can be a whole sentence on its own, but a sentence cannot be complete without a finite verb (except special *one-word sentences*).

"**Look**! Land ahead," said the sailor.

The word *Look!* is a complete sentence. The subject of the sentence is understood to be *you — You look!*

See also **argument: Advertisements; interjections**.

Information on different kinds of verbs is under the following headings:

Active and passive verbs
> *Active*
> *Passive*

Auxiliary verbs

Finite and non-finite verbs
> *Finite*
> *Non-finite*

Infinitives

Linking verbs

Regular and irregular verbs
> *Regular*
> *Irregular*

Simple and compound verbs
> *Simple*
> *Compound*

Singular and plural (number)

Tenses (time)
> *Present*
> *Past*
> *Future*
> *Special tenses*

Transitive and intransitive verbs

Active and passive verbs

Verbs can be *active* or *passive*.

Active

A verb is active when the subject of a sentence is doing the action.

> The lifeguard **saved** the swimmer.

The lifeguard is the subject of the sentence. *The lifeguard* is doing the action, so *saved* is an active verb.

Passive
A verb is passive if the subject of a sentence does *not* do the action in the verb. Instead, the action is being done to the subject.

The swimmer **was saved** by the lifeguard.

The swimmer is the subject of the sentence. *The swimmer* did not do the action *saved*. The *saving* was done to the swimmer. So it is a passive verb.

For information about how active and passive verbs affect your writing, see **active voice**; **passive voice**; **voice**.

Auxiliary verbs

Auxiliary verbs help to make compound verbs. They include words from the following list:

am, will, must, is, could, should, would, have, has, had, was, were, are, can, do, be, been, might, do, does, may

She **would have been running** in the marathon if her leg **had healed**.

The auxiliary verbs *would have been* make the participle *running* a compound verb. The auxiliary verb *had* adds to the participle *healed* to form the compound verb *had healed*.

So the mystery of the missing statue **had been solved**.

In this example, the auxiliary verbs *had* and *been* help to form the compound verb *had been solved*.

The younger generation **could be taught** to be more responsible in the type of products they buy.

In this sentence the auxiliary verbs *could* and *be* help to form the compound verb *could be taught*.

If they **had waited** longer they **might have caught** some fish.

This sentence has two compound verbs — *had waited* and *might have caught*.

See also **auxiliary verbs**; **participles**; WORD HISTORIES: **auxiliary**.

Finite and non-finite verbs

Finite
Finite verbs are verbs that make a complete sentence when linked with a subject.

The lifeguard **swam** towards him.

Other finite forms of the verb *swam* are:

> swim, swims, is swimming, has been swimming, will have been swimming, has swum

Non-finite

Non-finite verbs are those that do not make sense when linked with a subject, unless they have an auxiliary verb.

> The lifeguard **swimming** towards him.

The non-finite verb *swimming* does not make sense when linked to the subject *The lifeguard*. They do not form a complete sentence. Another non-finite form of this verb is *to swim*.

> The lifeguard **to swim** towards him.

Non-finite verbs need an auxiliary verb to make them complete. Then they make sense with a subject.

> The lifeguard **was** swimming.
> The lifeguard **is** swimming.
> The lifeguard **had been** swimming.
> The lifeguard **will be** swimming.
> The lifeguard **could have been** swimming.
> The lifeguard **had** to swim.

Infinitives

An infinitive is the simplest verb form. It is always introduced by another word (usually 'to').

> to swim, to be, to have, to think, to act

Infinitives are non-finite verbs — they need another verb if they are to make sense with a subject.

> The lifeguard had **to swim**.

In this example, the verb is *had to swim*.

Infinitives can be introduced by some other words besides 'to'.

> They **can** swim.
> We **should** swim.

In these examples, the verbs *can* and *should* introduce the infinitive *swim*.

Infinitives can be in the present or past tense.

> to swim, to be swimming (present)
> to have swum, to have been swimming (past)

See also **split infinitives**.

Linking verbs

Linking verbs are verbs that link the subject with other words in the sentence. It is a term used sometimes in grammar. Examples of linking verbs include:

> appear, sound, was, seem, grow, look, become, feel, get, smell, prove

> The orchestra **grew** louder.

The verb *grew* links the subject *The orchestra* with the adjective *louder*.

> Now the problem **seems** very clear to me.

In this text, the verb *seems* links the subject *the problem* with the adjectival phrase *very clear to me*.

See also **adjectival phrases**; **clauses**.

Regular and irregular verbs

Regular

Regular verbs form their past tense and past participle by adding *-ed*. For example, the verb *look* forms its past tense by adding *-ed* to make *looked*. Therefore the verb *look* is regular.

As well as *-ed*, regular verbs can have the suffixes *-s* and *-ing* added to them.

> I help.
> He help**s**.
> They help**ed**.
> Everyone was help**ing**.

See also **participles**; **suffixes**.

Irregular

Irregular verbs do not form their past tense and past participle with the suffix *-ed*. Instead, irregular verbs change their middle vowel sounds or the whole word to form a past tense.

> write, wrote, written
> go, went, gone

> No one **took** any notice of him.
> No one has **taken** any notice of him.

The verb *took* is an irregular verb — it has changed from *take* to *took* for the past tense, and *taken* for the past participle.

Irregular verbs are sometimes called 'strong verbs'. There are about 300 irregular verbs in the English language.

verbs

Further examples of irregular verbs:

     am, was, been
     have, had, had
     buy, bought, bought
     bring, brought, brought
     drink, drank, drunk
     swim, swam, swum
     sing, sang, sung
     shake, shook, shaken
     fall, fell, fallen
     hide, hid, hidden
     tear, tore, torn
     wear, wore, worn

See also **participles**; **suffixes**.

Hint

Irregular verbs

You can tell a verb is irregular when you write it in the past tense or use an auxiliary verb with it.

Today I **know** the answer.

Yesterday I **knew** the answer.

For a long time, I **have known** the answer — but I can't remember it!

Amazing but true!

Irregular regular verbs

Over hundreds of years, some regular verbs have become irregular. Here are two examples.

dig

The King James Bible was published in 1611. In that book, the past tense of *dig* was written as *digged*. Since then, *dug* gradually became more popular as the past tense form. Today, it would seem incorrect to write *digged*.

dive

In England, the past tense of *dive* has always been *dived*. However, in the USA, the word *dove* became popular. Today, American dictionaries show that the past tense of *dive* is *dived or dove*, but the most popular word is *dove*. The English language gained one more irregular verb, but in countries that do not speak American English, *dive* is still regular!

Simple and compound verbs

Simple
Simple verbs have only one part.
> The boar **turned** its head, **snorted** and **nodded**, then **ran** off.
The verbs *turned, snorted, nodded* and *ran* are all simple (one-word) verbs.

Compound
Compound verbs have more than one part. They have a participle together with auxiliary verbs.
> The boar **was snorting** as it ran away.
The verb *was snorting* is a compound verb. It has the auxiliary verb *was* and the participle *snorting*. Compound verbs can have more than two parts.
> **have been snorting**
> **would have been snorting**

Verbs in the future tense are compound verbs.
> I **will finish** the job tomorrow.
> We **shall win** the game.
> They **will be** surprised by the party.
See also **auxiliary verbs**; **participles**; **verbs**: **Future**.

verbs

Singular and plural (number)

Verbs have singular and plural forms to show number. The verb and the subject of a sentence must agree in number — they must both be singular or plural. The following table shows some of the singular and plural forms of some verbs.

Verb	Singular	Plural
to be	(I) am	(we) are
to have	(it) has	(they) have
to run	(it) runs	(they) run
to think	(she) thinks	(they) think
to play	(he) is playing	(they) are playing
to seem	(it) seems	(we) seem

See also **agreement: Agreement in number**.

Amazing but true!

-s makes plural nouns, but singular verbs

When you add -s to many nouns, it forms a plural noun.

> one table, two **tables**; a cup, many **cups**

When you add -s to many verbs, it forms a singular verb.

> They **run**. [*Run* is a plural verb to agree with *they*.]

> He **runs**. [*Runs* is a singular verb to agree with *He*.]

Some words can be either a noun or a verb (eg *drink, dance*). Therefore, when you add -s to these words, they become either singular or plural words depending on how they are used.

> She had a **drink** of milk. [*Drink* is a singular noun.]

> She had two **drinks** of milk. [*Drink* is a plural noun.]

> She **drinks** milk. [*Drinks* is a singular verb to agree with *she*.]

> They **drink** milk. [*Drink* is a plural verb to agree with *They*.]

Tenses (time)

Verbs have different tenses to show when something happened. English has three main tenses — *present, past* and *future* — and several special tenses.

verbs

Present
Verbs in the present tense tell about things that are happening *now*.
> I **play** sport. He **plays** sport.

This is called the *simple present* tense.
> I **am playing** sport. She **is playing** sport. They **are playing** sport.

This is called the *continuous present* tense.

Writing tip

Using simple present and continuous present verbs

Simple present and *continuous present* verbs are used in nonfiction reports and explanations.

- They allow you to write generally about a topic and express events or actions that are ongoing or happening all the time.

  Dolphins **are** mammals that **live** in the sea.

- They can give writing a feeling of authority because they sound scientific.

  The earth **spins** on its axis at the same time as it **is orbiting** the sun.

For examples of this in writing, see **report**: **Cause and effect, Classification, Question and answer — quiz**.

Simple present and *continuous present* verbs are used in stories when the writer wants to express an ongoing thought. For example, the moral in a fable describes an ongoing idea.

  Kindness **is** its own reward.

  One good turn **deserves** another.

See also **narrative**: **Fable**.

Past
Verbs in the past tense tell about things that have *already happened*.
> The dolphin **jumped**; he **turned** and **dived** with a splash.

The verbs in this sentence — *jumped, turned* and *dived*, are in the past tense. They tell about events that have already happened. Most stories are written in the past tense.

verbs

Writing tip

Using past tense verbs

Writers use the past tense when they recall events.

- Most narratives (fables, folk tales, fairytales, myths, legends, anecdotes etc) are written in the past tense. Storytellers often begin tales
with the words *long, long ago* or *once upon a time*.

- Non-fiction recounts (journals, biographies, autobiographies, oral histories etc) are written in the past tense because they are about events
that have already happened.

See **recount**.

Future
Future tense verbs tell about actions that have not yet happened. These verbs
are *compound* verbs because they have more than one part — they usually
have the verbs *will* or *shall* in them.

Perhaps one day, I **will travel** to other lands.
The future tense verb in this example is *will travel*.
Further examples:

We **shall travel** to other lands.
We **are about to travel** to other lands.
We **are going to travel** to other lands.

See also **shall / will**; **verbs**: **Compound**.

Special tenses
There are several special tenses of verbs in the English language. All of these
tenses have *compound* verbs — more than one word. The word groups that
form the special tenses are called *verb phrases*.

The English language has many tense forms that allow writers to express fine
shades of meaning. The following special tenses have slightly different
meanings about when (or if) the penguin eats the fish. Some people prefer to
give each tense form its own name. Other people who study grammar think
that these names are not a good way of describing how English verbs work.
The important thing is that you understand that English has many ways of
showing different meanings through the tense of verbs, and that you use these
accurately in your writing to express when events, processes or actions
happen.

- Continuous present tense
  The penguin **is eating** the fish.
- Continuous past tense
  The penguin **was eating** the fish.
- Continuous future tense
  The penguin **will be eating** the fish.
- Present perfect tense
  The penguin **has eaten** the fish.
- Past perfect tense
  The penguin **had eaten** the fish.
- Future perfect tense
  The penguin **will have eaten** the fish.
- Present perfect continuous tense
  The penguin **has been eating** the fish.
- Past perfect continuous tense
  The penguin **had been eating** the fish.
- Future perfect continuous tense
  The penguin **will have been eating** the fish.

Writers can even mix these tenses with modal verbs (would, could, should etc).

> The fish **would have been eaten** by the penguin.
> The penguin **could have been eating** the fish.
> The penguin **should have eaten** the fish.
> The fish **might be eaten** by the penguin.

It is not important to remember all the names of these tenses. It is important to know that the English language has tenses that let writers express exactly what they want to say.

See also **modal verbs**.

Transitive and intransitive verbs
Transitive verbs are verbs that have an object in a sentence. They pass the action from the subject to the object in the sentence. It is a term used in grammar.

> The dog **chased** the ball.

In this example, the verb *chased* passes this action from the subject (*The dog*) onto the object (*the ball*).

Intransitive verbs are verbs that do not pass on the action from a subject to an object.

> The dog **disappeared**.
> We **laughed** for hours.
> The dish **fell** to the floor.

In these examples, the verbs *disappeared*, *laughed* and *fell* do not have objects. The phrases *for hours* and *to the floor* simply tell when or where the actions happened. So *disappeared*, *laughed* and *fell*, in these sentences, are intransitive verbs.

viewpoint

See **point of view**.

vocabulary

The list of words people know and use is called their *vocabulary*. People increase their vocabulary by reading, listening to speakers, studying, watching television reports and documentaries, writing, following hobbies and new interests or jobs and by researching information. Reference books like dictionaries and thesauruses are helpful.

Amazing but true!

How many words do writers use?

It is impossible to know exactly how many words there are in the English language because it keeps growing. We do know that there are over 600,000 words listed in English dictionaries.

Of all these words, most people use very few in their writing. William Shakespeare was one of the greatest writers in the English language. Some scholars studied how many different words he used in his plays and poems. They discovered that even this great writer had a vocabulary of less than 20,000 different words in his writing!

---

voice

Voice is a term used in grammar to mean the kinds of verbs a writer uses — *active* or *passive*. The active voice makes the subject of a sentence sound more in control, active or decisive. The passive voice makes the subject sound weaker in some ways because the subject is being acted upon by something else. Whether the author chooses to use the active or passive voice can make a difference to how the audience thinks or feels.

See also **active voice**; **passive voice**; **verbs: Active and passive verbs**.

vowels

There are five *vowel letters* in the English alphabet — *a, e, i, o, u.* The other twenty-one letters are called *consonants.*

Vowel sounds are made with the lips and teeth open. There are short vowel sounds such as the *a* in *hat.* The vowels in the following words are all short vowel sounds.

> pat, pet, pit, pot, but

There are long vowel sounds such as the *a* in *hate.* The following words all have long vowel sounds.

> m**a**te, sp**a**, m**ee**t, m**ea**n, b**i**te, sk**i**, p**ie**, g**o**, gr**oa**n, fl**u**

Each vowel is used to represent more than one sound in English.

> **a**: cat, spa, wash, water, later, naval
> **e**: pet, scene, recipe, navel
> **i**: bit, bite, machine, ski
> **o**: rob, robe, to, onion
> **u**: cut, cute, busy, bury, bush, puny, rule

Vowels are sometimes used to represent consonant sounds.

> the **u** in **universe** has a /y/ sound as in 'yellow'.
> The **o** in **one** has a /w/ sound as in 'wonder'.

The consonant letter *y* can also be used to make vowel sounds.

> m**y**ster**y**
> sk**y**

See also **consonants**.

wagon / waggon

Either spelling can be used for this word. However, writers should stick to one spelling throughout any piece of writing.

> The horse was hitched to a **wagon**.
> The tractor pulled the **waggon** loaded with hay.

waist / waste

The *waist* is the part of the body just above the hips.

> She tied the apron string around his **waist**.

wait / weight

Waste can be a verb. It means 'to not make good use of something'. It can also be a noun meaning 'something that has been dumped', or 'something that is of no use'.

> **Waste** not; want not. (verb)
> Our society should not **waste** so many resources. (verb)
> **Waste** created by society is ruining our environment. (noun)
> Nuclear power stations produce radioactive **waste**. (noun)

wait / weight

Wait is a verb. It means 'to stay in one place'.

> My dog **waits** for me by the school gate.
> We had to **wait** for the ambulance to arrive.

Weight is a noun. It means 'how heavy' something is.

> The **weight** of the potatoes was too great for the bag.

war / wore

War is a noun. It means 'fighting between nations or groups of people, using weapons'.

> Red Cross protects and cares for people at times of **war**.
> Thousands of people fled to Turkey to escape the **war** in Iraq.

Wore is the past tense of the verb *to wear*.

> That evening he **wore** his best suit.
> Firefighters **wore** breathing masks, special helmets and clothing.

ware / wear / we're / where

Ware is a noun. It means 'any manufactured thing that is for sale'.
> The shops displayed their **wares** at the market.

Ware is used to make compound words to do with things for sale.
> warehouse, hardware, software

Wear is a verb. It means 'to put something on your body as clothing, cosmetics or jewellery'. It can also mean 'to have something, such as your hair, in a style or fashion'.
> I had to **wear** my old sneakers in the garden.

Wear is used to make compound words to do with things that are worn.
> footwear, travelwear, swimwear, sportswear

We're is a contraction of *we are*.
> My cousin will look after the house while **we're** away.

Where is used to make compound words to do with place:

> anywhere, everywhere, nowhere, somewhere, whereabouts, wherever

* to begin a question

  "**Where** is my book?" she asked.

* to begin an adverbial clause

  Black stumps showed **where the fire had travelled in the forest**.
  Let's go **where we can buy shoes**.

See also **adverbial clauses**; **compound words**; **contractions**; **interrogatives**.

---

wear or where?

People w**ear** **ear**-rings. (Look for the -**ear**.)

Wh**ere** is it? It is h**ere**, th**ere** and everywh**ere**.

---

way / weigh / whey

Way can mean 'a direction or path'.

> She couldn't find the **way** she'd come.

Way can also mean 'a method of doing something'.

> Coal is a dirty **way** of producing energy.
> The scientists tried another **way** of solving the problem.

Weigh means 'to measure how heavy something is'.

> **Weigh** the sugar to make sure it is the right amount for the cake.

Whey is a liquid that is left when cheese is made from milk.

> Little Miss Muffet
> Sat on a tuffet,
> Eating her curds and **whey**.

weak / week

Weak is an adjective. It means 'frail or not strong'.

> He felt **weak** after his illness.

Weak becomes a noun if the suffix -*ness* is added.

> Chocolate is my **weakness** because I can't stop eating it.

Week is a noun. It means 'the time period of seven days'.

> For the first two **weeks**, water the young plants every day.
> I am on holiday for three **weeks**.

well
See **good** / **well**.

were / where
Were is the past tense of *are*. It rhymes with *fir*.
> **Were** they late for school?

Where is an adverb meaning 'in, at or to what place'. It rhymes with *fair*.
> **Where** are they?

See also **ware** / **wear** / **we're** / **where**; **where**.

where
Where is used to make compound words to do with place.
> anywhere, everywhere, nowhere, somewhere
> whereabouts, wherever, whereupon

See also **ware** / **wear** / **we're** / **where**; **were** / **where**.

which
See **that** / **which** / **who**.

which / witch
Which is a word that begins a question or joins clauses in a sentence.
> This is a story **which** I have enjoyed for many years.
> **Which** story is that?

A *witch* is a person that people once believed was evil and did magic. Nowadays witches are more likely to be humorous or fantasy characters in stories.
> "But she's a good **witch**," said the blue fairy.
> "Why? Did she fail the evil exams?" laughed the red fairy.

who
See **that** / **which** / **who**.

who / whom

Who and *whom* are relative pronouns. They are often used to begin clauses that describe a noun.

Who is used as the subject of a sentence or clause.

> There was once a king **who** had twin children.

In this example, the word *who* means *a king*. It is the subject of the clause *who* [a king] *had twin children.*

Whom is used for the *object* of a sentence.

> In time the king had a daughter, **whom** he named Grace.

In this example, the word *whom* means the *daughter*. *Daughter* is the object of the clause *he named* [*the daughter*] *Grace*. So the writer used *whom*.

In English, *whom* is used after a preposition.

> To **whom** were you speaking?

This is the style that would be used in formal writing or speech. However, if this sentence ended with the preposition *to*, then the word *who* would be used.

> **Who** were you speaking to?

This is the style that would be used in informal speech and writing, and the trend is for this style to become more common. To many people, the formal *to whom* now sounds clumsy or awkward.

See also **adjectival clauses**; **object**; **pronouns**: **Relative pronouns**; **subject**.

Hint

who or whom?

Ask yourself, does the word refer to *he/she/*they or *him/her/*them?

If it refers to *he, she or they*, then use *who*.

> There was a king (he) **who** had twin sons.

If it refers to *him, her* or *them*, then use *whom*.

> In time the king had a daughter **whom** he named (her) Grace.

---

who's / whose

Who's is a contraction of *who is.*

> **Who's** going to clean up this mess?

Whose is a pronoun. It is the possessive form of *who* meaning '*who* owns something'.

This story is about people **whose** foolishness gets them into trouble. In this example, it is the *people* who own the *foolishness*.

See **contractions**; **possessive pronouns**.

will / shall
See **shall / will**.

word histories
See WORD HISTORIES: **English**.

words
Vocabulary
History
Spelling

Vocabulary
The English language has more words in its vocabulary than any other language. An important reason for this is that for hundreds of years English speakers have been willing to adopt or 'borrow' words from other languages. This means that English has a word or phrase for just about anything a speaker or writer wants to say.

History
English began as the language of the Anglo-Saxons, who migrated to Britain when the Romans left. Their language was *Old English*. However, England was also invaded and settled by peoples who spoke other languages; these invasions brought new words to English. English words have a fascinating history, which can help us to understand the meaning and spelling of words.

Spelling
Many people find English difficult because of its spelling system. English has words that look the same but can be said in more than one way; and words that sound the same but look different. It has words with letters that are not pronounced. Some people say that English does not have a regular system of spelling rules. Others think this is not entirely correct.

When English words were borrowed from other languages, the spellings were also often borrowed; for example, *reign* (Old French *regne*), *knight* (Old German *kneht*). Sometimes the spellings and the pronunciations were changed slightly. So English gained many words with silent letters, or unusual combinations of letters. It also gained many words that sound alike but have different spellings, such as *bare / bear*.

English writers also used to spell words in many different ways. Even the famous poet William Shakespeare spelt his own name in several different ways. People in various parts of England pronounced words differently (and still do)! So English has many words that sound alike, but are spelt differently (such as *bare/bear*). English also has words that use the same letters but are pronounced differently (such as *busy/bury*). And there are words with more than one pronunciation (such as *row, read, wind*). These things happened when the spelling of a word came from one part of England and the pronunciation from another part, or people gradually changed the sound of words over many years.

English spelling became more regular in the 1400s–1700s. This happened partly because of William Caxton and his printing press, the publication of the Bible in English and a dictionary written by Samuel Johnson. But by that time, English already had many ways to spell sounds and words, making its spelling very complex. It is an interesting topic, especially if you understand the history of words and why they are spelt the way they are — for example, why the word *answer* has a silent *w*.

See also **spelling**; WORD HISTORIES: **answer**, **English**, **knight**, **reign**.

would
See **could / should / would**.

would have (of)
See **could have (of)**.

wright
A *wright* is a person who makes, repairs or creates something. This word is sometimes used to create compound words.

> A person who writes a play is called a **playwright**.

Further examples:
> shipwright, wheelwright

writing process

Writing is a process with different stages. Professional writers usually go through six stages in their writing, to make sure that their work has the right effect when it reaches the audience.

Planning
Researching
Drafting
Revising
Editing
Publishing

Planning

Most writing needs careful planning. Some writing, for example short notes or letters, may be written without planning because writers know exactly what they want to say. But for writing that is meant to be read by an audience, authors need to know the answers to some basic questions.

These are some of the questions an author must answer before beginning to write:

* Who is my audience?
* What is the purpose of my writing? What do I want to do to the audience?
* What is the topic and what do I want to say about the topic?
* Do I need to research the topic to get further information?

Authors sometimes work with other people — partners or editors — to brainstorm ideas. In brainstorming sessions, people list all the ideas that come into their heads and then discuss them to see whether they are right for the audience and purpose of the writing. Sometimes they draw a plan or chart for the writing — a storyboard.

See also **audience**; **storyboard**.

Researching

When authors have ideas for writing, but do not have enough information to write about the ideas, they research their topic. It is easier for authors to write about a topic when they understand it well. Research makes authors more confident when they are writing.

Research is often needed for both fiction and nonfiction. In fiction, authors sometimes use facts to make their writing more believable. For example, a science-fiction story is based on facts about science or technology. In historical fiction, the author may need to describe the clothing or environment of the period, to give readers a feel for the past.

The following examples show how and why three different authors researched their topics:

- *Baleen*

Josephine Croser wanted to write a story that would explain why something is so. She chose whales as the topic. Her theme was 'why some whales have no teeth'. She needed to know about different kinds of whales to decide on her characters. She needed to know the kinds of things whales do so she could weave this information into her story and make it believable to the reader. This story has an appendix that shows the information the author researched.

- *The windmill*

This book is the first in a science-fiction trilogy (*set of three*). The author, Gary Crew, researched facts about nuclear waste, energy and the effects of nuclear radiation on animals, so the events in his story would make sense and be convincing to the reader.

- *Viewpoints on waste*

Rodney Martin was not an expert on the topic of waste disposal. So he interviewed people about their opinions and experience on different aspects of waste disposal. He also read reference books on the topic to get the facts he needed. These facts were checked with experts.

Drafting

After planning and researching ideas, the author writes a rough draft. The aim is to get the ideas into written form. This is easier to do if you have planned your work in a storyboard, and you have researched the topic of your writing.

Revising

The draft gives the author something to improve. Where the draft is unclear, the author changes the text. Words, sentences and paragraphs — even chapters — might be added, deleted, changed or shifted. At this stage it is important for the author to remember the audience and purpose of the writing. The author studies the revised draft to see if it says what was intended. Writers aim to communicate what they want to say to an audience as clearly and briefly as possible. There may be many revised drafts.

A useful technique at this stage is to put your writing aside for a day or two, then read it again. If something does not make sense, you are more likely to find it when you have had a rest from it for a while.

Editing

Most professional writers find it difficult to edit their own writing — they need an editor to give them another opinion.

Structural editing
The editor's first job is to think about the author's style and organisation of his writing, to see if the writing does what the author intended to the audience. The editor reads it and discusses with the author the style and organisation of the writing. This is called structural editing.

In nonfiction the editor looks at how the author has planned and written the chapters, headings, sub-headings, order of paragraphs and the text type or genre. In fiction, the editor looks at how the author has written about the setting, the characters, the plot and the theme of the story. The author usually revises the work again after the structural editing.

Copyediting
When the text has been revised, the editor checks the writing carefully to see if there is anything that might confuse the reader. At this stage an editor looks for ambiguities, tautologies, unclear grammar, and errors in spelling, punctuation, word usage and capitals. This is called *copyediting*.

Proofreading
Finally, after the text has been designed for printing and publishing, the editor carefully checks the work again. This is to look for any errors missed in spelling, punctuation, capital letters, pictures and any other problem that might have been missed, or that happened during the design process. This is called *proofreading*.

Often, each editing job — structural, copyediting and proofreading — will be done by different editors.

See also **ambiguity**; **capitals**; **grammar**; **punctuation**; **spelling**; **tautology**.

Publishing
The last stage of the writing process is to prepare the work for presentation to the audience. This is what *publishing* means — making the writing available to the public. The writing might be published as a newspaper, book, poster, magazine or letter, or put on the Internet. It might also be performed as a play, read out loud, or recorded on video or audio tape or CD.

yoke / yolk
A *yoke* is a wooden bar used to tie a work animal, such as an ox, to a cart or some other machine.

> The **yoke** was placed over the head of the ox.

Yoke can also be used as a verb.

>The horses were **yoked** to the old plough.

A *yolk* is the yellow part of an egg.

>The **yolk** is food for the bird as it grows inside the egg.

your / you're

Your is the possessive form of the pronoun *you*.

>'Anna,' he said. '**Your** mother's waiting for you.'
>Thank you very much for **your** lovely letters and flowers.

You're is the contraction of *you are*.

>'**You're** just jealous,' she said with a toss of her head.
>I hope **you're** satisfied!

See also **contractions**; **pronouns**: **Possessive pronouns**.

APPENDIX 1: WORD HISTORIES

abbreviation

The word *abbreviation* comes from the Latin word *abbreviatio* ('shortened'). It was used in this way in English for the first time in 1460. Before that time, other words related to this word came into English. The word *brief* came from Old French *bref*, which the French took from Latin *brevis* ('short').

Related words: *abridgement* (a shortened form of a text), *brief*, *briefs*, *brevity*, *breve* (in music in the 1400s meant 'a short note', but now means 'a long note').

abominable

The word *abominable* was first used in English in the 1300s. It was borrowed from the French, who had borrowed it from the Latin *ab* (a prefix meaning 'away') and *ominari* ('a bad omen'). From the 1300s to the 1600s, it was mistakenly believed that this word came from the Latin *ab* + *hominem* ('man'). For a long time it was even spelt by many people as *abhominable*. The word is perhaps best known in modern times because of its use in the *abominable snowman*, a mythical 'not human' beast. This popular use gave it the meaning 'terrible, horrible' which is common today.

Related words: *omen*, *ominous*

Achilles heel

Achilles was a hero in Greek mythology. When he was a baby, the gods told his mother that if she immersed him in water, his body would be indestructible. His mother held him by the heel and dunked him in the water, but the heel she was holding did not go under. When Achilles was a man, while he was fighting in a war, an enemy arrow hit him in the heel. Achilles fell and was killed. Today, the term *Achilles heel* means a person's weak spot.

Related word: *Achilles tendon*

acronym

This word was invented in 1943. It comes from two Greek words *akro* ('at the tip or end') and *onyma* ('name'). During World War 2, many new words came into the English language. Often these words were abbreviations of groups of words, formed from the first letters of other words; for example AWOL (**A**bsent **W**ith-**o**ut **L**eave). So many of these words were being invented at the time, that someone invented a new word for them — *acronym* (like *homonym*).

Related words: *acrobat*, *synonym*, *anonymous*

AD

This is an abbreviation of the Latin words *anno Domini* ('in the year of the Lord'). It was invented by the Christian church and meant the year in which Christ was born. The Christians based their calendar on this year; it is now used throughout the western world. The years after the birth of Christ are known as *AD*.

William the Conqueror won the Battle of Hastings in 1066 **AD.**

Adam's apple

Men have a bulge in their throat which is commonly called the Adam's apple. In the Bible, Adam (the first man) ate a forbidden fruit — an apple given to him by Eve. The bulge in a man's throat was named after the apple eaten by Adam, which supposedly got stuck there. The name *Adam* came into written English in 1569. The Bible was translated from ancient Hebrew scrolls. The Hebrew word *adam* meant 'one of earth' or 'the made/created one' meaning 'man'. (Some translations of the Bible, in Genesis, state that 'God formed man of the dust of the ground'.)

allegory

The old Greek word *allegorein* had two parts — *allos* ('other') and *agoreuein* ('to speak in public'). *Allegorein* 'other speaking' later became *allegoria* meaning 'a speech that has another meaning'. This word was borrowed from Greek by the ancient Romans, then the French, and finally the English in the 1300s as *allegory* — a tale with another meaning or 'voice' underneath.

Related words: *alias*, *alibi*, *else*

am

This is an abbreviation of two Latin words *ante* ('before') and *meridiem* ('midday' or 'noon'). It also meant 'siesta', so you can guess what life was like in Ancient Rome at noon! Therefore *am* means 'before midday'. It is often written with full stops (a.m.) but nowadays it is common to write *am* or *AM*.

among

This word comes from an Old English word *on-gemang* ('in a crowd'). In the 1100s the word had become *onmong*, then later *among*. This gives us a clue that the word *among* should be used when you are referring to more than two people or things.

Related word: *mingle*

ampersand (&)

In the 1830s, school children had to recite the alphabet, which at that time had the symbol & after the letter Z. As they finished the alphabet children would chant ' ... X Y Z and, per se, and'. Per se is Latin and means 'by itself'. So the children were really chanting '... and, by itself, and'. However, they must have had to chant it often and quickly, because they blurred the final phrase into one word — ampersand. This became the name of the symbol & which still means and.

anemone

An anemone is a wildflower found in Europe. It is sometimes called the 'wind flower', which makes sense because the word is believed to have come from the Greek anemos ('wind'). Some people believe that the word comes from Nemesis, the name of the Greek goddess of revenge. The word anemone was introduced to English in the middle 1500s. In the late 1700s, anemone began to be used for sea animals with long arms that move with the water. The swaying of the sea creature's arms with the current is similar to the wildflower in the breeze.

Related words: anemometer, anemoscope

annotation

The ancient Romans must have kept notes to remind themselves of thoughts or ideas, because they used the word annotare meaning 'to note'. This word came from another simpler word nota meaning 'a note'. During the 1500s English scholars borrowed many words from Latin when they needed new words in English. Scholars often made notes about their studies, so they created the words annotation (a noun) and annotate (a verb) from the Latin word annotare. Scholars and students still make notes in books and on computers and we still call these notes annotations. But English also gained a number of other words from Latin nota.

Related words: annotate, NB (Latin nota bene meaning 'note well'), note, notable, notation, notary

answer

In Old English, the word andswaru came from two parts: a prefix and- ('against') and swaru ('to swear' an oath). Andswaru ('and swear') was a reply made under oath by someone who had been accused of something. After many years it came to mean a reply to any question. The spelling changed to answer in the 1300s. The w was kept in the word, but we no longer pronounce it. It became a silent letter.

apostrophe

Apostrophe was a Latin word that came from the Greek word *apostrephein* ('to turn away'). This still makes sense today, because when we leave letters out of a word, we have 'turned them away'.

apostrophe of possession (')

In the Old English language there was no apostrophe mark. To show possession, writers would add -*es* to a singular noun.

> Alfred**es** broÞer
> (Þ = *th* in Old English.) This phrase meant 'the brother of Alfred'.

In the time of Shakespeare (1564–1616), writers used a simple -*s* to show possession.

> Alfred**s** brother

It was also common from Old English times up to the 1600s for writers to use the words *his* or *her* to show possession.

> Alfred **his** brother

Of course, using the words *his* or *her* was a clumsy way of showing ownership or possession. Also, when the writer just added -*s*, the reader could not be sure whether the writer meant a plural or a possessive.

But the history of the English language shows that there is always someone out there trying to solve such problems and improve the language. In 1692 a person called Ben Jonson wrote a book of English grammar. In this book, he used the apostrophe mark (') for the apostrophe of possession.

> Alfred**'s** brother
> Jonson said that his apostrophe mark (') showed that the *e* in *Alfredes brother* or the *hi* in *Alfred his brother* was missing. And so the apostrophe of possession had been invented, but it was really an apostrophe of contraction, showing that something had been left out!

appendix

This word was originally an ancient Roman word *appendere*. It was a verb with two parts — the prefix *ad-* ('to') and *pendere* ('to hang'). It was brought into the English language as *appendix* in the 1500s, meaning 'extra text added to the end of a book', or 'text hanging on the end of the main part of a book'.

Related words: *append*, *pending*, *pendulum*, *pendant*, *penthouse*

April

This word came into English in the 1300s from the Latin word *Aprilis* which was the name the Ancient Romans gave the fourth month of the year. Some think that it came from Aphrodite, the Greek goddess of love. Another opinion is that it comes from the Latin word *aperire* ('to open'): April in the Northern Hemisphere is spring — the time of the year when blooms open to produce new fruit.

arachnid

Arachnids (eight-legged creatures such as spiders and scorpions) were named after the Greek goddess Arachne, who was a very clever weaver. The spider's ability to spin fine webs was likened to Arachne's skill in weaving, so scientists named a whole class of animals after her.

Related words: *arachnophobia*

atlas

In 1636, a collection of maps was published in a book by a famous map maker called Mercator. In the front of the book was an illustration of the ancient Greek god, Atlas. The ancient Greeks believed that Atlas held up the universe, or the heavens. The book was popularly called the *atlas*, so from that time, any book that was a collection of maps was called an *atlas*.

August

The eighth month of the year was named after the Roman emperor Augustus. This word was used in Old English.

autobiography

This word was created by joining three different Greek words: *auto* ('self'), *bios* ('life') and *-graphos* ('write'). *Autobiography* simply means 'writing about the life of the self'. When you write the story of your own life, you are writing an autobiography.

See also WORD HISTORIES: **biography**.

auxiliary

This word came into English in 1601 from the Latin word *auxilium* ('help'). The suffix *-ary* ('belonging to') was added to change the Latin noun into an adjective. So the term *auxiliary verb* means 'helpful verb' — a verb which helps to create another verb.

babble

The Bible tells the story of people in the city of Babel. They built a tower to try to reach heaven. God punished the people for their pride by changing their language into many different languages, so they could no longer understand each other. The word *Babel* was a Hebrew word meaning the 'city of God'. This word came into English in the 1500s through other languages. The spelling changed to *babble* and the word was used to mean 'a mixture of sounds' or 'speech that cannot be understood'. In the 1600s the word began to be used for the sound of running water in a stream or brook.

Related words: *Babylon*

ballad

The ancient Romans used the word *ballare* ('to dance'). In Old French, this word was *ballade* ('a song or poem to dance to'). In the late 1400s the English borrowed *ballade* from the French, but dropped the *e* at the end of the word because it was not pronounced. Today, *ballad* means 'a type of song or poem'. English ballads have a strong rhythm, so they might still be suitable for dancing.

Related words: *ballet, ball (a dance), ballroom*

barbecue

This word came from the language of the Taino people, who lived in the West Indies. The Taino culture is now extinct, but its word *barbacoa,* meaning 'a wooden frame for sleeping on', was adopted by the people of Haiti. The Haitian people discovered that the wooden frame was also useful when they wanted to roast an animal such as a pig or a sheep.

Spanish people who had settled in North America, adopted this word. Then, in 1699, the English explorer and pirate, William Dampier, mentioned a *Borbecu* in his writing, meaning 'a wooden frame for sleeping on'. But, through their contact with Spanish people, the Americans adopted the word in the 1700s and early 1800s as *barbacue* and *barbecue*, meaning 'a festive occasion when an animal is roasted'. The modern meaning of the word in the USA can be: 1. any meat cooked over an open fire; 2. a gathering or restaurant at which barbecued meat is served; or 3. a portable cooking device for cooking meat outdoors. The outdoor barbecue (commonly called a *barbie*) became very popular in Australia because of the warm climate, but Australians did not limit the meal to just meat. *Barbecue*, in Australia, more often means: 1. outdoor cooking (including meat, eggs, fruit and vegetables) or 2. a gathering where a barbecued meal is eaten.

During the 1900s in the USA, restaurant advertisements introduced different spellings of *barbecue*, including *barbeque* and *BBQ*. The spelling *barbeque* became popular and is now listed as an alternative spelling in some dictionaries. However, *barbecue* remains the spelling used most often in formal writing.

BC

This is an abbreviation of the words *before Christ*. It was invented by the Christian church and meant the years before Christ was born. The Christians based their calendar on the year of Christ's birth, and this calendar is now used throughout the western world.

> The Romans invaded Britain in 43 **BC.**
> See **dates and time**: **Abbreviations of the date**.

BCE

This is an abbreviation of the words *before the common era*. People sometimes use *BCE* instead of *BC* when they want a term not so directly associated with Christianity. Unfortunately though, it is often mistakenly thought of as meaning *before the Christian era*. The English language has many examples of words that were 'mistakes'.

See also WORD HISTORIES: **abominable**, **ampersand (&)**.

beef

The ancient Romans called an ox a *bos*. The Old French language borrowed this word but changed it to *boef*. The Normans, who conquered England in 1066, spoke French. So when they ordered a meal of meat from this animal, they asked for *boef*. But the Old English Saxons, who looked after the animal in the field, called it a *cow*. This is why we have one word for the animal on the farm, and another word for its meat. The French now spell this word *boeuf*, and in English it gradually changed to *beef*.

Other food words like this that came into English for the same reason are:

> *mutton* (Old French *moton* became *motoun,* then *mutton* in English);
> *pork* (Latin *porcus*, 'a swine' became Old French *porc*, then English *pork*);
> *veal* (Latin *vitulus,* 'a calf', became Old French *veel*, then English *veal*).

between

In Old English, the Anglo-Saxons used the word *betweonum* to mean 'by two each'. Over many years, the sound and the spelling of this word changed to *between*. It is still used in an old form sometimes when we say *betwixt and between*. Some English dialects still use the word *betwixt*. The original meaning of 'by two' gives us a clue that the word *between* is to be used when writing about two or more distinct things.

Related words: *two*, *twins*

Bible

Paper was originally made from a reed the ancient Greeks called *papyrus*. As people found paper useful, there was a lively business for making and selling it. The place most famous for this was the ancient city of Byblos in Phoenicia. So the Greeks began to call papyrus *paper* and scrolls *biblos*, then later *biblion*. The Bible is made up of writings from a number of scrolls or books. When Rome became a centre for Christianity, the Romans adopted the Greek word *biblion* but used it in the plural to make the Latin word *biblia* meaning 'the books'. This word became *bible* in French and finally entered English in this form during the Middle English period (early 1100s–1400s).

bibliography

This word is from two Ancient Greek words: *biblion* meaning 'book' and *graphia* meaning 'writing or drawing'. The word *bibliography* came into English in 1678 when it was borrowed from the French word *bibliographie* or the Latin word *bibliographia*, meaning 'the writing of books'. In the mid-1800s it came to mean 'a list of books'.

See also **Bible**.

biography

This word is from two ancient Greek words; *bios* ('life') and *-graphos* ('write'). It came into English in the mid-1600s from the French word *biographie* or the Latin word *biographia*. It means 'writing about a life'. A *biography* is a record of a person's life.

See also WORD HISTORIES: **autobiography**.

biro

Laszlo Biro was a journalist in Hungary before World War 2. In those days, writers used ink and pens with nibs. The ink took time to dry and could be messy. Laszlo wanted a pen with ink that would dry quickly. So he designed a pen with a small ball that would spread the ink very thinly. This meant that the ink dried quickly. He registered this idea in 1943. During World War 2, the British Government bought Laszlo's design to make pens that would not leak when used in high-flying aircraft. The ballpoint pen was not available to the public until 1945 in the USA. They were expensive. In 1953, Marcel Bich of France made cheap disposable ballpoint pens which people called the *biro* after the original inventor, Laszlo Biro. These pens became popular in schools about 1959, but at first many teachers claimed that they would ruin children's handwriting!

bit

This word has several meanings, but most of them come from an Old German word *bitiz* meaning 'bite'. In Old English this word became *bitan* meaning 'to bite'.

A horse 'bites' the piece of metal, called a *bit*, that is placed in its mouth.

The *bit* of a drill 'bites' as it turns. This meaning came into English in the 1500s. About the same time, another meaning for this word entered English — 'a small piece of something'.

A completely new meaning for *bit* came into English in 1949 and it had nothing to do with *bite*. However, it did later have something to do with another new word, *byte* — they are both computer terms. While at lunch one day in 1949, John Tukey, an American computer scientist, invented the word *bit* by blending the words *binary digits* (reported in 'The New Hacker's Dictionary'). In computer language, 8 bits = 1 byte. A byte is the amount of memory a computer needs to store one letter or punctuation mark. The word *byte* was invented in 1956 by workers at IBM, an American computer company.

See also **portmanteau words**.

bloomers

Bloomers (long, baggy, women's underwear/pants) were named after an American feminist — Amelia Jenks Bloomer, from New York. In the early 1850s, she wore long, baggy pants as a symbol of liberation for women. They were actually designed by Mrs Elizabeth Smith Miller, also of New York.

blurb

It is traditional for publishers to add text to the jacket or cover of a book to encourage people to buy the book. In 1907, an American author named Gelett Burgess was a guest speaker at a booksellers convention. Gelett was also a practical joker. He made about 500 false covers for his new book, with a picture of a very attractive woman and words that said how wonderful his book was. He named the woman on the cover as 'Miss Belinda Blurb'. His practical joke was so successful that people began to use the name *blurb* to mean any text used to promote books, songs or movies. In 1914, Burgess wrote another book in which he gave his definition of the word *blurb*:

> Blurb
> 1. A flamboyant advertisement; an inspired testimonial. 2. Fulsome praise; a sound like a publisher …

brief

The ancient Greeks used the word *brakhús* ('short'), which is probably where the Romans got their word *brevis* ('short'). It became *bref* in Old French, then *brief* in English.

Related words: *abbreviation, abridge, breve* (in music), *brevity, briefs* (underpants in the 1900s)

bullet points (•)

Bullet points (the punctuation marks at the beginning of items in lists) were often asterisks in the days before computers. This is because typewriters did not have dot points, so people used the asterisk (*) key, although dot points were used in printed books. Once computers and word processors became common, people could create lists easily and add dots at the beginning of each item. They were originally called *dot points*, but the black dots reminded people of bullet holes. So before long, the metaphor *bullet points* became popular and has more recently been shortened to *bullets*.

capital

The ancient Roman word *caput* meant 'head' (of a person or animal). The English word *capital* came from another form of the Latin word — *capitalis*. Capital letters are taller than lower case letters (except small capitals). Since the head is at the tallest part of the human body, the old Roman word *capitalis* makes sense for 'taller letters', especially when we use capital letters in headings or headlines or at the head (beginning) of a sentence, paragraph or page.

Related words: *cap, captions, decapitate, chapter, cattle*

See also **small capitals**.

Cc

Cc is an abbreviation of the words *carbon copy*, from the times when inked paper (called *carbon paper*) was used to create copies of writing. The carbon paper was placed between two sheets of normal paper. As the writer pressed on the top sheet, the mark would be inked onto the sheet beneath. *Cc* is now used on letters, faxes and email, to mean that the message has been copied (sent) to other people besides the person to whom the message is addressed.

CD and CD-ROM

CD is an acronym for the words *Compact Disc*. Inventors named it this because digital information was stored or compacted onto a disc. The CD is used for music and other sound recordings. The word for a later invention, the CD-ROM, is an acronym for *Compact Disk Read Only Memory*. The CD-ROM became popular in the 1990s for storing sound, text and pictures for use on a computer.

Celsius

Anders Celsius (1701–1744) was a Swedish astronomer. In 1742, two years before he died, he wrote a paper describing the Centigrade thermometer. It was called the Centigrade thermometer because it measured boiling water at one hundred degrees. (The Latin word *centum* means one hundred.) We now call this *thermometer*, and the degrees it measures, *Celsius* after Anders Celsius. The measures are usually abbreviated, for example, 100°C. So Celsius is remembered more for his thermometer than for his astronomy!

cereal

This word came into English in the early 1800s from the Latin word *cerealis* ('of grain'). The Romans invented this word for the crops they grew (wheat, rye, barley etc). They named these things after their god of agriculture, *Ceres*. Now, in English, it means not only the grain crops that farmers grow, but also the breakfast foods made from these grains.

chant

In the 1300s, the English borrowed the word *chant* from the Old French word *chanter* ('to sing'). The French borrowed their word from the Latin word *cantare* ('frequent or often'). This word came from an even older Latin word *canere* ('to sing'). In English today, *chant* means to sing or recite something in a repetitive or monotonous way. Words especially suited to this type of speech or singing are called *chants*.

Related words: *canticle, incantation, descant, cantata, cantor, accent, shanty* (sailors' song)

chocolate

When the Spanish entered the Aztec world in the 1500s, they discovered a drink the Aztecs called *xocolatl*. It was made with cocoa beans, honey, chilli, vanilla and herbs mixed with water. The word came from two Aztec words, *xococ* ('bitter') and *atl* ('water'). The Spanish called it *chocolate* and took this drink back to Spain, but they changed the recipe and used sugar. Because the cocoa beans were rare, they kept it a secret. About a hundred years later, the French royals discovered the secret. They called it *chocolat*. Then in the early 1600s the drink became known in England. It was spelt in different ways, including *jocolatte*, but later became *chocolate*, as in the original Spanish spelling. Chocolate was also produced as a solid sweet as well as a drink.

chronology

This word came from two Greek words, *khronos* ('time') and *logos* ('speech, words'). It was introduced into English in the 1500s. The *ch-* spelling pattern in *chronology* came from Latin. So we have a word with Greek sounds and Latin spelling!

Related words: *chronological, chronometer, synchronise, chronicle*

circa

The ancient Romans called the place where they held their public games with gladiators and chariot races a *circus*. This is because the chariots raced around a circle, and circus meant 'circle' or 'ring'. *Circa* is another form of this Latin word, but it means 'about' or 'around'. It is used in English when referring to approximate dates. It is usually abbreviated to *c* (sometimes also *ca* or *circ*).

Related words: *circle, circuit, circulate, circum-* (prefix to *circumference, circumspect, circumstance* etc), *circus*

cliché

In the 1800s, French printing companies used the word *clicher* to mean 'stereotype' — type from a metal printing plate. In those days, printing type was made from molten metal poured into type moulds. It is thought that the word *clicher* is an imitation of the sound made during this process. A printing plate could reproduce the same text many times. The word *cliché* came to mean words or phrases that had been repeated often by people — like the words on a printing plate. The English word kept the French pronunciation /klee-shay/ and spelling.

comma

The Ancient Greek word *kómma* meant 'a part of, a piece cut off'. It also meant 'a piece of a sentence, a short clause'. The Romans used this word in Latin as *comma* to mean the same thing. In the 1500s, Latin scholars brought the word into the English language, where it also meant 'a part of a sentence'. When William Caxton began his printing press in London, he used a slash (/) to mark a pause in a sentence. By the early 1600s, the slash (/) was replaced by another mark (,) called a *comma* because it marked a part of a sentence.

could

In Old English, this word was *cuthe*, the past tense of *cunnan* meaning 'can' or 'know'. In the 1400s it was written as *couthe*, then *coude*. In the 1500s, some scholars added a letter *l* to the word, making it *coulde*. The scholars believed that the *l* was necessary because the word was in the same family as *would* (past tense of 'will') and *should* (past tense of 'shall'). This was a mistake, but it stayed. In Samuel Johnson's English dictionary of 1755, the word was spelt *could*. *Would* and *should* always had a letter *l* in Old English. *Could* did not. So the scholars mistakenly added yet another silent letter into English spelling.

See also **should**; **would**.

debt

The ancient Romans used the word *debitum* meaning 'something that is owed'. This word was borrowed by Old French and changed to *dette*. English then used the same word as the Old French. However, in the 1200s, scholars thought that the word should be spelt more like its original Latin word *debitum*, so they changed the spelling to *debte*, but kept the French pronunciation (without the /b/ sound). In the 1500s the letter *e* was dropped and the word became *debt* — still with a silent letter *b*.

Related words: debit, due, duty

December

To the ancient Romans, December was the tenth month of the year — their year began in March. The Latin word for *ten* is *decem*. Old French borrowed this word as *decembre*; English borrowed it from the French as *December* in the 1200s. (No one knows what *-ber* means.) So December, which is our twelfth month, really means 'tenth month'.

desert

This word came into English from the Latin word *deserere* meaning 'to abandon'. It had two parts: a prefix de- ('not' or 'out of') + *serere* ('to join'). A past tense form of this Latin verb was *desertus*. It was used first in English in the 1200s as *desert*, a noun meaning 'a dry or barren area'. This is why it is spelt with only one *s*. In the 1400s it was used as a verb meaning 'to abandon'.

Related word: *serried* (serried ranks)

design

English borrowed the word *design* from the Old French word *designer* meaning 'to be a mark of'. Old French had borrowed its word from the Latin word *designare*: *de* ('out' or 'down') + *signare* ('to mark'). The French later changed their word to *dessin,* meaning a drawing or pattern. In the 1600s, English speakers used this meaning for the word, but kept the Latin spelling — *design*.

Related words: *designate, sign, signal, signatory*, *signature*

dessert

Dessert is usually the last course of a meal. Traditionally, in France and England, people cleared away dishes from the table and even the table cloth when the main meal was finished. Then bowls of fruit and other sweet foods were brought to the table and people helped themselves. The French word for this was *desservir*. It had two parts: a prefix *des-* ('not') and *servir* ('to serve') — the course that was 'not served'. This is why the word *dessert* has a double *s*. The word was later used to mean the last course of the meal. The English borrowed the word from the French in 1600, but gave it the meaning 'a sweet dish', because the last course of a meal was usually sweet.

Related words: *deserve*, *serve*, *servant*, *service*

dialect

In the 1300s, the English borrowed an Old French word *dialecte* meaning 'discussion, debate'. The French had borrowed the word from the Latin *dialectus*. The ancient Romans took the word from the Greek word *dialegthai* ('to have a conversation'). The Greeks invented this word by adding their prefix *dia-* ('with each other') to the word *legein* ('to speak'). Over many years, in English, this word came to mean 'a way of speaking', and later 'a particular local way of speaking'. For most of the 1900s, people thought of dialects as being incorrect or poor forms of speech or writing. However, by the end of the 1900s, dialects were thought of as important varieties of language that made English richer, not poorer.

Related words: *lecture*, *lectern*, *legend*, *lesson*

dialogue

The word *dialogue* came into English from French in the 1200s. It originally came from the Greek word *dialogos* meaning 'to have conversation'. The word came from *dia-* ('with each other') and *logos* ('words'). The *-gue* spelling on the end of the word is a French form of the Greek spelling. English copied this spelling in the 1500s and 1600s.

Related words: *monologue, catalogue, prologue, epilogue*

dinghy (also dingey, dingy)

This word entered English as a result of that country's trade with India in the early 1800s. It comes from a Hindi word *dingi* meaning 'a small rowing boat used on rivers'. It was given various spellings in English, including *dingey* and *dingy*. The *gh* spelling in the English word was introduced to show that the letter *g* was to be pronounced /g/ as in *go* so the word would not be confused with *dingy* (pronounced /din-jee/) meaning 'dirty, dark'. *Dinghy* became the most common spelling.

dollar symbol $

An old Mexican-Spanish coin called a *Reale*, has an image of two pillars with ribbon winding around them. These pillars were symbols of the *pillars of Hercules*, a name given to the Straits of Gibraltar in Spain (the entrance to the Mediterranean Sea). The ribbon pictured on the coin flowed in the shape of an S. The symbol for a dollar ($) was modelled on this image — a letter *S* with the pillar running through it.

Mexican-Spanish Reale coin and diagram of dollar sign taken from its design

drama

The ancient Greeks and Romans loved theatre. The Greeks had a verb *dran* meaning 'to do or act'. From this word they made the noun *drama* which meant 'a deed or action'. On stage, actors act out a story for an audience, so the Greeks used the word *drama* to mean 'something which is acted or done'. The English borrowed this word in the 1600s.

Related words: *dramatic, melodrama, drastic*

eg

This is an abbreviation of the Latin words *exempli gratia* ('for the sake of an example'). In modern English, it means 'for example'. It is sometimes written with full stops (e.g.).

elegy

The ancient Greeks originally used the word *elegos* ('song'), but later changed its meaning to 'song of mourning' — something that might be sung at a funeral. The ancient Romans borrowed this word from the Greeks and added it to their language, Latin. The French borrowed it from Latin, then in the 1500s, the English borrowed it from the French as *elegy*. In English it meant a poem written to mourn someone who was dead.

English

After the Romans had left England, in the 400s and 500s people called Jutes, Angles, Saxons and Frisians invaded the country. These people came from places now known as Denmark and north-western Germany. The peninsula of Denmark is curved and reminded people of a fishhook. An ancient Germanic word for fishhook was angle, so the people from this region called themselves the *Angles*. The native Celts, however, called all these invaders *Saxons*, but so many Angles went to live in the new settlements that by the year 601 the invaders were generally called *Angli* and the country was called *Anglia*. In the Old English language this word had become *Engle* and the language was called *Englisc*. (In Old English the letters *sc* were pronounced /sh/.)

Related words: *angler*, *angling* (fishing)

entrée

This word has more than one meaning in English, but they are all similar to the original meaning of this word when its spelling and pronunciation /**on**-tray/ was borrowed from French in the late 1700s. It means 'the action of entering'. In the middle 1800s, English people began to use it to mean one of the courses served at a meal. The *entrée* was the small dish that was the 'entry' to the main meal. However, in America, the word came to mean 'the course that followed the appetiser'. So, today, if you order an entrée in the UK, Australia, New Zealand and Singapore you will be served a small dish before the main meal. If you order an entrée in the US, you will be served the main meal — but the word still has its French spelling and pronunciation in both forms of English.

epitaph

When a body was buried in ancient Greece, someone gave a speech. The Greek word for 'tomb' was *taphos*; the word for 'over' was *epi*. So the speech was described as an *epitaphios* ('speech over the tomb'). The Romans changed this word to *epitaphium*; in Old French it became *epitaphe*. In the 1300s, it entered the English language as *epitaph*. It also came to mean words written on a tombstone.

Related words: *epicentre*, *epilogue*, *episode*

etc

This is an abbreviation of the word *etcetera*. It comes from two Latin words *et cetera* ('and so on'). It is sometimes written with a full stop (etc.).

euphemism

This word was borrowed in the 1600s from the Greek word *euphemismos*. The Greeks formed their word from two other Greek words, *eu* ('good, well, pleasant') and *phémé* ('speech'). It meant 'to speak pleasantly'. Later, it was used in English to mean 'words that express something in the most polite, pleasant or positive way'.

exclamation mark (!)

The exclamation mark used in English today was once called the *note of admiration* meaning 'mark of wonder'. It was written in old manuscripts as a slash and two points (/..) and was used to show when a reader should stress the reading of text. Printers later printed it as an upright line with one dot below (!) perhaps to save space or to make the ending of a line neater? The ancient Romans shouted the word *Io*, which meant joy, but could also be used to mean *Hurrah! Ouch! Hey!* Some people believe our ! mark came from the Latin word *Io* — the *o* was written beneath the *I* and later became a dot.

Fahrenheit

Gabriel Fahrenheit (1686–1736) was a German scientist who lived mostly in England and Holland. He improved the method of making thermometers. He also invented the scale of measures used in thermometers at that time. On his scale, water boiled at 212 degrees and froze at 32 degrees. This thermometer and its scale of degrees were named after him. The measures are usually abbreviated, for example, 212°F.

February

On the fifteenth day of the second month of the year, one region in ancient Italy had a festival of purification or cleansing. Their word for 'purification' was *februum* and the festival was called *februarius*. So the second month came to be known by the name of this festival. The Old French language borrowed this word as *feverier*; then in the 1200s, the English borrowed it from the French as *febrarius*. In the 1300s it changed back to the old Latin spelling by adding the letter *u* again — *February*.

Ferris wheel

In 1892, a great exhibition was held in Chicago, USA. A man named George Ferris designed and built a large, rotating wheel with chairs in which people could ride. This machine was called, naturally, the Ferris wheel. Since then, such wheels may have become bigger and fancier, but they are all named after the inventor.

font

The English word *font* means a set of type. It came from the French word *fonte* in the late 1500s. The French took this word from another French word *fondre* meaning 'to melt'. This is also where we get the word *foundary* — a place where metal is melted and cast into various shapes and forms. The blocks of type used by the first printers in Europe to form words were made from metal.

Related words: *fondu, foundary*

foreword

Foreword comes from the two words, *fore* ('front') and *word*. It was first used in English in 1842 and was translated from the German word *vorwort*. It is simply a statement made at the front of a book.

Friday

This word comes from the Old English word *frige-dæg* ('Frig's day'). Frig was the old Scandinavian goddess of love.

-gh

Many English words have the letters *gh* as silent letters. In Old English some words like *might* were spelt *miht* or *myht*. After the Normans conquered England (1100–1300s), French-speaking writers used their French spelling rules and changed the *h* to *gh*, and so it became *might* — but the *gh* was not pronounced. Some words like *licht* were also changed to *light*. In Old English the *ch* in *licht* was pronounced, but in *light*, the gh was not. So more silent letters came into English because of the French.

They also added the *g* and changed the Old English words *genoh* ('enough'), *toh* ('tough'), *ruh* ('rough'), *theah* ('though'), *thoht* ('thought') and *thurh* ('through', 'thorough'). So English gained another group of irregular spellings. In some words the *gh* in *ough* was pronounced and at other times it was silent.

In the 1500s, scholars tried to make English spelling more regular by changing words like *delit* (borrowed by Old English from Old French) to *delight*. So the letters *gh*, which are not really English at all, became a common problem to people trying to learn how to spell English words.

goodbye

The word *goodbye* came from the phrase *God be with ye*. It was a common saying as people parted to go on a journey — and it was quite a mouthful. Imagine saying *God be with ye* if several people were going on a trip! So naturally, people shortened the phrase over the years to *God be wi' ye*, then *goodbye*. Even now, *goodbye* is shortened further, to *bye*. Oddly though, people sometimes lengthen the expression again by saying *Bye-bye*! It is not only English speakers who shorten expressions. The Italians have a five-syllable word for *goodbye* — *arrivederci* /ah-ree-ve-**der**-chee/ but the shorter Italian word *ciao* /chow/ tends to be more popular.

Granny Smith apple

In the early settlement days of Sydney, Australia, there was an old widow, Mrs Smith, who used to act as a nurse for women and children in her area. She was given the nickname 'Granny Smith'. Granny Smith used to throw her kitchen scraps in the backyard of her home. One day, she noticed a young apple tree growing in this part of the yard. Eventually the tree grew and produced a strange, green type of apple with a special taste of its own. Granny Smith harvested the apples and took them to market, and they soon became popular. The apples were named after her, and are now found throughout the world.

grateful

Grateful comes from a Latin word *gratus* ('pleasing or thankful'). The word became *gradevole* in Italian. This is why the word was spelt *grate-* + *-ful* in English when it entered the language in the 1500s. The Latin word *gratus* also entered English in several other words during the 1400s and 1500s.

Related words: *congratulate*, *eg*, *gratify*, *gratitude*, *gratuity*, *grace*, *gratis*, *ingrate*

See also WORD HISTORIES: **eg**.

guillotine

From the 1500s, the different peoples of Europe used machines for beheading people. In the 1700s, a French doctor named Antoine Louis invented a machine with improvements. For a while it was called the *Louisette* after its inventor. In 1789, the French Revolution began and the authorities beheaded those who were out of favour. Another French doctor named Joseph Guillotin recommended that the Louisette be used as the official method of beheading people. His suggestion was accepted. However, by 1792, the machine had a new name — *guillotine*, after the doctor.

Today, the word is used in several ways:

* a machine for cutting paper
* a surgeon's knife for cutting the tonsils
* to cut off discussion in a debate, for example in government

handicap

In the 1600s, there was a popular gambling game in which the players bet with personal possessions. An umpire decided the value of the possessions. The players and the umpire would put their hands in a cap then pull them out to show if they wanted to go on with the game. The game was called 'hand in cap'. This gradually came to be pronounced *hand i' cap*, then shortened to *handicap*. In the 1700s the word was used for a horse race, in which an umpire decided the weights horses should carry to make a race more even. It was not until the 1800s that the word was used for a race or competition (for example, golf) in which some contestants were disadvantaged to make the contest even. *Handicap* is still used for horse racing, but it also means 'disadvantage' or 'disability'.

herb

The English borrowed this word from the French *herbe* which was pronounced /erb/ The Old French took the word from the Latin *herba* which meant 'grass', 'fodder (animal food)' or 'herb'. Until the early 1900s it was usually pronounced /erb/ as in *French*. Today, English speakers are tending to pronounce the *h* as it was in its original Latin form; so history repeats itself.

See **a / an: Use with words beginning with the letter h**.

hiccough / hiccup

This word is onomatopoeic — it sounds like the thing it names. However, it has two different spellings which are both pronounced the same. The word was first used in English in the late 1500s as *hiccup*. This imitated the actual sound of a hiccup. English spelling was not consistent then, so the word was spelt in many ways, including *hicket*, *hickock*, *hickop*, *hickup*, *hikup*. In the 1600s the spelling *hiccough* was invented — the act of a hiccup was compared to a cough. So the compound word *hiccough* ('hic' + 'cough') became a common spelling, but people continued to pronounce it /hic-cup/ as they always had. The spelling *hiccough* is now disappearing and the original *hiccup* has again become popular.

hippopotamus

This word came into English in the 1500s from a Latin word, which came from the old Greek words *híppos ho potámios* meaning 'horse of the river'. So a *hippopotamus* is a river horse. The clipped word *hippo* was used back in the mid-1800s.

holiday

This was once two words in Old English — *halig dæg* ('holy day'). Holy days were for religious festivals. It later became one word, *haligdæg*. In the 1300s it came to mean 'a day of no work' because people did not work on holy days. The two words merged over many years to become *holiday* and there are many more holidays now than there were holy days in Anglo-Saxon times!

hotel

This word was borrowed from the French *hôtel* in 1644. At first, the word meant a mansion or an official building such as a town hall. In 1765 it began to mean a very classy inn or place where travellers could stay. The French do not pronounce the letter *h* in this word, and so it was often pronounced '*otel* in English.

hyperbole

Hyper- was a prefix used by the ancient Greeks to mean 'over, above, in excess'. *Bole* was a Greek word meaning 'a ball'. *Hyperbole* was the arc a ball would follow if thrown high. English borrowed *hyperbole* to mean words which an author or speaker used in an 'over-the-top' manner — an exaggeration. In English, the *e* on the end of the word is pronounced, just as the Greeks pronounced it in their word *bole* — /hi-**per**-boh-lee/.

Related words: *hyperactive*, *hype*

ie

This is an abbreviation of the Latin words *id est* which meant 'that is'. It is sometimes written with one full stop (*ie.*) or with two (*i.e.*) The modern trend is to use no full stops.

interjection

In government, people are accustomed to politicians hurling interjections at each other — words or comments that interrupt another person's speech. In grammar, an interjection is a particular part of speech — words used to express an emotion and often 'thrown in' amongst other words in a text or conversation. This is very appropriate because it comes from two Latin words; *inter* meaning 'between' and *iacere* meaning 'to throw'. The Romans used the word *interiectio*, which the Old French changed to *interjection*; it was then 'thrown among' the English words in the 1500s.

island

An ancient German word *aujo*, meaning 'land next to water', became *ig* in Old English meaning 'island'. Later, this Old English word was joined to the word *land* to become *igland*. During the 1400s, Norman (French) writers in England changed the spelling to *iland*. In the 1500s, other scholars confused this word with the word *isle*, and added the letter *s* to make it *island*. The scholars believed that the word had come from the Latin word for *island* (*insula*) but this was incorrect. This error gave us a silent letter *s* in the word *island*.

January

On New Year's Eve people remember the year just gone and look forward to the year ahead. Perhaps this is why the ancient Romans named this month *Ianuarius mensis* ('the month of Ianus'). Ianus was one of the Roman gods. His head had two faces — one looking backward and the other looking forward. He was supposed to protect doors, arches or entrances (the Latin word *ianua* meant 'door' or 'entrance'). The Latin language did not use the letter *j*. So when the Latin name for this month was brought into English in the 1300s, the letter *i* was changed to *j* and the word became *January*.

jargon

The words *jargoun* and *gargon* were used in the Old French language to mean 'chattering bird sounds'. These words probably mimicked bird sounds. The English created *jargon* from the French in the 1300s. The old poet, Chaucer, used the word *jargon* in a poem called *Canterbury Tales*, to compare someone with chattering birds. It soon became commonly used to mean 'idle chatter'.

By the late 1500s, it meant a language that could not be understood by someone outside a special group.

Related words: *gargle*

July

In ancient Roman times, the calendar had only ten months. In 46BC, the Roman emperor Julius Caesar (100–44BC) changed the calendar by adding two months, and inventing the leap year. Caesar was assassinated two years later in 44BC. One of his assassins, Mark Antony, dedicated the seventh month to Caesar by giving it his name Julius, which in English is *July*.

kangaroo

When Captain Cook and his botanist, Joseph Banks, explored Australia in 1770, they asked the Aboriginal people the name of a large hopping mammal they had seen. In their journals they recorded the word *kangooroo*. Of course, the Aboriginal peoples of Australia had many languages and cultures, so Captain Cook had really learned only one of the Aboriginal words for the animal in Queensland. That language now records the word as *gangurru*, but in English it has been spelt for about two hundred years as *kangaroo*.

khaki

Khaki has an unusual spelling, and is used to name an unusual colour — the colour of dust or dirt. This is because it comes from an Urdu word *khaki* meaning 'dusty', a form of the word *khak* meaning 'dust, earth'. The Indian army had uniforms this colour in the middle 1800s because it was good for camouflage. So, at the end of the 1800s, the British army also used this colour for their uniforms in the South African wars, and the word came to mean a particular colour in English, but it kept its Urdu spelling translated into English script.

knight

This is an Old English word. It used to be spelt *cniht* and was pronounced /k-nik/tuh/. It originally meant 'young man'. By the 900s it meant 'man servant' but by the 1000s it meant 'soldier'. During the Middle Ages (about 1000–1400) in England there was a system where men who fought battles on behalf of their lord or landowner, were granted land; such men were then called *knights*. In the 1400s it meant someone who became a noble because of service in the military. In modern times (from the 1500s) it was used for someone who had been given recognition by a monarch (king or queen) for services to the country — not necessarily military service. Throughout these changes in meaning, the sound and spelling of the word have also changed. The spelling became more like the Old German word *knecht*, then *knight*. (Many *-cht* words changed to *-ght* in English). The *k* became silent, as it did in some other Old English or Germanic words (*knapsack*, *knife*, *knot*).

See also WORD HISTORIES: **-gh**.

koala

This was originally an Australian Aboriginal word *gulawang*. It was first spelt in English as *koolah*, but was later mistakenly changed to *koala*. It means 'no water'. The koala does not drink water, but gets its moisture from the eucalypt (gum tree) leaves and dew on the leaves it eats.

kookaburra

This was originally an Australian Aboriginal word *gugubarra*. The word imitates the loud call of this bird. The word was spelt *kookaburra* in English.

leading

This word, pronounced /*ledding*/, means the space between lines of text on a page. In the days when printers prepared type with letters on blocks of metal, they could add extra space between lines by inserting thin lengths of lead. Therefore the space between lines of text became known as *leading*.

limerick

In the early 1800s, Edward Lear wrote and illustrated a book of nonsense verse using an AABBA rhyming pattern. His book made this form of verse popular. In the mid-1800s in England, a common party activity was to sing silly songs. The songs had an AABBA rhyming pattern and always ended with the line *Will you come up to Limerick?* (a region and town in Ireland). In 1896, the name *limerick* meant the type of verse written by Edward Lear, who was dead by that time. Such poems have been called *limericks* ever since.

lower case

In the early days of printing, printers prepared the type for a newspaper or book like a jigsaw puzzle — the letters were put in place one by one. To save time, printers kept their sets of letters in alphabetical order in large wooden trays or cases, with each letter and punctuation mark in its own compartment. These cases were placed on a sloping rack while the printer used them. The small letters, which the printer had to reach for more often, were kept closer in the lower section of the cases, so they were called *lower case* letters. This term is used even today in word processing and typesetting software.

See also **upper case**.

March

The ancient Romans named the third month of the year *Martius*, after their god of war *Mars* — it was 'the month of Mars'. The Old French language borrowed this name as *Marche*, then in the 1100s, English borrowed it from Old French as *March*.

Messrs (plural form of Mr)

This is an abbreviation of the French word *messieurs* (plural of *monsieur*) 'Misters'. It was first used in English in 1447. The English borrowed the French word because they could not add the letter *s* to form the plural of the abbreviation *Mr*, or it would have been confused with *Mrs*.

Miss

Miss (the title of a woman) is an abbreviation of the word *Missus*. *Missus* was a pronunciation of the word *Mistress* in the late 1500s. At that time it meant 'a married woman'. Later it came to mean 'an adult woman or a married woman'. In the 1800s, the meaning *of Miss* changed to 'unmarried woman, or young girl'.

See also **Mrs**.

Monday

In Old English this word was *monandæg* ('moon day') or 'the day of the moon'.

Mr

In 1447, *Mr* was an abbreviation of the word *Master*. However, during the 1500s and 1600s it gradually came to be pronounced *Mister*. It originally meant 'an adult man' — married or unmarried. By the 1800s the word *Master* as a title came to mean 'an unmarried man, or a young boy', whereas *Mister* meant 'a married man'. Today, *Mr* is once again used for the title of a man — married or unmarried.

Mrs

In 1582, *Mrs* was an abbreviation of the word *Mistress*, which meant 'a married woman'. The abbreviation came to be pronounced /missuz/. In the 1600s and 1700s it could have two meanings — a married woman, or an adult woman.

Ms

Ms (pronounced /mz/) is an abbreviation of the word *Mistress*. It is used as a title for a woman — married or unmarried. It is believed that this abbreviation was first used in the 1930s, but did not become popular until the 1960s, and only became more widely accepted in the 1980s. Many women preferred the title *Ms* to *Mrs* or *Miss*, because it does not tell whether they are married or not — like the title *Mr* for men. However, there is still some debate over the use of this term.

See also **Mrs**; **Miss**.

mutton

See **beef**.

name

The ancient Greek word *ónoma* ('name') became the Latin word *nomen* and was borrowed by many other languages. It came into Old English as *name* from an Old German word *namon*. Because the word went into so many languages, it has many related words.

Related words: *acronym*, *anonymous*, *antonym*, *eponym*, *homonym*, *nominate*, *noun*, *synonym*

noun

The ancient Roman word *nomen* meant 'name'. Old French adopted this word but changed it to *non*. The Normans, who spoke a dialect of French, changed it again to *noun*. In the 1300s, when the people who studied grammar needed a word for the group of words that name things, they chose the word *noun* — because it meant 'name'. So nouns are words that name things, people, places and ideas.

November

To the ancient Romans, *novembris* was the ninth month of the year — their year began in March. The Latin word for *nine* is *novem*. *November* came into English in the 1200s. So November, which is our eleventh month, really means 'ninth month'.

October

To the ancient Romans, *octobris* was the eighth month of the year — their year began in March. The Latin word for *eight* is *octo*. *October* was used in the Old English language. So October, which is our tenth month, really means 'eighth month'.

OK

OK (also *O.K.* or *okay*) was an American word that became one of the most-used words in the English language, and has even become a part of other languages. However, the history of this popular word is not clear — there are many opinions. Perhaps the most popular and likely opinion is that it came from Boston (late 1830s) where a group of people liked to play with the language by creating humorous spellings and phrases. One such phrase was *orl korrect* or *oll korrect*, which was funny because the spelling of the words was not correct. (The phrase also exists in German as *alles korrecht*.) This phrase became an acronym, *OK*. It was first used in print in a Boston newspaper in 1839. In the following year, the Americans had a presidential election, and as usual, the candidates had slogans. One candidate, Martin van Buren, was born in a Dutch community of New York called Kinderhook; so his nickname was 'Old Kinderhook'. During his election campaign, he used the slogan 'You're OK with Old Kinderhook'. Van Buren lost the election in 1840, but *OK* won a popular place in the English language since that time.

O' (O'Brien)

The letter *O'* in many Irish family names is an abbreviation of an old Gaelic term meaning 'son of'. So John O'Brien would be John, the son of Brien.

pm

This is an abbreviation of the two Latin words *post meridiem* meaning 'after midday'. The abbreviation is sometimes written *p.m.* or *P.M.*

pork

See **beef**.

portmanteau words

French kings and princes sometimes had a *portemanteau* — an official servant who carried their mantle (clothes). The word came from *porter* ('to carry') and *manteau* ('a mantle or cloak'). The English borrowed the word from the French in the late 1500s. They changed the spelling to *portmanteau* and used it to mean a case or bag for carrying clothes. Lewis Carroll used this word to describe strange words he invented for his poem 'Jabberwocky'. In this nonsense poem, Carroll bundled pairs of words into single words as if he were squeezing clothes into a portmanteau. He called his strange words *portmanteau words*. The following example is the first verse of Carroll's 'Jabberwocky'.

> 'Twas brillig, and the slithy toves
> Did gyre and gimble in the wabe;
> All mimsy were the borogroves,
> And the mome raths outgrabe.

First verse of 'Jabberwocky', by Lewis Carroll

Lewis Carroll's portmanteau words did not become popular in the English language (but his nonsense poem did). However, his idea of blending words did become popular, and many portmanteau words like brunch (breakfast + lunch) are now part of the English vocabulary.

posh

In the 1830s *posh* was a slang word for *halfpenny* and later for money generally. It is believed that it may have come from the Romany word *posh* which meant 'half'. Rich people were therefore called 'posh' because they owned a lot of money. There is also another explanation about rich people, but this has not been proven to be true: rich passengers on the ships sailing between England and India used to pay extra to have cabins on the ship's side facing away from the sun. These cooler cabins happened to be on the port side going out from England, and on the starboard side coming home. So the story grew that *posh* was an acronym for *portside out, starboard home*.

pounds (£)

The £ symbol for English money (*pounds*) comes from the first letter of the Latin word *librae*. *Librae* were coins used by the ancient Romans. The word *librae* meant 'pound weight'.

PPS

PPS means *Post Post Script* — an afterthought after the afterthought.

See also **PS**.

pram

Pram is a clipped form of the word *perambulator*. In the 1600s, *perambulator* meant 'a person who walks'. The word came from the Latin word *ambulare* ('to walk'). In the 1820s, a perambulator was the name of a machine used to measure distances. It was not until 1857 that the word began to mean the small carriage for young children. By 1884, people had become tired of saying the long word *perambulator*, and so, as is the custom in English, the word was clipped to *pram*.

PS

PS is from the Latin words *post* ('after') and *scriptum* ('write'). A *post script* is an afterthought that a writer adds to the end of a letter. It used to be written with full stops, but the computer age has made it more popular without stops.

pun

In the 1600s and 1700s, it was common for people to shorten long words to one syllable. *Pun* is believed to be a shortened form of the word *pundigrion*, meaning 'quibble'. This word was probably borrowed in the 1600s from the Italian word *puntiglio* meaning 'nice point' or 'quibble'. Today a pun means a 'funny or clever point'.

Qantas

The word *Qantas* is a proper noun — the name of an Australian airline company. It is one of the few words in the English language in which the letter *u* is not placed after the letter *q*. This is because *Qantas* is an acronym for the original name of the company — *Queensland and Northern Territory Aerial Services* — when it started in 1920. (Queensland is a state, and Northern Territory is a territory, in the northern part of Australia.) In the 1930s the name changed to Qantas Empire Airways, then in 1947 to just QANTAS. Today it is written either in full capitals (QANTAS) or with a capital (Qantas).

qu-

In Old English, words beginning with a /kw/ sound were spelt *cw-* (*cwen* for 'queen'). After the French (Normans) conquered England in 1066, French writers brought their spelling system with them and used it to represent Old English words. At that time, the French used the letters *qu* for the /kw/ sound. So they changed words like *cwen* to *queen*.

question

The ancient Romans used the word *quaerere* meaning 'to seek' or 'to ask'. From this word, the Romans also formed the word *quaestio* ('a quest'). The Old French took this word from Latin as *quest*; then English borrowed the word in the 1400s from the French as *question,* meaning 'something that is asked'.

Related words: *acquire, enquire/inquire, inquiry, inquest, query, quest, request, require*

re

Re is often used in business letters and faxes to introduce the subject or topic of the letter. It means 'concerning, regarding'. Many people believe that it is a clipped form of the word *regarding* but this is not so. It is an abbreviation of a Latin word *res* meaning 'thing, matter'. It was used in the phrase *in re* which meant 'in the matter of'. This phrase has been reduced in modern times to simply *re*. It is often followed by a colon when introducing the topic of a business letter.

See also **procedure**: **Directions in a letter**.

reign

The ancient Romans used the word *regnare* meaning 'to be king, to rule'. Old French borrowed this word from Latin, but changed it to *reignier*. They did not pronounce the *g*. In the 1200s, English borrowed this word from the French, but changed it to *reign*. They kept the French pronunciation, which is why the letter *g* is silent in English.

Related words: *rector*, *regal*, *regent*, *royal*

RIP

RIP has been written on tombstones in churchyards for hundreds of years. It is commonly thought that RIP is an acronym for the words *rest in peace*, but this is incorrect. Latin used to be the language in which church services were spoken. *RIP* is an acronym for the Latin words *requiescat in pace* (which just happens to mean 'may he/she rest in peace').

See also **acronyms**; **obituary**.

RSVP

RSVP is an acronym from the French words *Répondez s'il vous plaît* which means 'reply if it pleases you' or 'please reply'. It is sometimes written as *R.S.V.P.*

Saturday

In Old English this word was *Sæterdæg*, which was short for *Sæternes dæg*. Old English took this word from the ancient Roman phrase, *Saturni dies*, which meant 'Saturn's day'. Saturn was the ancient Roman god of agriculture.

scuba

In 1943 Jacques Cousteau and Emile Gagnan invented something to replace the clumsy diving equipment of that time. They wanted equipment that would allow them to swim freely underwater without being attached to their boat. So they invented a *self-contained underwater breathing apparatus.* The acronym SCUBA was formed from these words. This word is now usually written in lower case (*scuba*).

sentence

This word came from an Old French word *sentence* in the 1200s. The French took this word from the Latin word *sententia*, which meant 'feeling'. The English words *sense, sensitive* and *sentiment* still have this meaning. It was not until the 1400s that the word began to mean 'a group of words that made sense'.

Related words: *sense, sensible, sensitive, sensory, sentiment, sentimental*

September

To the ancient Romans, *mensis september* was 'month seven' of the year — their year began in March. The Latin word for *seven* is *septem. September* was used in the Old English language. So *September*, which is our ninth month, really means 'seventh month'.

serial

The ancient Romans used the word *series* to mean 'a number of things connected in a line'. In the 1600s, this word came into the English language with the same meaning used by the Romans. In 1841, the word *serial* (from *series*) was invented to mean stories that were published one part at a time. Such stories were often published in newspapers to entertain readers and keep them buying the newspaper regularly. Charles Dickens wrote serials.

Related words: *assert, insert, series*

shampoo

To shampoo your hair, you rub a liquid into your scalp and massage your head. This is, in fact, the original meaning of the word, 'to massage' or 'to press', from the Hindi word *champna*. European travellers discovered this word in India in the 1600s. It came into English as *champo* in the 1700s, meaning 'to massage or rub a person's limbs'. In 1848, Charles Dickens used the word with this meaning, but spelled it *shampoo(ed)*. The word kept its meaning of 'massage' until the late 1800s, but it was also used as a noun to mean a liquid used to wash the hair. In the 1900s *shampoo* was used as a verb again, but this time meaning 'to wash the hair', and as a noun to mean a liquid for washing the hair, the carpet and even the pet dog!

should

In Old English this word was *scolde* or *sceolde*. It was the past tense of the verb *scal*, which became *shal* and later *shall*. (The *sc-* in Old English was pronounced the same as *sh* today.) *Scolde* meant 'obliged to do something', and the letter *l* would have been pronounced. During the period of 1200–1400, the French conquerors of England changed the spelling to *scholde* and then to *sholde*. During the 1500s, the letter *l* became silent as people no longer pronounced it, but they kept the spelling. In Samuel Johnson's English dictionary of 1755, it was spelt *should*, but also had the form *shouldst*. At that time the words *should* and *blood* rhymed.

See also **could**.

slash mark (/)

The slash mark and brackets were the first punctuation marks used in printed English. They began to appear in the first half of the 1500s. The first English printer, William Caxton (1422?–1491) used the slash mark to separate word groups. The comma was used to replace some of the slash in some ways in the early 1600s.

See also **solidus**.

slogan

A *slogan* is an advertising statement used by businesses to help people remember them. Sometimes these slogans are 'shouted' at the public on billboards, TV and radio advertisements and any other form of advertising. This word came from the Gaelic (Irish) word *sluaghgairm*: *sluagh* ('crowd') + *gairm* ('shout'). It meant 'war cry' — something the warriors or clansmen shouted as they went into battle. In Scotland, the word became *slughhorne* and *slogurn*. From there, it was borrowed into English in 1513. By the 1700s it was spelt *slogan* and was used for advertising, which some people would say is a modern form of warfare — fighting for the customers' attention.

solidus

The ancient Romans must have liked hard cash! They had three coins. The Latin words for their coins were:
- *libra* (this also meant 'a pound weight' or 'a pair of scales')
- *solidus* (this also meant 'solid'.)
- *denarius* (a silver coin)

The English took the symbols £., s., and d. for their old currency (pounds, shillings and pence) from these three Roman words. Up to the 1800s the letter s was shaped more like the letter f. When the English wrote a sum like 'two shillings and sixpence' in numerals, it was written as *2f6* (2s6). It is believed that the f gradually became a single stroke or slash mark (2/6) called the shilling mark. This mark began to be used as a punctuation mark for separating words, and was renamed after the Roman coin, the *solidus.*

Sunday

The ancient Romans called this day *dies solis* ('day of the sun'). (This means they named the day after the sun — not that it was a sunny day.) The ancient Germans used the Roman system of naming days after gods and bodies in the solar system. In their language 'day of the sun' was *sunnuntag.* Old English took this word from the German as *sunnandæg.* In the 1300s, this three-syllable word changed to the two syllables in *Sunday.*

sword

An ancient German word *swert* meaning 'pain', gave several European languages their word for a weapon that certainly caused pain. In German it became *schwert,* Swedish *svard,* Danish *svoerd* and in Old English it was called a *sweord.* The letter w was pronounced in Old English. Over hundreds of years English speakers gradually 'dropped' the w so it was pronounced /sord/. However, writers dropped the e and kept the w, which meant this word then had a silent letter.

tab

The word *tab* meaning 'text indented from the left margin' is a clipped form of the word *tabulator* or *tabulation.* Old typewriters had locking keys so that a typist could indent text to a set mark, by hitting the tabulator key on the keyboard. The word *tabulator* is too long to print on the key of a keyboard. So modern computer keyboards often have the word *Tab* printed on the key. This made *tab* more common than *tabulator,* so the larger word was clipped.

See also **clipped words**.

tea

The Chinese discovered the drink tea, and called it *te.* The Malays adopted the drink from the Chinese and called it *teh.* In the 1600s, the Dutch traders discovered the drink, called it *thee* and took it to Europe. The English took the word from the Dutch and called it *tea,* but pronounced it as /tay/ or /tee/, but /tee/ became the popular sound.

television

The word *television* is made up of two words: *tele-* from Greek ('far away') and *vision* from the Latin *videre* ('to see'). The English borrowed the word *television* from the French in 1907. In the early 1940s, people began to use the clipped word *telly*. By 1948, the acronym *TV* was also being used.

tense

Tense has been used in English to mean 'the time of a verb' since the 1300s. It came into English from an Old French word *tens*. Before that, the French took the word from the Latin word *tempus* meaning 'time'. In English, we keep the original Latin meaning of time when we speak of the tense of verbs, but the spelling was influenced by the French. We kept the Latin spelling in our word *temporary*.

Tense, meaning strained or pulled tight, came from the Latin verb *tensus* meaning 'stretched'. It came into the English language in the 1600s, when it meant 'stretched tight'. In the 1800s people began to use the word *tense* to refer to their nerves being stretched tight or strained. Another word that comes from the same family of Latin words is *tension*.

Thursday

The ancient Romans called this day *Iovis dies* meaning 'day of Jupiter' (Jupiter was the Roman god of war). The ancient Germans took on the Roman system of naming days after gods and bodies in the solar system. They named the second day of the week *donnerstag* after Thor, their god of thunder. In Old English this word became *thunresdæg*. Later it was compared to an old Scandinavian form *thórsdagr* which meant the same thing, and changed to the modern form of *Thursday*.

Related word: *thunder*

Tuesday

The ancient Romans called this day *dies Martis* meaning 'day of Mars' (Mars was the Roman god of the sky). The ancient Germans took on the Roman system of naming days after gods and bodies in the solar system. However, they named this day *tiesdei* after Tiu, their god of war. In Old English this word became *Tiwesdæg*. Later, the spelling was changed to the modern form of *Tuesday*.

two

The word *two* has a very ancient history, going right back to the Indo-European language which language scholars believe was the beginning of many languages throughout Europe and the Middle-East. The Indo-European word *duwo* became Greek *dúo*, Latin *duo* and Russian *dva*. Old English had different forms of this ancient word — a male form *twegen* and a female form *twa*. *Twa* eventually became the English word *two*, but the pronunciation changed and the *w* became silent. *Twegen* became the English word *twain*.

Related words: *between*, *twain*, *twelve*, *twenty*, *twice*, *twin*

type

The ancient Greeks used the word *túpos* to mean 'a blow or the mark left by a blow'. The Romans changed this word to *typus*. In the 1700s this word was used in English to mean letters on printing blocks which left an impression on paper. So, the machine that made tiny blocks of type hit against a ribbon and leave letters marked on paper, was called the *typewriter*. With modern word processors, writers can use many styles of type called *fonts*.

upper case

In the old days, printers prepared the type for a newspaper or a book like a jigsaw puzzle. The letters were put in place one by one. To save time, the printers kept their sets of letters in alphabetical order in large wooden trays or cases — each letter and punctuation mark in its own compartment. These cases were placed on a sloping rack while the printer used them. The capital letters were kept in the top or upper section of the cases because they were used less often than the small letters. So they were called upper case letters. This term is used even today on modern word processing and typesetting software.

See also **lower case**.

veal

See **beef**.

viz

This is a contraction of the Latin word *videlicet*. When this word was used to explain something in Latin, it meant 'namely'. Scribes abbreviated this word by using the symbol 3 instead of the *-et*. The symbol 3 looked a bit like the letter *z*, so the modern abbreviation of *videlict* became *viz*.

Wednesday

The ancient Romans called this day *Mercurii dies* ('day of the planet Mercury'). Mercury was also the ancient Roman messenger god. The ancient Germans and Norse people took on the Roman system of naming days after gods and bodies in the solar system. However, they named this day *óðinsdagr* after Odin, their chief god. In Old English, Odin was known as *Woden*, so this word became *Wodnesdæg*. In the 1200s the spelling was changed to *Wednesdei* and later to the modern form of *Wednesday*. The first letter *d* is no longer pronounced as it used to be long ago, so it joined the list of silent letters in English spelling.

who

The Old English word for *who* was *hwa* (both the *h* and the *w* were sounded). During the period 1200–1400 in the south of England, writers spelt this word with a *w* or *wh* but it was still pronounced /hwa/. From the 1400s, the pronunciation and spelling of the *a* changed to *o*. At about the same time, writers settled on the *wh-* spelling, but the *w* was no longer sounded. So the word *who* was pronounced as /hoo/ but it began with a *w*.

The same story is true for the words *whom* (Old English *hwaem*) and *whose* (Old English *hwaes*). For no real reason, between the years 1400 and 1600 several other English words with an /h/ sound before the letter *o* were also changed to *wh-* (*whole, wholly, whoop*). This is why English has this strange group of words beginning with a silent *w*.

window

The Vikings, who invaded England after the Romans left, came from very chilly lands. They built holes in the side of their houses and ships to let air in, but did not have glass to fit into the holes. So the wind blew through the hole and, no doubt, cracks in the wooden shutters. They called the hole in the wall *vindauga* from two words, *vindr* ('wind') + *auga* ('eye'). So the hole in the wall was the 'eye of the wind' or the 'wind-eye'. Through the 1100s and 1200s this word gradually changed to *windoze*, and then in Modern English to *window*.

would

In Old English this word was *wolde*, the past tense of *willan* meaning 'will'. The letter *l* would have been pronounced in Old English. The word kept this spelling until scholars in the 1500s in England changed it to *woulde*, but during this time the letter *l* was no longer pronounced. Shakespeare, in the early 1600s wrote it as *would* or *wouldst*. In Samuel Johnson's English dictionary of 1755, it was spelt *would* but it also still had the form *wouldst* and *wouldest*.

APPENDIX 2: BOOKS AND AUTHORS CITED

The following books have been cited within this guide. The books make it possible for you to see the full context of many of the language samples used. For details, go to **www.erapublications.com**.

A children's medical encyclopedia, Betty Zed, Era Publications
Alex and the glass slipper, Amanda Graham
Amazing landforms, Janeen Brian
Antarctic journal, James Hasick
Baleen, Josephine Croser, David Kennett
A checkup with the doctor, Katherine Smith
Consumer guide to toys, Sue Mahony, Lynne Badger, Barbara Comber
Deadly & dangerous snakes, Ted Mertens
Dream of a bird, Nga Bach Thi Tran from *Poems not to be missed*, Susan Hill
Entertainers, Kevin Comber
Fables: A short anthology, Janeen Brian, Lisa Herriman, Lesley Scholes
The first lunar landing, Rodney Martin
Hannah, Josephine Croser, Steven Woolman
How cows make milk, Katherine Smith
Investigating fungi, Gwen Pascoe
Issues, Rodney Martin
Letters to Leah, Josephine Croser, Amanda Graham
Life in a rainforest, Rodney Martin
The life of a duck, Josephine Croser
Looks like lunch, Amanda Graham
Making puppets, Josie McKinnon
Me, an author? An authobiography, Amanda Graham
Memories: An autobiography, Mem Fox
The mystery of the missing garden gnome, Leone Peguero, Amanda Graham
Natural disasters, Janeen Brian
One week with my grandmother, June Loves, David Kennett
One wild weekend with my grandmother, June Loves, David Kennett
The penicillin puzzle, Rodney Martin
Perseus the gorgon-slayer, Jane O'Loughlin, Katherine Stafford
Pilawuk: When I was young, Janeen Brian
Poems not to be missed, Susan Hill, Debbie Strauss
Rescues, Janeen Brian
Seb & Sasha, Josephine Croser, Amanda Graham
The tiger, the Brahman, & the jackal (a play), Margrete Lamond, Bill Wood
'Tomorrow' is a great word, Janeen Brian
Viewpoints on waste, Rodney Martin
Voices, Edel Wignell, David Kennett
Which is which?, Josephine Croser
Wise & wacky works, Rodney Martin, Steven Woolman